AF279452

RACE
426 N. Varney St.
← SHOP
12
10
2
OON
CHAMPION

VINTAGE SPEED PARTS

The Equipment that Fueled the Industry

TONY THACKER

CarTech®

SPEED & POWER
EQUIPMENT

CarTech®

CarTech®, Inc.
6118 Main Street
North Branch, MN 55056
Phone: 651-277-1200 or 800-551-4754
Fax: 651-277-1203
www.cartechbooks.com

Edit by Bob Wilson
Layout by Monica Seiberlich

ISBN 978-1-61325-697-8
Item No. CT682

Library of Congress Cataloging-in-Publication Data Available

Written, edited, and designed in the U.S.A.
Printed in China
10 9 8 7 6 5 4 3 2 1

All photos are provided by Tony Thacker and the Tony Thacker Collection unless otherwise noted.

Publisher's Note: In reporting history, the images required to tell the tale will vary greatly in quality, especially by modern photographic standards. While some images in this volume are not up to those digital standards, we have included them, as we feel they are an important element in telling the story.

DISTRIBUTION BY:

Europe
PGUK
63 Hatton Garden
London EC1N 8LE, England
Phone: 020 7061 1980 • Fax: 020 7242 3725
www.pguk.co.uk

Australia
Renniks Publications Ltd.
3/37-39 Green Street
Banksmeadow, NSW 2109, Australia
Phone: 2 9695 7055 • Fax: 2 9695 7355
www.renniks.com

Canada
Login Canada
300 Saulteaux Crescent
Winnipeg, MB, R3J 3T2 Canada
Phone: 800 665 1148 • Fax: 800 665 0103
www.lb.ca

TABLE OF CONTENTS

ACKNOWLEDGMENTS

I wasn't planning to write this book. I wanted to do a book about chopping tops, but my buddy Scotty Gosson, who had started this book with 736 photos taken at Speedway's Museum of American Speed, got sick and was unable to finish what he'd begun. So, I dived in.

Thankfully, a few years ago I acquired the collection of racing photographer Dan Shannon, who in turn had acquired the photos of Charles Strutt. At one point, I almost sold the collection, but the offer was ridiculously low, and I didn't—thank goodness, as it proved invaluable in telling this story with great action shots of race cars equipped with the speed equipment written about here. I never met Charles or Dan, but I owe them a huge thanks because I couldn't have finished this book without their photographs.

Other drag racing photographers and car guys who gave of their work and knowledge include Philippe Dahn, Lou Hart, Carl Olson, Lynn Park, Steve Reyes, Greg Sharp, and Dave Wallace. In the corporate world, I want to thank Nick Arias III at Arias Components, Donovan Engineering, Ford Motor Co., General Motors, Bill Tichenor at Holley, Smitty Smith at Edelbrock, Mike Hermann at H and H Flatheads, Indianapolis Motor Speedway, Chico Kodoma and Shige Suganuma at Mooneyes, Clive Prew at Stromberg, and Mike Thermos at Nitrous Supply. Likewise, thanks to Jessie Belond of the Belond family, Bobby Green of Old Crow Speed Shop, Roger Harrell of the Harrell family, Marc Rozman of the Ramchargers, and Alex Xydias of the So-Cal Speed Shop for access to their archives.

I also owe a debt of gratitude to David Steele, director of the American Hot Rod Foundation; his wife, Katie Sloan-Steele; and archivist Jim Miller (son of Eddie Miller Jr.). All three were invaluable: David for answering endless questions, Katie for her investigative skills in digging up long-lost names and addresses, and Jim for his knowledge and images of his grandfather.

Finally, I want to thank my wife, Kailay, who is patient with my obsession and handled all the cutouts when the photographs were just not up to par. If I have missed anyone, I truly apologize. It was not intentional; put it down to age.

INTRODUCTION

When she was about 3 or 4 years old, I asked my daughter, "What came first, the chicken or the egg?" She shot back, "The rooster." I thought that was a pretty sharp response. When I sat down to work on this book, I remembered that moment and equated that the chicken was the car, the egg was the speed equipment, and the rooster was the racer.

It has been written many times that the minute the second automobile was produced, the race was on, and that may well be true. Humans seem to have an innate inclination to race, and good ole Henry Ford gave every man and woman the means to go racing with the Model T. Not only did the T revolutionize the automobile industry but it also initiated an aftermarket industry that supplied every widget imaginable to make your T more versatile, look snappier, and go faster.

I first became aware of this phenomenon in the early 1960s while delivering *Hot Rod* magazine on my paper route as a kid in England. It didn't seem possible back then to be involved in any way, until I bought an old rigid-frame Triumph motorcycle that I customized. That got me and my friend Robin Ditcher in the door. We opened Rat Motors, making and selling chopper parts. Ditcher ran the business, and I did the marketing, but after a year or so we took down our shingle.

The next effort was another motorcycle business with Guy Carter called Big Bike in South London. We dealt mainly with Kawasaki fours, and importing a lot of American speed equipment taught me more about the business.

In 1988, at the behest of my friend and mentor Pete Chapouris, I moved to California and went to work at the Specialty Equipment Market Association (SEMA). He said, "Come down, have lunch, and start networking." I had no idea what networking meant, but nine years with SEMA taught me. I met George Bush, Billy F Gibbons of ZZ Top, and everybody in between. I learned what networking meant and how the industry worked from the inside. I also learned how it was changing as the traditional jobber went away and the industry shifted from a three-step system to a two-step system and is now heading almost toward a one-step system, where manufacturers sell direct to the consumer.

At one time, a customer ordered a catalog, went to the nearest speed shop, and purchased the parts they needed. If they were not in stock, the customer ordered them and waited. Today, a customer orders them, and quite often, they are shipped overnight with free shipping. It's a different world to what it was 10 years ago—let alone 50 or more years ago—and it's perhaps that instant gratification that has enabled the industry to grow into a $46.2 billion industry in 2019, according to SEMA.

It's sad that free, overnight delivery has rendered the traditional speed shop almost obsolete. We have lost that place to hang out, meet like-minded enthusiasts, and hopefully get good information. It's impossible to halt that progress. Those days are gone, but I hope this book reminds us all of those halcyon days and the companies that built the industry.

CHAPTER 1

1908-1932
MODEL Ts, MODEL As, AND CHEVROLETS

It's generally believed that Henry Ford abhorred racing, but that's not exactly true. Ford understood the "Win on Sunday, sell on Monday" philosophy all too well, but he didn't appear to like to lose.

It Was All Henry Ford's Fault

Henry Ford's very first race came on October 10, 1901. He raced *Sweepstakes,* a 26-hp contraption, in a 10-lap sprint around a 1-mile dirt oval at Grosse Pointe, Michigan. The race was sponsored by the Detroit Driving Club, and Ford trounced the American racing champion, Alexander Winton, who was driving his own Winton *Bullet.* Ford won $1,000, which was enough money to start the Henry Ford Co.

The following year, Ford embarked upon two more race cars: the red *Arrow* and the yellow *999.* They had huge 1,156-ci 70- to 100-hp 4-cylinder engines, a truck-like frame, spindly wire wheels, and a single seat. There was no body, rear suspension, or differential. In typical fashion, Ford, who had sold interests to bicycle champion Barney Oldfield and Tom Cooper, walked away from the project when the cars failed to start at a test session two weeks before the race.

The rematch with Winton came on October 25, 1902, again at Grosse Pointe. There were four other cars in the race, but Oldfield, who had never driven a car before testing, won the 5-mile Manufacturers' Challenge Cup in the record time of 5 minutes and 28 seconds. Ford's deal with Cooper and Oldfield allowed him to take credit but not share the purse.

Ford got behind the tiller once again on January 12, 1904, when he drove the *Arrow* (previously named the *999*) on frozen Lake St. Claire just northeast of Detroit. With Ford on the stick and Edward "Spider" Huff working the throttle, they hit 91.37 mph over the measured mile. It was a record.

Meanwhile, Ford was busy with the Ford Motor Co., which had been incorporated on June 16, 1903. The first production car, a 2-cylinder Model A, was completed at the Mack Avenue plant on July 23. By the summer of 1904, Frank Kulick was Ford's new driver, winning races in a flat four made of two Model As bolted together. It only had 20 bhp, but they

Henry Ford's very first race was a 10-lap sprint on a dirt oval at Grosse Pointe, Michigan, sponsored by the Detroit Driving Club. Driving his 26-hp #4 Sweepstakes, he beat Alexander Winton in his 70-hp Bullet to win $1,000. (Photo Courtesy Ford Motor Co.)

Henry Ford is behind the wheel of Sweepstakes in 1901 with ride-on mechanic Edward "Spider" Huff on the running board. Sweepstakes was powered by a fuel-injected twin cylinder that recorded a speed of 72 mph, beating the existing world record speed of 65.79. (Photo Courtesy Ford Motor Co.)

eventually cut the weight to 881 pounds, so it enjoyed a great power-to-weight ratio, which was an attribute of most early Fords.

In June 1907, Kulick and Bert Lorimer raced a production version of Ford's new 6-cylinder Model K on a 1-mile oval at the Detroit Fairgrounds in a 24-hour race for stock cars. They covered 1,135 miles and won the event, but they used two different cars, something apparently allowed by the rules. Unfortunately, that October, Kulick crashed the *666*, a race version of the Model K, and broke his leg in several places. Ford had the race car scrapped, and he declared a ban on building race cars that lasted until 1910.

In 1908, Ford was busy cranking out Model Ts. Meanwhile, Kulick raced and won in stripped-down, tuned-up versions. He even thrashed Bob Burnham in the great *Blitzen Benz* in a 1-mile oval sprint at the Detroit Fairgrounds on September 11, 1911.

The following year, Kulick licked his highly modified Model T across frozen Lake St. Claire and reached 107.8 mph. Reaching 107 mph was quite amazing since the car was nothing more than a stripped-down T with an engine, a pair of seats, and wooden wheels. Safety equipment was comprised of goggles and a necktie.

The Model T, nicknamed Tin Lizzie or Lizzie, had an advantageous power-to-weight ratio that was proving to be the winning formula. Ford had unwittingly (or perhaps even wittingly) given every man the means to go

The 200-hp 1,312-ci German Benz was clocked at 125.95 mph at Brooklands in 1909. It was then shipped to the United States, where the renamed Lightning Benz went 131.275 in the hands of Barney Oldfield. In 1911, Bob Burnham bumped the renamed Blitzen Benz speed to 141.37.

Henry Ford sits in back of the Arrow on a frozen Lake St. Claire in 1904 while mechanic Edward "Spider" Huff perches on the running board feeding fuel into the carburetor. They managed a staggering 91.37 mph (39.4 seconds for 1 mile). (Photo Courtesy Ford Motor Co.)

racing, and go he did. It was a classic case of "build it and they will come" or, in this case, "build it and they will go."

Kulick's race cars were highly modified, and some contemporary reports said they were factory tuned with setback 4-cylinder engines, Bosch magnetos, and short exhaust stacks. An industry was being born.

In 1913, Ford attempted to enter Kulick and the Model T in the Indy 500. Apparently, officials refused the entry unless Ford added 1,000 pounds to the car. Ford famously opted out, saying, "We're building race cars, not trucks."

An original Miller-Schofield high-speed head was created for the 1928-1934 Ford 4-cylinder. It positioned both the inlet and exhaust valves in the head rather than the block. New billet versions are available. (Photo Courtesy Scotty Gosson)

Harry A. Miller

You can't mention Indianapolis without mentioning Harold Arminius Miller, known as Harry Miller. Born in Menomonie, Wisconsin, in 1875, Miller worked in the auto industry in Michigan and became a mechanic for Ransom E. Olds. He was a riding mechanic for Ernest Keeler in the 1906 Vanderbilt Cup Eliminating Trials, but the car only completed one lap. As a consequence, Miller upped and moved back to Pasadena, California, where he worked at the Pasadena Auto Co. In 1907 or 1908, he opened his own shop that specialized in carburetion.

After a stint at the Master Carburetor Co., Miller filed a patent for his own carburetor design in 1909. He received it that December, just five days after his 34th birthday. His carburetors soon employed a new and original blend of aluminum, nickel, and copper that Miller christened Alloyanum. Prior to that, carburetors had been made out of brass or bronze alloy. Not only was Alloyanum good for carburetors but it was also ideal for casting pistons. Miller's lightweight pistons were soon in great demand for race cars and airplanes.

In 1915, Miller opened the Harry A. Miller Manufacturing Co., at 219 E. Washington Blvd., just a few blocks southeast of downtown Los Angeles, California. According to *The Automobile* issue on August 17, 1916, they were "turning out 50 carburetors a day." Apparently, Miller, with some 50 employees, was making $1 million per year through sales of his carburetors and other components.

There was also a race shop that built and serviced race cars and built their first complete racing engine. *The Automobile* went on to say, ". . . a great many of the racing drivers make headquarters at the Miller plant. There is now a department given over entirely to them where their cars are kept and where they have all the machinery."

Miller was just one brand of carburetor. There was also Kingston, Newcomb, Master, Schebler, Stewart, Stromberg, and Zenith. However, Miller dominated the racing world at that time.

According to the late author Mark Dee's writing in his book *The Miller Dynasty*, sometime in 1922, Col. Harry Hooker commissioned Miller to build a 16-valve dual overhead camshaft (DOHC) head for Hooker's *Hooker Special* Modified.

Leo Goossen designed the head, and apparently Hooker was almost killed his first time out because it was so fast. Hooker turned over driving duties to Fred Frame, who demolished stock Ford cranks every seven laps. The *Hooker* was considered the fastest Model T in the country, although Eddie Meyer, Edward Winfield, and Frank Lockhart were all able to beat it. Nevertheless, the Miller DOHC made an impression.

Ford's introduction of the Model A in 1928 revolutionized the fledgling speed industry. At 40 hp, the Model A had double the horsepower of the Model T and offered the would-be racer a better start. The industry jumped on the Model A, knowing that it was a blank canvas on which to paint speed and could easily be improved upon. Even Harry Miller could see the writing on the wall.

In 1928, Miller, George L. Schofield, and several other backers formed Miller-Schofield to mass produce carburetors, lightweight pistons, and a pushrod-operated OHV cylinder head for the Model A designed by Leo Goossen.

The OHV head alone apparently added some 28 hp to the A. "Adding a 1½-inch Winfield carburetor and boosting the RPM to 3,000 netted 82 to 86 hp. Not bad for a $100 investment," wrote Art Bagnall in his book *Roy Richter Striving for Excellence*.

The following year, Goossen designed a DOHC head for the Model A, but only three were made. It was not so with the OHV head that was made in quantities of 50 per day until Black Tuesday on October 29, 1929, and the start of the Great Depression. By mid-1930, Miller-Schofield was bankrupt. To the rescue came Harlan Fengler, boy wonder of the board tracks, who persuaded plumbing magnate Crane Gartz to buy the patterns.

The new company was called the Cragar Corp., an amalgam of Crane and Gartz, and was located at 940 North

In 1929, owner/builder Chris Ripp campaigned Miss Daytona, a 16-foot step hydroplane powered by a centrifugal supercharged Miller 151-ci DOHC. It was raced by Indy legend Wilbur Shaw in Florida and Cuba. It is currently owned by Bruce Meyer.

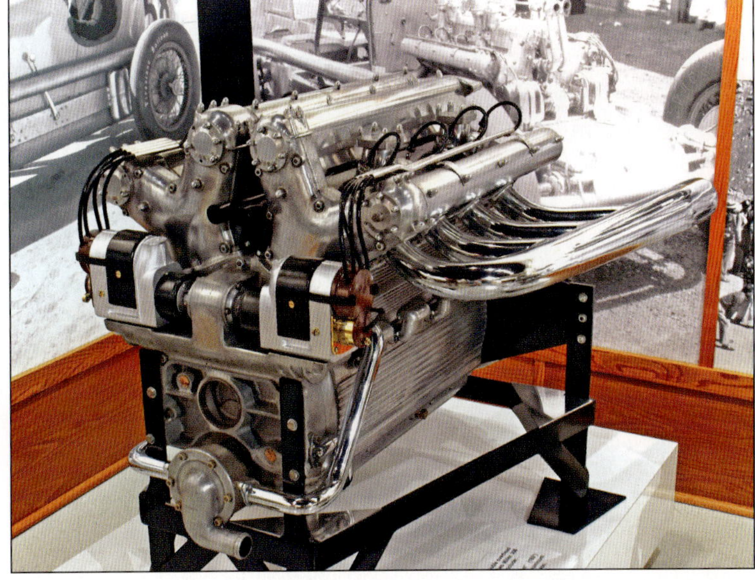

One of only two 1932 Miller 308-ci DOHC V-8s ever built was designed by Harry Miller and Leo Goossen. They were destined for a pair of four-wheel-drive race cars that were unfortunately not particularly successful. (Photo Courtesy Scotty Gosson)

This 272-ci DOHC V-16 was designed in the 1920s by Leo Goossen for Harry Miller. This is the second engine built, and it was raced in 1947 with Shorty Cantlon driving. Unfortunately, Cantlon was killed on lap 40 while trying to avoid an accident. (Photo Courtesy Scotty Gosson)

The rear view of a 4WD Miller DOHC V-16 shows a beautiful crank-driven integral supercharger. The engine is a fantastic piece of design and engineering that was actually four 4-cylinder engines joined at the hip. (Photo Courtesy HarryAMillerinc.com)

A cutaway of a Model A block fitted with a Miller-Schofield rocker arm head was photographed at Speedway's Museum of American Speed. Fitted with a pair of Winfield Model S carburetors, it could produce more than 80 hp. (Photo Courtesy Scotty Gosson)

Orange Dr. in Hollywood, California. Cragar advertised Experimental Engineering and built race cars, engines, and Cragar OHV heads for Ford Model A and B engines.

Vogue Tire

Although not a performance accessory as such, one cannot deny the impact that Vogue Tire and Rubber Co. had on the performance market. The company was founded in 1911 in Chicago, Illinois, by chauffer Harry Hower. Around 1918, Hower approached the wealthy Woodbury family, who invested in his concept for a whitewall design that was initially on both sides of the tire. The winged logo says Hower Vogue Cord.

In 1926, Hower was approached by Loyd O. Dodson of MacDonald-Dodson Tire Co., which began distributing Vogue tires from two stores in Los Angeles, the first of which was located at 1317 S. Hope St. MacDonald-Dodson serviced the affluent Hollywood set that could afford tires—often six per car—and with whom Vogue tires proved popular. Their patronage helped Vogue ride out the Depression.

Edsel Ford had whitewalls on all of his special-built speedsters, and an endorsement of sorts came in 1933 when Ford demonstrated the benefits of its three-point suspension using a Model 40 three-window coupe fitted with Vogue tires. The following year, Vogue tires were

Although they were not strictly a performance accessory, Vogue Tires were in vogue, especially after World War II. That was when Coachcraft Ltd. built the 1941 Mercury-based Carlton Coupe for Peter Stengel. It was fitted with fancy Vogue whitewalls.

offered as an option on the 1934 Ford. Indeed, actress Joan Crawford sported a set on her 1934 roadster that also sported chrome-plated wheels.

Loyd Dodson purchased Vogue Tire in 1942 for $50,000 and remained its chairman until his death in 1996.

JC Whitney and Eastern Auto

There's an old saying, "Where there's muck there's brass," meaning that there's money in scrap. In 1915, after fleeing religious persecution, Lithuanian immigrant Israel Warshawsky proved it was true by opening a wrecking yard at 1915–1935 S. State St. on Chicago's south side. It was the city's first large-scale salvage yard.

Warshawsky & Co. began by selling the salvage take-offs, but during the Depression it graduated to buying and selling new old stock (NOS) parts from the many bankrupt auto business and parts stores. These new parts were sold through a new retail store and a mail-order catalog. Model A cylinder heads were just $3.15.

In 1934, after graduating from the University of Chicago, Israel's son Roy joined the company. He soon talked his dad into expanding the business by making their own accessories and parts. Roy also persuaded his

dad to change the slightly tongue-twisting Warshawsky to something more manageable, and so it became JC Whitney.

Obviously, like all mail-order catalogs, JC Whitney had to cater to the common denominator, but even in 1972, when the aftermarket was in a state of transition, JC carried an impressive array of real speed equipment.

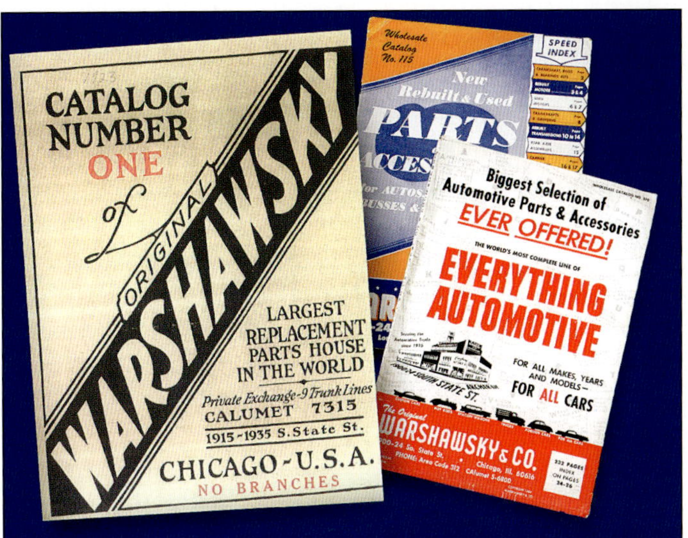

Originally founded in 1915 by Israel Warshawsky as a wrecking yard, Warshawsky & Co. gradually morphed into JC Whitney when Israel's son Roy took over. By 1972, its catalog contained almost 200 pages and more than 100,000 parts and accessories.

Around 1942, JC Whitney purchased its first advertisement for $60 in *Popular Mechanics*. The company asked readers to send 25 cents for a "giant auto parts catalog," enabling the company to sell nationwide and become a household name akin to JCPenney.

Founder Israel died in 1943, but under Roy's leadership the company continued to grow along with the post–World War II America boom in all things automotive. The mail-order catalog soon boasted more than 100 pages, listing everything from acorn nut covers to cylinder heads. Indeed, Jim Donnelly writing for *Hemmings* said that Andy Granatelli, founder of Grancor Speed Equipment with brothers Joe and Vince, credited Warshawsky with the growth of Grancor. By 1947, the retail store occupied an entire city block.

Over on the West Coast, Eastern Auto was founded by Joseph Kraus in 1919. Kraus began to develop parts for Model T Fords and did particularly well during the Depression when folks couldn't afford a new car but needed to keep rollin'. During the mid- to late-1930s, as the effects of the Depression abated, business improved and demand for individuality increased.

Meanwhile, Joe's son Alex graduated from UCLA in 1939 and joined the company. Like Roy Warshawsky in Chicago, Eastern Auto embarked upon a program of aggressive expansion.

Located at 3319 S. Grand Ave. in Los Angeles, Eastern Auto started to produce specialized customizing products that it advertised heavily. Different styles of ripple disk hubcaps, inspired by the Cadillac knock-off hubcaps, were also among the first items they developed especially for the custom car enthusiast. Trim pieces to decorate the fenders and running boards, special grille moldings, solid hood sides for the Model T to 1936 Fords, fender skirts, and later more and more hop-up parts were developed and marketed, specifically aimed toward customization.

Cal Custom

Kraus had many customers who wanted neat add-on parts. At first, he sold simple bolt-on stuff, such as voltage regulator covers, suicide knobs, curb feelers, etc., but then he decided to start producing custom body panels. At that time, body shops, let alone custom body shops, were few and far between, and few people had the money to pay for custom work when they found a shop. Kraus started with solid hood sides for 1932–1936 Fords, then added smooth trunk lids, smooth hood ornaments (later called a bullnose), as well as long shackles and lowering blocks.

Many people wanted to brighten up the appearance of their cars that had little chrome due to the war

Joseph Kraus founded Eastern Auto in 1919 and began making parts for the Model T. After World War II, Kraus's son Alex joined the company, and it began to produce customizing products that were advertised heavily in magazines, such as Hot Rod.

effort. One of the best sellers was a chrome dash panel for 1942–1948 Fords. In 1949, Eastern Auto celebrated its 30th anniversary and decided to put out a catalog loaded with aftermarket parts (shaved door handle kits, hubcaps, skirts, etc.) as well as a large selection of speed equipment to trick out in-lines and flatheads.

The introduction of the first new bodies since before World War II helped business pick up as well. In late 1957, business was going so well that Eastern Auto began to advertise heavily in magazines. This was due to a decision to drop the retail operation and concentrate on product development under a new name: California Custom Accessories Manufacturing Company.

By the end of the 1950s, Cal Custom's line included many parts that are now classics, such as aftermarket Caddy bullets, dummy spots, Kandy Apple spray bombs, wheel spiders, and Baby Moons. It was always on the lookout for new stuff, and it even bought the rights to teardrop dash knobs from Bob Hirohata, and possibly some rights to parts designed and produced by George Barris. It was a great time for cool aftermarket parts.

Cal Custom's manufacturing operation was always on a small scale, usually farming out its designed products to local shops for production. This helped keep production costs down and left more money for the development of new products.

In 1969, Cal Custom, Hollywood Accessories, Matco Products, and Hanson Instruments merged to become a new corporation named Orion Industries. Three years later, the Cal Custom and Hansen Hawk divisions were consolidated. Before the end of 1972, Cal Custom/Hawk had also absorbed the high-performance line of Segal Automotive Products. Then, around the early 1980s, Mr. Gasket bought it and started putting the Mr. Gasket name on all its products.

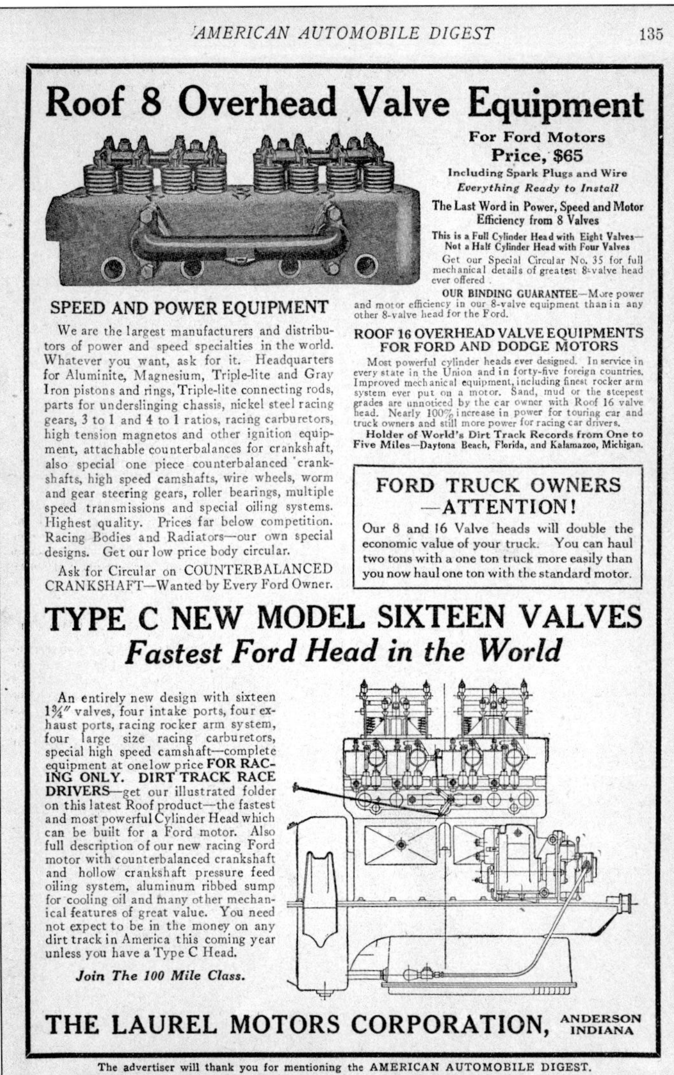

Robert M. Roof merged with the Laurel Motors Corp. and in 1923 ran this advertisement in American Automobile Digest *for 8- and 16-valve cylinder racing-only heads for both Ford and Dodge.*

Robert M. Roof

Of course, the epicenter of the automobile industry was Detroit and its environs. It stood to reason that an accessory industry would blossom in the Midwest where there were a lot of small manufacturers and suppliers, some already supplying the fledgling auto industry. Robert M. Roof was one such engineer, and in 1916, he figured that there was a market for a high-performance cylinder head for the Model T.

As it transpired, Roof somewhat confusingly, decided to call his Model T head the "Model A." His design, based on the European hemi-head Peugeot and advertised as such, bolted directly to the Model T block and employed the stock cam to operate 16 valves.

Advertised in the *Fordowner* magazine, the head was a hit with Model T racers, of which Roof was one. It was so popular that in 1917 the Roof Auto Specialty Co. introduced its similarly engineered Model B head for road cars and trucks.

By now, Roof had merged with Laurel Motors, which not only developed the line of polished nickel cylinder heads but also other speed equipment, including Aluminite and Lynite pistons and rings, parts for under slinging (lowering) chassis, 3:1 ratio nickel-steel gears, racing carburetors and ignitions, crank counterbalances, and high-speed cams.

Laurel also offered complete Model T–based racing cars to "lovers of fast cars." The stylish speedsters were of their own design but were just one of numerous speedsters or speedster bodies offered by a booming aftermarket industry.

As Henry Ford and his production engineer Charlie Sorenson got into their stride and began cranking out those Model Ts at the rate of some 750,000 a year, the aftermarket boomed. Everyone, including Roof-Laurel, benefitted from the sheer volume of Model Ts. Roof introduced more products, including a cross-drilled five-bearing crank, hot cams, and in 1925 a line of superchargers.

By that time, Roof-Laurel was exporting to 50 countries around the world. However, in 1924, Roof joined with Myron Reynolds to form R & R Manufacturing. The company designed speed equipment for Ford, Chevrolet, and other marques. For the Chevy 4, it made the Giant Super Power Head and obviously did not hold back on the marketing hyperbole.

Times were changing though, and Ford reluctantly discontinued his beloved Model T and replaced it with the Model A in 1928 and the Model B in 1932 alongside the new monobloc V-8. Reynolds left the partnership in 1929, and Roof continued alone, producing the

The 1928 Roof 101 Cyclone 4-port valve-in-head features overhead intake valves and in-block exhaust valves for the 1928–1934 Ford Model A and B. They are still in limited production.

Cyclone F head and the SOHC RCO Flash heads in 1931 for the Model A and Model B. In testing, Roof's own Cyclone-equipped 1929 roadster hit 100 mph.

Born in 1882, Roof was already middle aged by the time his inventions and his nine patents became popular. Eventually, he retreated to his home garage, where he cast and machined his parts. Roof died in 1949, but R & R was sold to Ray Duckworth, a one-time Roof apprentice, who continued to manufacture Roof speed equipment for some years.

"Rajo" Joe Jaegersberger

An unfortunate truism of the aftermarket is that once someone has done the hard work of inventing, designing, engineering, manufacturing, and paying for a part, no matter how significant or even insignificant, it's very simple for someone else to come along and copy that part, investing the bare minimum. Sadly, it happens regularly, and it happened to Robert Roof.

Of course, there were several outfits that thought nothing of copying Roof's design and did so, as did J.R. Craig and W.L. Hunt of Indianapolis. While Craig-Hunt concentrated on the racing world, another entrepreneur, Joe Jaegersberger of Racine, Wisconsin, developed a head very

similar to Roof's. Introduced in 1919, the "Rajo" Model 30 valve-in-head was nigh on identical to Roof's that in itself was stated as being derived from a Peugeot design. The Rajo Model 30 bolted atop the Model T block and used the stock cam to operate eight overhead valves.

Cheap and cheerful, the catchily named Rajo was aimed squarely at road cars and was distributed initially by the Trindl Sales Corp. of Chicago. However, Rajo soon took on the sales task using a dealer network.

While Rajo was not specifically designed for racing purposes, anything that improved the Model T was bound to find its way onto the track. They made marketing hay when privateer Noel Bullock won the 1922 Pikes Peak Hill Climb in his Rajo-equipped Model T speedster.

The 23-year-old Bullock assembled *Old Liz* in a blacksmith's shop in Madrid, Nebraska. He raced and developed his car for six years, but it was rough. The press variously described it as a contraption, a low-caste tin can, an unpainted hoodless burlesque of an automobile, and unpainted bug, and a home-brewed flivver, which it was. It was also fast, sporting an 8-valve crossflow rocker arm head, and it is known that Bullock installed the latest Rajo racing head just a few weeks before Pikes Peak. A new carburetor was also on order, but it didn't arrive in time. The bottom end and the oiling system was all stock Model T, but the cam was apparently Bullock's own grind.

Lacking funds to ship the car, Bullock drove the 300 miles from his home to Colorado Springs, Colorado, where

Accomplished motorcycle and cross-country auto racer Erwin "Cannonball" Baker, inspiration for the legendary Cannonball Run, *is behind the wheel of a Model T-based Rajo-equipped racer at Ascot in the late 1920s. (Photo Courtesy Old Crow Speed Shop)*

Noel Bullock won the 1922 Pikes Peak International Hill Climb is his Rajo-equipped home brewed flivver. The organizers disqualified him but later reinstated his victory. (Photo Courtesy Old Crow Speed Shop)

In 1919, "Rajo" Joe Jaegersberger made this aluminum OHV conversion for the Model T Ford. It was likely based on the Roof conversion. This is the Model 30 with four exhaust ports and one intake all on the right side.

he slept under his car. Bullock's 975-pound, low-slung flivver was met with derision. No one expected him to make it up the 12-mile hill and told him so in no uncertain terms. But make it he did, and he won in a very respectable 19.5 minutes.

Bullock eventually moved to California, where Ted Horn raced *Old Liz* adorned with various logos including Dow Metal Pistons and Simms Motor Oil. Meanwhile, in 1923, the Pikes Peak organizers initiated a minimum weight rule after newspapers ran headlines such as "Nebraska Kid Mechanic Built Flivver out of Junk – Won Pikes Peak." Bullock's win was retroactively disqualified. However, it was later reinstated.

Rajo continued in the business of speed, and as late as 1952, advertised a "Sensational High Compression Compound Induction Head for Chevrolets." Basically, it was a secondary induction—carburetor and intake—independent of the primary factory induction. It came in at 40 mph and gave an additional charge. I'm not sure it took off, as I have never seen one.

Ed Winfield

Businessmen often complain about hiring employees and training them only to have them leave and start up in competition. Well, it happened to Harry Miller with Edward A. Winfield. Born in 1901, Winfield was a natural engineer, who by age 13 had built his own hot rod Model T.

According to Ed Almquist in his book *Hot Rod Handbook #129* circa 1951, "Ed was quite friendly with Sam and Harland Durand, and one day they got curious about the Durand family's new 1910 Model T. After stripping it down to the bare chassis and engine, 11-year-old Ed drove it out onto the street where he hit 60 mph, which was quite fast for 1912. Apparently, the family used the stripped-down T, with Pa hanging onto the wheel and Nellie, his wife, hanging onto his shirt tails. Everybody sat on the gas tank because there was nowhere else to sit."

Two years later, Winfield built his first hot rod, tuning the engine,

Once in California, Noel Bullock's *Old Liz* was raced by Ted Horn. It provided a rolling billboard for companies such as Dow Metal Pistons and Simms Motor Oil. (Photo Courtesy Old Crow Speed Shop)

It is circa 1914, and 13-year-old Ed Winfield is behind the wheel of his first Model T-based hot rod. It was apparently good for 80 mph. The following year, he went to work for Harry Miller. (Photo Courtesy Old Crow Speed Shop)

Ed Winfield is behind the wheel of his infamous #1 "Two up and two down" race car at Los Angeles's Ascot Speedway on February 6, 1927. Winfield is generally regarded as the father of hot rodding. (Photo Courtesy Old Crow Speed Shop)

improving the ignition, and working over the valves. He apparently hit 80 mph. The following year, at age 14, Winfield went to work for Miller, where he learned to calibrate carburetors, earning $0.60 per hour.

Pretty soon, Winfield was building complete engines. By 1920, he quit Miller and, according to court documents (law.justia.com), formed a partnership with Sam Durant in a machine shop and automobile repair business in Glendale under the name Winfield and Durant. They also did business as Winfield Inventions Ltd., and the Winfield Carburetor was developed soon after the formation of that partnership. It has been known by that name ever since. The partnership was discontinued about 1923, and Winfield went into business in La Cañada, under the name "Edward A. Winfield."

At this time, there was a company in Glendale by the name of Winfield Carburetor Company owned by one Morrow who was licensed by the plaintiff to manufacture the Winfield carburetor on a royalty basis. In 1937 or 1938, the plaintiff moved to his present place of business, which he owns. In 1939, the plaintiff acquired all the interest in the Winfield Carburetor Company and, thereafter, caused a sign to be painted on the front of his building and one on the side, each of which read: "WINFIELD Carburetor & Manufacturing Co."

On June 26, 1926, Winfield filed a patent for a downdraft carburetor. Part of the description said: "The general object of the invention is the provision of a carburetor of such nature that an internal combustion engine equipped therewith may be operated with maximum speed, power." Winfield's patent was granted on August 8, 1933.

Over the years, Winfield received a number of patents and is generally regarded as the "father of hot rod-

ding." While Miller had developed speed equipment and complete engines, his market was primarily big-time racers, whereas Winfield appeared to cater more to the average person racing a Model T with a marketing slogan of "Winners of the Field."

Essentially, Winfield made three basic models of carburetor: the Model H and V series with H being sidedraft and V being updraft (discontinued in 1927), the Model M series that was also updraft, and the Model S (silent) and SR that were both updraft and downdraft. An entire book could be written about all of the various Winfield carburetors, as there were so many variants and special builds for racing.

An updraft Winfield S-R carburetor fed a Latham supercharger attached to a Lincoln V-12 in Bruce Wanta's 1936 Packard Mulholland Speedster built by Troy Ladd's Hollywood Hot Rods.

Later in life, Ed and Paul Frome look on as a mechanic wrenches on Ed's 7:1 rocker arm head on a Model A block. The car was driven by Rex Mays but protested as illegal by the Miller racers. In fact, it was only 183 ci. (Photo Courtesy Old Crow Speed Shop)

In 1919, Winfield's mother gave him enough money to buy a used grinding machine. He set it up in her garage and was able to convert it to grind cams for Model Ts. It could be said that pretty much every aftermarket cam owes its legacy to the grinder of Ed Winfield and his mom.

More or less self-taught with only an eighth-grade education, Winfield was always experimenting and trying the seemingly impossible. For example, in the early 1920s, Winfield built his famous "two-up, two-down" Model T engine.

Unhappy with the way the Model T performed and breathed, delivering unequal charges to the cylinders, Winfield ground his own revolutionary 180-degree billet steel crank and his own camshaft. He also changed the firing order so that each cylinder received an equal charge and increased the compression ratio to 6:1. According to Dean Batchelor in his book *The American Hot Rod,* Winfield said, "It had a little vibration." It was darn fast though.

Winfield may have made his reputation with carburetors, but he was equally good with camshafts. At age 16, he changed the cam duration of his single-cylinder motorcycle. Using hand tools, he also skimmed the head and enlarged the intake, saying, "I could climb any mountain road around here in high gear."

Winfield was an accomplished racer, and his exploits at the new Legion Ascot 5/8-mile speedway in Alhambra and other Southern California tracks gave him the opportunity to promote his products. In 1925, Ralph de Palma switched to a Winfield Model V carburetor on his

Aside from his carburetors, perhaps Ed Winfield's most popular product was this cast-aluminum head for the 1928-1931 Ford four. He also made a Super Winfield head. New versions of this head are still available.

This well-patinated Hodge-headed Model T with twin distributors and twin Winfield downdrafts sat in the window of a garage in Huntington Beach, California, for many years before it was extricated and unfortunately "restored."

Another manufacturer of early racing carburetors besides Winfield and Riley was Walt Flynn, who owned Enterprise Machine in Indianapolis. Flynn carburetors were purported to be improved Rileys.

While Ed Winfield was on his way to winning the 1927 Ascot Match Race, Eddie Meyer was upside down in the #6 Redlands Special. However, John R. Lucero in his book Legion Ascot Speedway *said the driver was Harry Jacquez. (Photo Courtesy Old Crow Speed Shop)*

match-race Miller, and his nephew Pete de Paolo fitted an updraft Winfield to his supercharged Duesenberg and won the Indy 500.

From that point on, Winfield produced the go-to carburetor. His younger brother William "Bud" Winfield worked as a field rep, working the West Coast tracks as well as Indianapolis. Eventually, Bud went out on his own and is most renowned for his involvement in the famous Novi straight–8 engine.

In 1927, Ed Winfield won the Ascot Match Race (it was during this event that Eddie Meyer crashed the *Redlands Special*). He also won the Helmet Dash and the 50-mile Ascot Classic that same year and went on to win the 100-mile classic at Ascot.

Ingenious Ed was equally adept at cam design and grinding, and according to Dees in his *Miller Dynasty* book, "Ed Winfield was the only source who could be depended on to furnish an aftermarket performance camshaft not only with a profile designed on proper engineering principles, but with each lobe ground to match the other." Buyers had to be patient though; Ed was not to be hurried.

William H. Jahns Sr.

In 1912, William H. Jahns Sr. opened a foundry at 2662 Lacy St. in Los Angeles, just northeast of what is now Dodger Stadium. The Jahns

Pistons tagline was "Nothing but Pistons," and it made them for both OEMs and the aftermarket. To kick things off, it made a showing at that year's Indy 500.

In 1947, one of Jahns's sons, William Jr., left the family business and opened Jahns Racing Pistons in Santa Ana, California, specializing in high-performance aftermarket pistons (the other brother was Robert Jeffrey). In 1948, William Sr. retired and leased the Los Angeles factory to a Mr. Brandine.

Meanwhile, in Santa Ana, Jahns was going gangbusters, and Bill's nephew Jeff joined the company. Jeff

Founded by William H. Jahns Sr., Jahns Pistons became an industry leader. This shot shows the factory located at 2662 Lacy St. in Los Angeles. William Sr. retired in 1948, meanwhile, his son started Jahn's Racing Pistons in Santa Ana.

was a racer, first at the lakes and then at the nearby Santa Ana drags. Jeff got his farm license at age 14 and honed his racing skills on old Highway 395 that led directly to El Mirage, 70 miles due north. Jeff raced a 1927 roadster there in 1949. The following year, he raced a 296-powered 1940 coupe that went 91.90 mph.

Then, one day in 1953, Uncle Bill failed to show up for work and never came back. That chapter in the Jahns's story closed. However, in 1955, Uncle Bill resurfaced at 825 S. Date Ave. in Alhambra, California, and opened a new shop called JE Engineering Corp., which we know today as JE Pistons.

Sales of performance pistons must have been brisk, as the company appeared to do only minimal advertising. The only mention I found was a listing in a So-Cal Speed Shop advertisement in *Hot Rod* from August 1948. So-Cal also gave JE Custommade Racing Pistons a full-page listing in its catalog. Other than that, Jahns flew under the radar until 1970, when it advertised its involvement with Jack Lufkin's Bonneville Modified sports car. It also advertised its involvement with "TV" Tommy Ivo in the 1970s and, of course, "Big Daddy" Don Garlits. JE Pistons, albeit with different owners, may be one of the oldest, more or less continuous brands in the performance aftermarket.

George Riley

Born in 1895, in Seattle, Washington, George Riley was an adventurer, sailor, soldier, miner, and inventor. His first patent was awarded in 1918 for an expanding mandrel for lathe work. That was followed in 1919 after a move to Los Angeles with a patent for the Riley Multi-Lifts. It was his first automotive product, and it was a doozy.

Actually, it was for a Lizzie, as Riley correctly surmised that the Model T needed more steam. According to the patent filing, the Multi-Lift was a valve-operating mechanism for internal combustion engines. The device was bolted to the side of the Model T block and the accelerating mechanism extended into the tappet chamber. A combination of lifters effectively doubled the valve lift and therefore increased performance.

Riley began advertising his Multi-Lift for $35 in the November 1920 issue of *Ford Owner and Dealer*. At its peak in the late 1910s, *Ford Owner and Dealer* contained more than 200 pages of Model T accessories and such. Incidentally, by 1923, there were an estimated 15 million cars and trucks in the world and half of them were Model Ts. The market was vast.

Riley was advertising his Multi-Lift contraption for $35 and established a dealer network with Hammel-Gerke Co. in Los Angeles, handling the distribution alongside Winfield Carburetors from $20 each.

The October 1924 issue of Ford Owner and Dealer *carried this ad from Hammel-Gerke Co. advertising George Riley's Multi-Lifts that increased valve lift. They also carried Winfield carburetors.*

In the late 1920s, George Riley put driver Walt May behind the wheel of the Model T-based Multi-Ford racer to promote his products. Sadly, May died in 1931. (Photo Courtesy Old Crow Speed Shop)

Lifelong hot rodder Jim "Jake" Jacobs works on the exhaust systems of his Model A roadster powered by a Riley two-port-headed banger. Note the split valve covers and the Riley water neck.

In one of his letters, Riley suggested that the Multi-Lift increased performance, "providing the ignition and compression was in first class working condition." He went on to suggest "that for maximum power mileage, and freedom from vibration, we recommend a 1-inch or better yet 1¼-inch carburetor, and one of the following ignition systems, or their equal, Bosch battery, Atwater Kent, Mallory or Uni Coil." Of course, a proper tune-up will make any engine run better, Multi-Lift or not.

Another Riley Racing four-port conversion dated 1949 complete with 2-inch Riley carburetors on a Riley log intake is powering Max Herman Jr.'s Model T racer.

In 1960, this 220-ci four-port Riley-equipped Model B-powered dragster set the X-Dragster record at 107.65 mph at the Detroit Nationals. It's owned by Gary Kind and Sandra Gardner.

To promote his invention, Riley fielded the *Multi-Ford* T-based race car driven by Walt May. Sadly, May died in 1931 at San Jose, but prior to that he was one of the "Ascot Dirt Thrillers" and also known as one of the "Three Musketeers of the Speedway" with Jimmy Sharp and W. Hartwell "Stubby" Stubblefield.

Seeing the success of Winfield's carburetors, Riley made his own. One aspect of Riley's carburetor business often overlooked is that of motorcycles. It seemed, for a while at least, that every drag bike and hill climber was fitted with not one but two Riley carburetors. What made them ideal for motorcyclists, especially hill climbers,

Chet Herbert's The Beast *Harley drag bike featured Riley carburetors with the unattached spherical brass floats that made them insensitive to angles and thus perfect for hill climbers.*

In 1947, Bob Rufi, famous for his streamliner, was running this Riley four-port Ford in a belly tank. It got some attention, and on October 19, he ran 131 mph. (Photo Courtesy Old Crow Speed Shop)

Their catchy name was in the vernacular of speed.

Founded in 1914, the company was named after the 17th-century governor of France's North American colonies, Louis de Buade de Frontenac. In the early days, there were three versions of the Fronty head: R for race cars, S for speedsters, and T for trucks and touring cars. The cross-flow design featured a single intake port with three exhaust ports.

Apparently, a Fronty Model T head increased horsepower from the Model T's stock 20 hp to an impressive 33. However, that was inadequate for racers, and the remaining Chevrolets (Arthur and Louis; Gaston had been killed not long after the 1920 Indy 500) had Van Ranst redesign the R head with two intakes rather than one. Called the S-R, the head was tested in the 1923 Indy 500. With an average speed of 85 mph, the Fronty Ford finished a credible fifth behind four Miller 122s.

For the 1924 Indy, Frontenac likewise developed a DOHC, 16-valve head called the Model D-O that outperformed the 1923 S-R with an average speed of 88 mph for the final 300 miles of the Brickyard. Three Barber-Warnock Frontys were entered, but their best placing was Bill Hunt in 14th followed by A.E. Moss in 16th and Fred Harder in 17th.

Incidentally, Henry Ford was the referee. Each driver won just less than $1,000, and the adage "Win on Sunday, sell on Monday" was never so appropriate. It is reported that the brothers went on to sell around 10,000 cylinder

were their spherical floats that were not attached inside the carburetor. They just floated, making them insensitive to angles.

Made from heat-treated 356 aluminum, Riley carburetors were fitted with Ford Stromberg main jets and idle tubes and Chandler Groves needle seats and adjusting screws.

The Chevrolet Brothers and "Fronty" Frontenac

Auto racing brothers Arthur, Gaston, and Louis Chevrolet recognized the potential market for speed parts and retained C.W. Van Ranst to design an overhead valve conversion for the Ford four. The "Fronty," as it was called, wasn't the first OHV conversion for Lizzie, and it wasn't the best performing. However, Gaston won the Indy 500 in the Frontenac in 1920, and a Frontenac won again in 1921 with Tommy Milton driving.

This small advertisement for the Frontenac Cylinder R Head designed and built by Arthur and Louis Chevrolet appeared after the 1922 Indy 500. It was redesigned and called the S-R for the 1923 race.

The Fronty was designed to improve the Model T, and this one with a Hudson carburetor and Bosch magneto powers a race car hauler built by Lloyd Fisher in 1930 from a 1919 Model T. (Photo Courtesy Scotty Gosson)

Lloyd Fisher's race car was powered by a Model T engine fitted with a rare Frontenac DOHC racing head. It was also fitted with twin Winfield Model O downdraft carburetors mounted outside the body because there was no room under the hood. (Photo Courtesy Scotty Gosson)

The Frontenac was a crossflow design with the single inlet port on the left-hand side. It is shown here with a single downdraft carburetor.

heads, including those for Model As, Chevrolet fours and sixes, and Whippets.

Smithy's, Porter, and the Muffler Boom

Founded in 1920 by Harold Duane Smith, Smithy's mufflers were said to offer less backpressure, extra mileage, and extra power. In 1936, Smithy's was located at 210 E. 16th St. at the corner of South Los Angeles St. just south of downtown, but very little is known or has been written about the company. It does appear that Smithy's provided the gene pool for all the muffler shops that followed. Indeed, Archie Porter started there as a welder circa 1931 before building his own muffler empire with his brothers.

The first Porter Mufflers shop appears in the 1941 Los Angeles City Directory at 5401 Sunset Blvd. That said, both Smithy's and Porter Mufflers appear to have had several locations during the ensuing years, adding to the confusion.

In 1941, Porter Mufflers ran a small advertisement in *Throttle* selling blow-out proof, leak-proof steel-packed mufflers and straight pipes for lakes racing. In fact, the Porter Mufflers logo was emblazoned on a brace of Deuce roadsters that raced the lakes in 1940 and 1941. Porter Mufflers ran an ad on the back cover of the Southern California Timing Association (SCTA) Racing Program of June 15, 1941, when the address was listed as 5109 Sunset—possibly another location. Besides Porter Mufflers, Sandy's Muffler Shop, Edelbrock, Cannon, Fritz, and Bell Auto Parts all advertised on the back covers of the *SCTA Racing News* programs with artwork by Eldon Snapp.

By the late 1940s, Smithy's "Home of V-8 Duals" offered custom-built mufflers and deep tone duals for Ford V-8 and Mercury. Its advertisement in the 1949 Hot Rod Show program depicts a range of round can mufflers for all cars and even duals for Ford and Mercury. Apparently, the cans were initially filled with steel chips that were later replaced with stainless steel wool.

When *Hot Rod* magazine came along in January 1948, there were muffler ads from Douglass, Elmer's, and Smithy's. By year's end, they had been joined by Ralph's and Clarke Exhaust—there was obviously money in cans.

In 1951, a fire devastated one of the Smithy's locations, probably a manufacturing facility, at 1716 Naud St., East Los Angeles, causing an estimated $100,000 worth of damage. In the November 1951 permit to repair the damage, the owner was listed as A.G. Smith (possibly

Founded in 1920 by Harold Duane Smith, Smithy's had several locations. This ad from the Second Hot Rod Show program shows its manufacturing facility located at 1716–20 Naud St. in Los Angeles.

Harold's wife, Adelaide). Then, in the 1956 city directory, Smithy's was located at 214 E. 16th St. while Porter Mufflers now occupied the old address of 210 E. 16th St.

Curiouser and curiouser, and making matters more complicated is a newspaper report from 1957 that says Leroy Enterprises Inc. took over the facilities of Smithy's Manufacturing Corp. and Smithy's Muffler Co. It appears they moved to 6891 Suva St., Bell Gardens, and apparently went bankrupt in 1969 when Wershow Real Estate Auctions sold everything, including the building.

Smithy's disappeared for a time but was resurrected by three-time America's Most Beautiful Roadster winner Ermie Immerso, who in turn sold the brand to PerTronix around 2000. There's no doubt that the name Smithy's was eventually corrupted into the more common Smitty's.

Typical of the times, the street legal Smithy's rod featured a Model A roadster body mated to a Deuce grille shell. Note the hefty belly pan that might have aided streamlining. (Photo Courtesy Belond Family)

Porter Mufflers fielded not one but two Deuce roadsters at the dry lakes during the 1940–1941 seasons. It looks like they drove to the lakes (as did most), pulled the headlights, and raced. (Photo Courtesy Belond Family)

The back cover of the mimeographed SCTA Racing News program from June 15, 1941, carried ads from Edelbrock, Porter Mufflers, Ted Canon, Fritz, Sandy's, and Bell Auto Parts. (Art by Eldon Snapp)

Originally, Sandy Belond's muffler shop was in back of Karl Orr's Speed Shop in Culver City, but by 1941, he had moved to this neat shop at 5701 South Western in Los Angeles.

Meanwhile, Sandy Belond, a member of the Road Rebels in 1939 with a Deuce roadster that ran 94 mph in 1941, also learned the muffler business from Archie Porter. Belond was initially in business in 1938 at South Figueroa St. and West 41st St. in Los Angeles, before moving at the end of 1940 to 5701 S. Western in Los Angeles.

In 1938, Belond offered "Steel Wool Mufflers for Model A and V-8 Fords. Complete with pipe [for] $4." Later, at the new location, he offered everything from Edelbrock manifolds to complete dual exhaust systems and race car headers. Sandy ran a quarter-page every month in *Throttle* magazine until it ceased publication.

George Wight and Bell Auto Parts

In the spring of 1923, George Wight opened Bell Auto Parts, a wrecking yard at 3633 E. Gage Ave., in the city of Bell about 10 miles south of Los Angeles. A racing fan, Wight pulled the specialty parts from the wrecked cars and developed a thriving business. It was thriving enough to build a small brick building to house the parts and a machine shop. Wight became an active supporter of lakes racing.

Bell Auto had a few good years until Black Tuesday, October 29, 1929, and the Wall Street crash. The Great Depression took a terrible toll, and in 1932 Cragar went out of business. When George Wight heard the news, he reached out to Crane Gartz and made an offer Gartz couldn't refuse. Wight had faith in the future of amateur racing, and by early 1933, he owned Cragar. Wight and his successor at Bell, Roy Richter, developed it into one of the great aftermarket brands.

Here are the two Porter Mufflers cars in line at El Mirage. The #348 car was possibly driven by Gus Rollins, who turned 104.16 mph. The #31 roadster in the foreground belonged to Randy Shinn.

Forty-six-year-old George Wight opened a wrecking yard in Bell, a suburb of Los Angeles, in 1923. It went on to become one of the very first speed shops when he began selling the take-offs. George eventually took over the Cragar brand.

According to Art Bagnall, "Some people looked at George (Wight) as just a 'backyard' mechanic, but the truth was, he was a 'sharp old cookie.'" Indeed, Wight redesigned the original Cragar head that had both intake and exhaust ports on the same side to a crossflow design. He was then able to raise the compression ratio from 5.75:1 to 8:1, which greatly improved performance.

The 1928 introduction of the Model A, with twice the horsepower of the Model T, relegated the Model T for the most part to the trailer. In 1932, Ford put a nail in the coffin of the Model A with the introduction of the 4-cylinder Model B and to a lesser extent, at least initially, the flathead V-8.

The Model B was nothing more than an "improved" Model A, which is what they called it in England. It had the same 200.5-ci capacity as the Model A, but it was 26 pounds lighter and more powerful, pumping out 50 hp at 2,000 rpm. It had larger bearings, balanced internals, a new higher-lift cam, forced lubrication, a redesigned cylinder head, and 4.6:1 compression compared to the Model A's 4.2:1. Machined intake ports were matched to a larger manifold and a bigger, improved Zenith carburetor was now fed by a fuel pump rather than gravity. Ford engineers believed they had "the perfect four." There was no doubt, the Model B was better than the Model A, and canny racers made the most of it.

By this time, there was a plethora of speed equipment available, albeit primarily for Ford engines. Some of the lesser-known brand names included Acme; Alexander; Coisson; Dreyer of Indianapolis; John Gerber of Iowa (Chevy); Pop Evans; Fargo; Howell; a SOHC Model A head built by Harry Hoffsterman in Ohio; Ray McDowell of

This receipt from Bell Auto Parts dated July 27, 1936, appears to be made out to actor Clark Gable for a complete Cragar head, four valve springs, and two valves. The total was $107.32, including tax.

Hollywood then Burbank; the Morales brothers that was later produced by Joe Gemsa; Hal of Ohio; Morton-Brett; Ray Day out of Seattle, Washington; Roose Bros. of Baltimore, Maryland; Rucker out of San Francisco; Slim Rutherford; the Simons Super Power Head; Art Sparks, who made both OHC and rocker-arm versions, etc.

Scintilla and Bendix

Scintilla was founded in Zuchwil, Switzerland, in 1917. Its magneto ignition system, known simply as the Magneto, was eventually used in Charles Lindbergh's *Spirit of St. Louis* that flew across the Atlantic in 1927. The magneto was deemed reliable.

Meanwhile, Laurence R. Wilder, a Chicago promoter, obtained the American agency and brought Scintilla to

Chicagoan Laurence Wilder obtained the American agency and brought the Swiss-made Scintilla magneto to the United States in 1921. It took two years before Scintilla received its first order for just six units. (Photo Courtesy Scotty Gosson)

the United States in 1921. It took two years before Scintilla received its first order in 1923 for just six magnetos from Wright Aeronautical.

Fearing that the small company might fall into American hands, Robert Bosch S.A. acquired the majority of shares in Scintilla AG in a hidden acquisition in 1935. A Swiss bank acted as the middleman, but the purchase was not announced until 1954. In 1924, Scintilla opened a combined assembly plant and sales office on 57th St. in

This beautifully illustrated Art Nouveau-style Bosch Magneto ad from the brass-era reflected not only people having fun in their Model T but also interest in the newly explored Middle East and mystical things such as magnetos.

Another magneto used on early Offenhauser and Ford racing engines was this shaft-driven Bendix Scintilla magneto. However, they had to be reworked when used on a Ford that had a different firing order.

Described in a 1914 brochure as the Bosch-Ford High Tension Magneto, this high-performance aftermarket device cost a hefty $48 and was gear driven by the crank. It was a good racing addition, seen here on a HAL-equipped banger.

New York City. However, the Bendix Aviation Corporation purchased Scintilla in 1929, adding this division to their group operations.

As America went to war, military production ramped up, and by January 1942, 17,000 magnetos a month were produced. Over the years, Scintilla was owned by several corporations, including Ronco. In 1993, it was purchased by Taylor Cable Products, which continues to produce this piece of hot rod history.

HAL

The HAL engine company evolved when Harold "Hal" Hosterman, an Akron, Ohio, speed equipment dealer, started manufacturing OHV conversions for the Model T engine in the 1920s. Hosterman's "Akron Hed" design used ball bearings inside curved tubes to replace the traditional OHV pushrods and rocker arms assembly. Williams Foundry in Akron cast the heads.

Hosterman started making the heads around 1926, producing 1,500 to 2,000 of them over several years. Hos-

Another DOHC HAL was installed in Max Herman Jr.'s Model T racer. Note the alky-tuned Stromberg 97s mounted on the side, the shaft-driven water pump, and the Offenhauser mag converted to Ford firing order.

terman once said that he and his friends would hop up their cars with his head designs. Then, they would wait at the foot of a hill in town for owners of big cars to start up the incline. After allowing them a "third of the way" lead, they would take off and pass them as though the other cars were standing still.

Hosterman sold the heads with special exhaust manifolds through various distributors, including the Montgomery-Ward catalog. Twin-cam cylinder heads for Ford Model As and Model Bs followed, and HAL heads started to garner quite a buzz.

Muroc and the Dry Lakes

Around the time that Legion Ascot Speedway opened in 1924, the dry lakebeds to the north of Los Angeles were discovered on the other side of the San Gabriel Mountains. It was a long, hot drive either over the Grapevine to the west or through the Cajon Pass to the east. It was more than 100 miles each way when the roads were terrible. Nevertheless, the lakes gave racers the vast, unpoliced open spaces on which to test their mettle, and it cost nothing to do so.

In the very early days, Muroc in the Mojave Desert was the place to race. In 1920, the Corum brothers settled the land and opened a store next to the lake. Another California town was called Coram, so to keep the post office happy, the brothers reversed their name and the area became known as Muroc.

An AAA-timed event took place in 1923. There's also good photographic evidence in Dee's *Miller Dynasty* of

On display at the Speedway Motors Museum of American Speed, this DOHC conversion by Harold Hosterman known at the "HAL" remains highly sought after. This one is fitted with a pair of downdraft Winfield SR carburetors in the valley. (Photo Courtesy Scotty Gosson)

On April 4, 1924, Tommy Milton took his 183-ci single seater to a new record of 151.26 mph at Muroc. Using ethyl-doped gasoline, he was 6 mph faster than the existing land speed record. (Photo Courtesy Old Crow Speed Shop)

Tommy Milton's 183-ci single seater running for another AAA-sanctioned record on April 4, 1924. Electronically timed, Milton hit 151.26 mph using ethyl-doped gasoline. He was 6 mph faster than the land speed record of 146.16 mph, which was set by Ernest Eldridge in the 1,320-ci Fiat Mephistopheles at Arpajon, France, in July 1924.

Despite the rigorous journey, Muroc was soon attracting other speed merchants. The first organized amateur event was on March 25, 1931. Sponsored by the Gilmore Oil Company, the entry fee was $1. Other sponsors appear to have included Ed Winfield, Dunham Ford, Colyear Motor Sales, and George Wight.

That first meet had a great report in the March 1948 issue of *Hot Rod* magazine. No winner is listed for the first race, but Ike Trone was listed as the winner of the April 19 race in a Riley-headed Model A, and *Hot Rod* later reported that Jonnie Fameralo clocked 112 mph in April 1931 with a "Model A Winfield flathead job."

According to Gilmore records, 16-year-old Glen Smith won the Gilmore Oil Co. trophy for the main event at the race on June 14, 1931. Smith and his father, Boyd Smith, who owned a salvage yard in San Fernando, constructed the car using a modified Model T chassis fitted with a Model A engine and transmission mated to a Model T rear axle. Smith's car was actually fitted with an aluminum touring body with a wraparound cowl that resembled an expensive Auburn or Duesenberg.

Aftermarket parts on the car included "dental drive" 19-inch Dayton wires with chrome-plated lock rings and Racine Racing tires, split front radius rods, and upgraded brakes. Most racing Model Ts had already made the switch to Model A or Model B engines.

As a result of the Muroc expedition, the Muroc Racing Association was formed, and a set of rules were formulated.

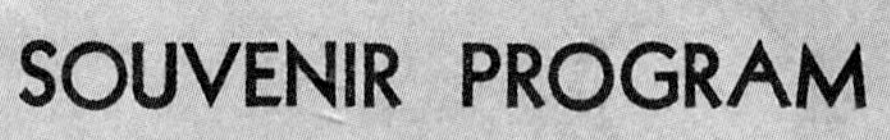

Amateur races began to be organized in 1931 by the Muroc Racing Association. The Gilmore Oil Co. was joined by Ed Winfield, Dunham Ford, Colyear Motor Sales, and George Wight in sponsoring the events. (Photo Courtesy Old Crow Speed Shop)

It's 1935, and Bill and Tom Spalding, who just got their driver's licenses, are kicking up dust at Muroc dry lake in their Model A Phaeton. They were soon in the ignition business. (Photo Courtesy Old Crow Speed Shop)

Cars ran in the following classes:

- Model T Rajos
- Model T Flatheads
- Model T Chevies and Frontenacs
- Model A Overhead Valves
- Model A Flatheads

During the winter of 1932, the rules were revised.

Lee Chapel

In 1930, Lee Chapel worked at a wrecking yard at 3265 San Fernando Rd. in Los Angeles. Chapel had built a one-man Chevrolet that he raced at nearby Ascot. When he wasn't racing, the car was pushed outside the yard to attract customers. Eventually, Chapel put a sign on the seat advertising speed parts for sale and painted the address on his race car.

According to the May 1948 issue of *Hot Rod*, within three months, Chapel had taken over half the building for a speed shop that his brother Herman took care of. Herman also drove the race car. In 1933, Chapel relocated to 4557 Alhambra Ave., where he stayed until 1937 when Ascot burned down. He then toured the country midget racing until he eventually settled in Oakland, where he resumed the speed

According to the writing on the back of this photograph, this is Herman Chapel, brother of Lee Chapel. Herman operated one of the very first speed shops in the world. (Photo Courtesy Old Crow Speed Shop)

Dual-Plane Intake Manifolds

Rather than having overlapping intake pulses coming into the plenum every 90 degrees as with a single-plane intake manifold, each side of a dual-plane intake manifold gets a much cleaner induction pulse every 180 degrees of crank rotation. That's why a dual-plane intake is often referred to as a 180-degree manifold.

With the induction pulses coming into the carburetor every 180 degrees (or actually only half of the carburetor in a divided plenum two-plane), the induction pulse seen at the carburetor is greatly enhanced, especially at low air speed. This translates to further improved lower-RPM carburetor booster function and atomization, resulting in better low-end output, enhanced drivability, and economy.

Certainly, a race-prepped V-8-powered Deuce roadster may well have been fitted with Tommy Thickstun's dual 180-degree intake. Sadly, Thickstun died in 1946 at age 34 while vacationing with Frank Baron and friends.

shop business at 1143 E. 14th St. in Oakland. It was from that location that Chapel developed the Tornado line of speed equipment after World War II.

Tommy Thickstun, Vic Edelbrock, Et Al.

Compared to his contemporaries, Tommy Thickstun was a mere pup. Born in 1912, when most of the others were already in business, Thickstun grew up in Los Angeles and harbored an interest in the engineering side of hot rodding.

According to Paul D. Smith in his book *Merchants of Speed*, Thickstun took pattern making and sand-casting while in high school and in 1930 made a dual-carburetor intake for a Chrysler straight-8. He quickly followed this with a similar but high-rise dual-intake for the flathead Ford V-8, which was a bold move considering that the early flatties were not particularly popular with the racers. It wouldn't be until the late 1930s that the V-8 caught on and pushed back the bangers.

Thickstun opened a small shop at 2002 W. Washington Blvd. in El Segundo, California, just south of what is now Los Angeles International Airport (LAX). Working with mechanic friend Frank Baron, who opened his own shop in 1937, the intake they developed has what is known as 180-degree porting.

Like most Los Angeles–based speed and machine shops, Thickstun and Baron were eventually pressed into war work. Thickstun became an aviation engineer.

Now, reading between the lines because it was never spelled out in those days, Thickstun's manifold was far from perfect. Smith wrote, "The sharp angles of the manifold's runners where they entered the engine ports impeded the natural flow of the fuel mixture." Smith

Tommy Thickstun's design for his dual high-rise intake was criticized for its poor runner design, evident here with the sharp angles between the risers, the runners, and the ports. Thickstun was not about to amend his design.

Vic Edelbrock's Breawood Garage is pictured in 1939. From left to right: Duke Harding, Pee Wee Gallant, Wes Collins, Edelbrock, Tommy Thickstun, and Ray (unknown last name) discuss Thickstun's high-rise manifold. Vic had his own ideas. (Photo Courtesy Edelbrock Corp.)

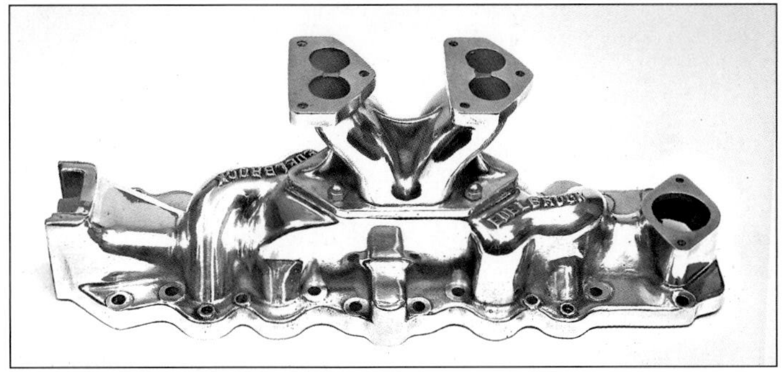

Vic Edelbrock was not impressed with the way Tommy Thickstun's runners had such sharp angles. When Thickstun refused to modify his intake, Edelbrock went ahead and cast his own "Slingshot." (Photo Courtesy Edelbrock Corp.)

This nifty illuminated traveling display was towed behind a 1940 Ford pickup from Los Angeles to the 1947 Indy 500 by Bob Tattersfield. It beautifully displayed all their wares.

Found at the Kennedy brothers' shop, this Tattersfield high-rise dual intake with dual oil-bath air filter is quite different in runner design from the Thickstun intake.

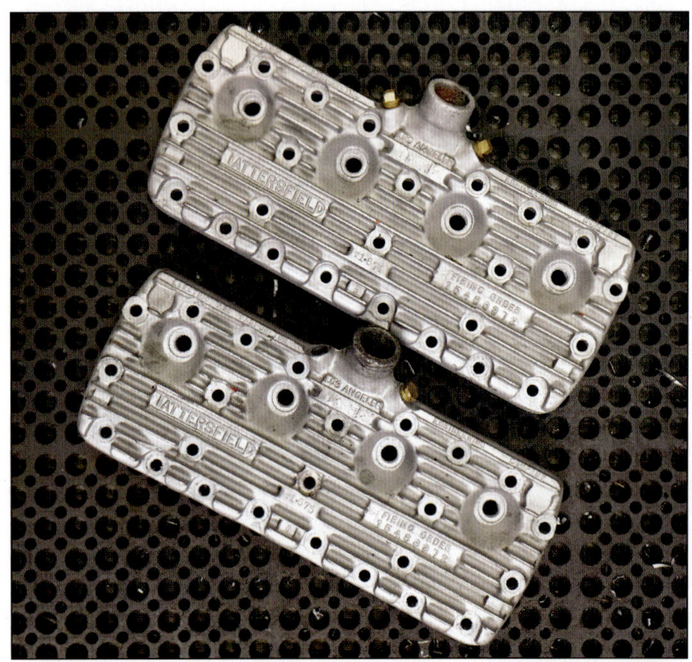

These Tattersfield heads for a 24-stud 59A Ford flathead V-8 were found at H and H Flatheads. Note the words Electric and Carburetor Engineering Company above the top fin. They're busy heads.

Tattersfield also made speed equipment for Ford's 4-cylinder engines. Its parts included finned side plates and finned dual downdraft intakes. This banger has a Winfield head.

went on to say, "This design flaw eventually led one of his friends to develop an intake manifold that would be the basis for an extremely successful aftermarket business."

Several accounts indicate that the friend was Vic Edelbrock Sr. According to Don Montgomery in his book *Hot Rod Memories Relived Again*, "The story is that after Edelbrock failed to get Thickstun to improve the manifold then Vic Edelbrock built his first manifold."

In a way, we were off to the races. Once one person made a copy, it was free rein, and intakes were offered by Edelbrock, Meyer, and Thickstun to name but three. Then, according to Montgomery in his book *Authentic Hot Rods*, "Jack Henry began advertising his new manifold in 1940."

Henry used a stock Ford intake that had the central carburetor mounting plugged. He then machined two areas either side to accept a pair of carbs. Henry's shop was on Firestone Blvd. in South Gate, California, where he did general hot rod work and engine swaps.

Stromberg 97

The Stromberg Motor Devices Company got its start in 1909 when Alfred Stromberg and Adolph Carlson injected much-needed capital to the carburetor designs of John Goldberg. After that, production of carburetors for automobiles, motorboats, and aircraft increased from 1 a week to 10 per day. By 1928, 12,000 employees were delivering 4,000 carburetors a day. Unfortunately, both Carlson and Stromberg died; Stromberg in 1913 and Carlson in 1929, when the company was sold to Bendix Aviation Corp.

With the strength of Bendix behind the brand, Stromberg's dual-downdraft or 2-barrel 48s became original equipment on the 1934 Model 40 Ford and the 1935 Ford Model 48 (Note: 1933 Fords had the Stromberg "40" carburetor). Ford literature said, "[With] the adoption of a dual downdraft carburetor with dual intake manifold, engine power has been increased approximately 12 percent." The 97s were offered on the 85-hp V-8s from 1936 to early 1938, and the 81s powered the 60-hp V-8s in 1937 and 1938.

Although the 97 had a smaller venturi (15/16s compared to the one-year-only 48's 1^{1}/$_{16}$), the 97 became the Ford replacement carburetor and the performance carburetor of choice. From a performance standpoint, multiple Strombergs worked well, and the jets were easy to change, so tuning was simple and they were plentiful. Indeed, they are still in production.

Some say you can't have too many Stromberg 97s, and four would be a good number, as seen on Davis Finch's flathead-powered rail. Note that he has a homemade intake as well as homemade billet aluminum heads.

Over the years, there have been many air filters designed to fit the Stromberg 97 carburetor. However, these Mel Scott ram tubes are actually a fuel injection conversion.

CHAPTER 2

1932-1942
THE FORD V-8

It didn't happen overnight, but the world of high performance was about to be hit upside the head. At the end of March 1932, Ford introduced the revolutionary monobloc, low-cost Ford V-8.

As we have seen, a good hopped-up four-banger could outrun an early Ford V-8 most days. Engineers at Ford knew they were on the right track, and it was only a matter of time. According to Ford engineer Emil Zoerlein, "We tried various camshafts and carburetor adjustments, and we finally smoothed the engine out, and the first reading we got was 65 bhp maximum." That was a good improvement over the stock Model A's 40 bhp.

The one-year-only 1932 Ford quickly gave way to the 1933 Model 40 that boasted 75 hp at 3,800 rpm. According to Ford, "The increase in power is obtained by the introduction of cylinder heads made of aluminum . . . of higher compression (6.3:1 compared to 5.5:1)." The new engine was also lighter due mostly to the aluminum heads that weighed in at 13 pounds, 1 ounce, whereas the cast-iron heads weighed 22 pounds each. There were also hardened exhaust valve seats.

More changes came for 1934. The big improvement was the introduction of a dual-throat Stromberg 48 that helped push output to 85 hp and torque to 147 ft-lbs at 1,250 rpm.

Ford continued to improve on the V-8, and for the 1937 model year, it took care of one big problem: overheating. This was improved by moving the water pumps from the cylinder heads (where they sucked) to the block (where they pushed). It was a huge improvement, and the cars were rated at 85 hp. There were also full insert main bearings replacing the previous Babbitt type: a new Stromberg 97 carburetor. However, there was a return to cast-iron heads.

The other big news from Ford in 1937 was the introduction of the V-8-60 that offered a less expensive, more fuel-efficient alternative to the larger V-8. With 136 compared to 221 ci, the V-8-60 produced 60 hp at 3,500 rpm and 94 ft-lbs of torque at 2,500 rpm. Not a particularly popular engine with the general racing crowd, the V-8-60 did find favor in midget racing circles. As a consequence, plenty of speed equipment was developed

For a long time, at least until 1937, racers preferred a hopped-up four-banger to the newfangled V-8. This little Model A with a Deuce grille at Bonneville in 1951 might well have been banger powered. (Photo Courtesy Dan Shannon Collection)

It is a boat anchor by today's standards, but when it was introduced in 1932, the Ford flathead V-8 one-piece monobloc casting was revolutionary. Like the T before it, it provided racers with nearly a century of fun.

The Model 40 was identified by the curved hood louvers and front grille. Aluminum heads first appeared on the car in 1933. A compression ratio of 6.3:1 compared to 5.5:1 helped increase horsepower from 65 to 75.

In 1937, Ford introduced the 136-ci V-8-60. This one powers Jim Stroupe's 1927 Model T and is fitted with an Italmeccanica supercharger and a pair of Strombergs.

A new old stock (NOS) 59A replacement block is on display in the Don Garlits Museum of Drag Racing. The 1939 flathead had 221 ci, whereas the equivalent Mercury engine had a 3.1875 bore, 3.75 stroke, and 239 ci.

Hot Rods As They Were, the rate of acceptance of the V-8 engine was slow, but it's obvious that by 1937 it had increased rapidly.

Year	Percentage of V-8 Entries
1932	0
1933	0
1934	5
1935	6
1936	12
1937	29
1938	33
1939	31
1940	47
1941	62

from cylinder heads by Eddie Meyer to superchargers by Italmeccanica.

The following year, Ford made more significant strides in the development of the 221-ci engines by increasing the number of cylinder head bolts from 21 to 24. The compression ratio remained 6.2:1.

In 1939, the Mercury (Merc) version of the Ford V-8 offered 239.4 ci with a stock compression ratio of 6.3:1. The new Model 99A offered 95 hp. V-8 production passed the 6 million mark during this year. Finally, here was an affordable engine produced in significant volume that hot rodders could sink their teeth into. Soon, a hopped-up Merc became the engine of choice.

According to Don Montgomery writing in his book

In an effort to reduce the cost of racing during the Depression, the organizers of the Indy 500 introduced what became known as the "Junk Formula" in 1930. It was structured for modified two-seater production cars with a minimum weight, a maximum capacity of 366 ci, and no supercharging.

Although introduced in 1932, the real debut of the class came in 1933. In 1934, the Bohn Aluminum & Brass Co. entered a stylish 1934 roadster laid out by Ford engineer Don "Sully" Sullivan and powered by a hot 21-stud engine also built by Sullivan.

The engine was fitted with Bohnalite aluminum racing heads, 0.30 oversize pistons with an 8.5:1 compression ratio, a racing cam, and a Bosch ignition. It also sported a sophisticated looking twin-carburetor intake designed by Sullivan, made by Bohn, and fitted with a pair of Stromberg 97s mounted sideways, lining up the fuel bowls with the centrifugal force of the turns. Apparently, the engine produced an impressive 140 bhp at 4,400 rpm.

In the hands of driver Chet Miller and mechanic Eddie Tynan, the car qualified at 109.252 mph. Unfortunately, it sailed over the wall on the

This engine with Bohnalite heads and a stock 1934 aluminum intake with a single Stromberg duplex carburetor powered C.O. Warnock's "junk class" entry driven by Doc Williams in the 1933 and 1934 Indy 500. (Photo Courtesy Indianapolis Motor Speedway)

Also running in the 1934 Indy was the Bohnalite Special driven by Chet Miller. Its Ford V-8 was fitted with aluminum heads and twin Stromberg 97s sideways atop a dual intake designed by Don Sullivan. (Photo Courtesy Indianapolis Motor Speedway)

11th lap after hitting a patch of oil spilled by Wilbur Shaw. Eventually, Sullivan's intake was put into production. Initially, it was unbranded, but after World War II, it was made and marketed by Hexagon Tool & Engineering Corp. at 23830 Harvard St. in Dearborn, Michigan. However, not many are known to exist.

In 1934, Preston Tucker persuaded Edsel Ford to field a fleet of FWD 221-ci flathead-powered roadsters at Indy. The cars, designed and built by Harry Miller, were beautiful with wrap-under grilles styled after the 1935 Ford. Unfortunately, they were underfunded and built in a hurry. Because of that, they suffered overheating (naturally) and steering problems caused by the location of the steering box being too close to the hot exhaust.

Because they were FWD, the Ford blocks were reversed and faced backward. Apart from some porting, racing cams, and non-stock four-ring pistons, the bottom ends were fairly stock. They even had Babbitt bearings. Between the Bohnalite heads, some of the engines were fitted with four Winfield SR carburetors, while some supposedly had experimental Stromberg 97s that wouldn't go into production until 1936. One car was even fitted with a Sullivan intake and twin Strombergs with hot rod–style stacks sticking up through the hood. According to Mark Dees, the engines "were good for about 150 hp at 5,000 rpm." It was good news for hot rodders.

Despite the fact that the flathead Ford V-8 did not perform very well at Indy, other racers could see that the V-8 had potential well beyond the bangers. It was just a matter of time. Besides, Sullivan had shown the way with his dual-carburetor manifolds. It wouldn't be long before someone copied that good idea.

Chet Miller drove the attractive Bohnalite Special with 0.030-inch-over pistons and an 8.5:1 compression ratio. Horsepower was estimated at 140. Chet qualified at 109.252 mph but sailed over the wall after just 11 laps. (Photo Courtesy Indianapolis Motor Speedway)

Three of the FWD Miller-Fords were fitted with a Don Sullivan-designed log manifold for four carburetors, but it apparently did not perform well. Sully knocked out a 180-degree high-rise for 48s.

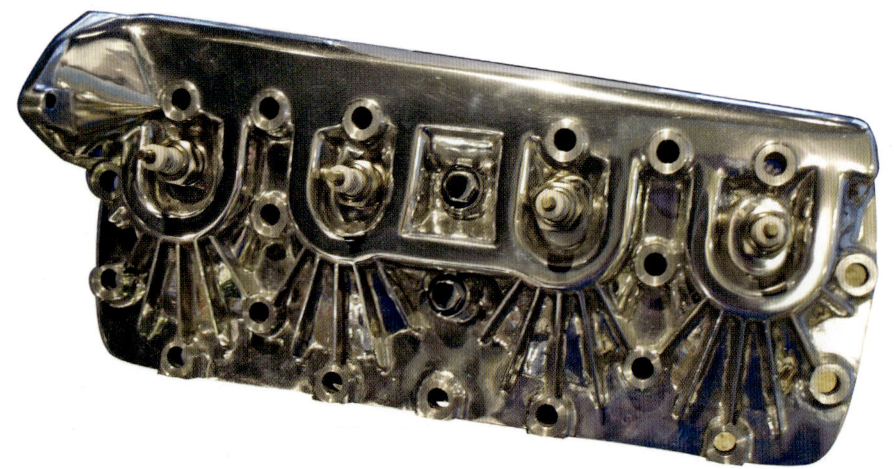

According to Speedway Motors Museum of American Speed, these 9.5:1 Bohnalite aluminum heads were fitted to the 1935 21-stud 221-ci Miller-Fords. However, I was unable to find an image of them installed. (Photo Courtesy Scotty Gosson)

Eventually, Dearborn's Hexagon Tool & Engineering adapted the Don "Sully" Sullivan intakes made for the Bohnalite Special and marketed them in the 1940s. Note the carburetors were mounted backward.

It was not much more than a fender and windshield-less 1934 Model 40, but nevertheless, driver Al Gordon thought he had won the 1934 Mines Field Gold Cup Road Race. Instead, "Stubby" Stubblefield was given the win. (Photo Courtesy Old Crow Speed Shop)

The most beautiful Ford-based car at the 1934 Indy 500 was the Don Hulbert Special built by Floyd "Pop" Dreyer, but it failed to qualify. In 1946, Andy Granatelli acquired the car and installed eight jet-assisted takeoff (JATO) rockets. (Photo Courtesy Old Crow Speed Shop)

Some years later, Don Sullivan partnered with Andy Hotton to produce these Hotton & Sullivan Engineering cast-aluminum cylinder heads for the 1938–1948 Ford. They also produced intakes.

It pays to advertise, and Vic Meleo's Model T Modified carries "Jim's Speed Shop" lettering on the body. It was early 1939 and Vic, a member of the Road Runners, had just broken another shaft. (Photo Courtesy Harrell Family Collection)

Jim Harrell's younger brother Nick joined the engine building team full time in the early 1940s. Jim, meanwhile, worked the swing shift at the shipyards before joining Douglas Aircraft. (Photo Courtesy Harrell Family Collection)

Jim Harrell: Jim's Speed Shop

The business of speed was starting to grow, and Jim Harrell, who also went by the name Jim White, opened an auto repair business near the corner of San Pedro and 99th Street in South Central, Los Angeles. It was 1932, and the Depression was still affecting everyone, but Harrell felt optimistic. While the business was called Jim's Auto Parts, Harrell and most people referred to it as Jim's Speed Shop.

According to Roger Harrell's book *Harrell Engines & Racing Equipment*, "The shop was in front, and the family lived in a small house in the rear of the property. They lived and worked there until mid-1933, when they bought a more suitable place on the corner of Main Street and 109th Place (11006 S. Main St.). The location had a storefront facing Main Street, a comfortable house and a large garage facing the alley off 109th Place that was the home of Jim's Speed Shop that in turn became the home of Harrell Engines until 1976."

In 1946, Harrell, a member of the Albata Club, ran a Mercury-powered Modified Model T

This photo of Nick Harrell was taken in the late 1950s, as indicated by the Chevy W-series engine behind the little boy and the duals on the shelf behind Nick. (Photo Courtesy Harrell Family Collection)

With World War II behind them, Jim and Nick got on with developing a line of speed equipment that included dual and triple intakes and finned heads. Initially, they were named "Tornado," but that was soon dropped in favor of "Harrell Los Angeles."

equipped with his own heads and intake at 126.40 mph to take second place in an SCTA event at El Mirage. The Modified also had a Spalding ignition and a Winfield full-race cam.

You might remember Harrell as the first name on the door of the infamous *Winged Express* AA/Fuel Altered of Harrell, Borsch, and Muse.

The Great Muroc Race

To explain the impact that racing at the dry lakes was having on society in general, let's take a look at the 1980 *Automobile Quarterly* article "Madness at Muroc – The Great Duesenberg-Mercedes Match Race" by Griffith Borgeson. It transpired that Phil Berg, described as the business manager of actors Clark Gable and Gary Cooper (well-known car guys), bet actor Zeppo Marx of the Marx brothers that his 265-hp Model J Duesenberg was faster than Marx's Mercedes-Benz SSK—to the tune of $10,000.

Drivers were hired, Eddie Miller for the Duesenberg and Mercedes authority Joe Reindl in the Mercedes. In the end, more than $25,000 was wagered and thousands of people turned up on October 2, 1932, to watch the action. That was a lot of money in the height of the Depression. The movie stars flew there in their private planes, 200 or more friends came in four private buses, and the plebs arrived in their own cars.

Perhaps as many as 2,000 journeyed to the dry lake to watch the two cars race in a giant 5-mile circle—it was a circular drag race. Both cars were stripped of their fenders, bumpers, running boards, trunks, tops, factory windshields, and mufflers. The Duesenberg had a fabricated shield in front of the driver, as did the Mercedes, but Zeppo, riding in the passenger seat, appears to have had no protection other than goggles and an aviator helmet.

"Our big worry was tires," said Eddie Miller, "and I threw treads constantly in practice. The afternoon before the race, we had a new lot of Vogue tires sent up from L.A. We sat up until three in the morning whittling the tread off the tires with butcher knives."

Joe Reindl in Zeppo Marx's Mercedes SSK raced Eddie Miller driving Phil Berg's Duesenberg. The 15-mile circular drag race was eventually won by Miller and Berg, who collected $10,000.

The afternoon before the race, a batch of Vogue tires was shipped from Los Angeles. Miller spent the night cutting down the rear treads with butcher knives. The wheels were balanced with lead wire wrapped around the spokes.

Joe and Dellie Reath opened Reath Automotive in January 1957 and campaigned this heavily drilled, front-blown Model A V-8 at Bakersfield circa 1959. I can't be certain, but I'd guess Clay Smith Cams was involved in some way. (Photo Courtesy Dan Shannon)

The start was set for 6:30 a.m. to avoid the heat. Reindl took the inside line and accelerated away, but Miller caught him at about the 3-mile mark on the first lap. It was then that Miller knew he had it in the bag.

"I was doing about 108 or 109," Miller said. "He wasn't running so well." Miller looked back, but Reindl was lost in Miller's dust.

If nothing else, "Madness at Muroc" cemented the reputation of the Duesenberg as one hell of a fast car, Miller as one heck of a driver, and Muroc as the place to race.

Pierre "Pete" Bertrand and Clay Smith Cams

Despite his French-sounding name, Pierre "Pete" Bertrand was born in 1902 in Pinos, Zacatecas, Mexico. However, he and his brother Ernie grew up on the family farm in Franklin County, Nebraska. Like many kids, they didn't like farming and instead dabbled in extreme sports of the day, such as gliding and auto racing.

Eventually, Bertrand moved to Los Angeles, where he pursued his racing career driving a Fronty-headed Model T around Southern California. Driving for such luminaries as the Morales brothers, he finished eighth in the 1934 AAA Pacific Coast Championship. Unfortunately, early in 1935, Bertrand was seriously injured in a racing crash, and his wife-to-be, Esther, who was expecting, persuaded him to give it up.

Needing work, Bertrand decided to go into the cam-grinding business. According to Paul Smith in his book

No doubt one of the most famous and popular drag cars to carry the Clay Smith Cams "Mr. Horsepower" logo was the 1934 five-window coupe #554 of Mooneyham & Sharp. This photo was taken at Baylands Raceway circa 1986.

Merchants of Speed, Bertrand ground cams on a grinder he made from a lawnmower sharpener. Because the grinder was hand operated, Bertrand earned the nickname "Popeye" because of the muscular left arm he developed working the grinder. His Speed Specialty Shop was located at 1829 E. 6th St. in Long Beach, California.

Sadly, in 1942, Bertrand died at the age of 40 from pneumonia. His employee Clayton Sherman "Clay" Smith was able to buy the business from Bertrand's estate. Smith, of course, established a brand that lives on today, even though he died in 1954 at the age of 67.

Robert Paxton McCulloch's Supercharger

Stanford University engineering graduate Robert Paxton McCulloch inherited a substantial amount of money from his multimillionaire grandfather. The inheritance enabled him to start the McCulloch Engineering Co. in Milwaukee, Wisconsin, developing engines and superchargers for aero and auto applications.

The first product was a 60-ci two-stroke racing engine.

The second product of engineer Robert Paxton McCulloch was this in-line centrifugal supercharger mounted between the Stromberg carburetor and the stock intake and driven by three V-belts. (Photo Courtesy Scotty Gosson)

Improvements resulted in a cleaner version for 1938, shown here on Kevin Helsdown's engine. Improvements included a new intake, allowing for engine oil lubrication, but production halted in the early 1940s.

In the mid-1950s, McCulloch developed a more compact general-purpose, variable-ratio McCulloch-Paxton supercharger: the VR57. It enjoyed better airflow capabilities and therefore greater boost.

It was followed in 1937 by a centrifugal supercharger for the flathead Ford V-8. Belt-driven, the supercharger was mounted horizontally on top of the intake with the carburetor mounted on top. The pulley turned a shaft that turned the impellor and generated about 4 psi.

According to Don Montgomery in his book *Hot Rods As They Were*, the kits that sold for $84 were advertised to boost horsepower from the stock 85 to 124 hp, which seems optimistic. Montgomery went on to say that annual changes made by Ford to the V-8 caused constant redesigns of the supercharger, and the price soon jumped to $125.

Despite the price and the lack of significant boost, more than 5,000 units might have been sold before World War II. However, the war saw a significant increase in sales, and in 1943, McCulloch sold out to BorgWarner for $1 million. After the war, in 1951, McCulloch resurrected his supercharger business under the Paxton Engineering brand.

SCTA

By 1937, racing activity at the lakes was growing, and dozens of car clubs attended en masse. The activity grew to such a level that Dean Batchelor said, "After the last meet of the year, seven clubs (Desert Goats, Night Flyers, 90 MPH Club, Ramblers, Road Runners, Sidewinders and the Throttlers) proposed a merger of all Los Angeles–area clubs."

On November 29, 1937, clubs gathered at the Throttlers' clubhouse on Santa Monica Boulevard in Hollywood and formed the Southern California Timing Association (SCTA). The members wanted to bring some organization and safety to racing at the lakes, but what really precipitated the move was the exodus of organizers George Wight of Bell Auto Parts and George Riley of George Riley & Co., who owned the timing equipment. Writing in *Throttle* issue number one in January 1941, Ed Adams, president of the SCTA, said that by May 1938 timing equipment had been purchased for $350. Top speeds then were typically in the 100- to 120-mph range.

The SCTA's first sanctioned event was held on May 15, 1938, at Muroc. Unfortunately, strong winds mitigated any racing, and a crowd of 10,000 spectators became unruly. Nevertheless, it was obvious to Adams that they had "something on the ball." Yes, 10,000 spectators. To keep this group informed of activities, the *SCTA Racing News* was published. It is now the oldest racing magazine still published in the United States.

Toward the end of 1937, seven lakes racing car clubs gathered together and formed the SCTA. By May 1938, the new group had its own timing equipment. They were off to the races. (Photo Courtesy Old Crow Speed Shop)

Given the military attire, this shot was probably taken postwar. The 544 car is a typical mishmash of early Ford parts as well as speed equipment, such as a dropped I-beam axle and finned aluminum heads.

Before and after World War II, the SCTA Racing News *was produced by Eldon Snapp and Wally Parks, who were members of the Road Runners. There was just three mimeographed double-sided pages that listed about 200 racers.*

According to Batchelor, there were soon 20 clubs in the SCTA, and Don Montgomery said that by mid-1938 there were 38 member clubs.

Eddie Meyer

In 1919, 26-year-old French-born Eddie Meyer won his first-ever race at Ontario, California, in a home-built Model T. That same year, he also opened a garage in Redlands, California, about 60 miles due east of Los Angeles. Meyer specialized in repairing Model Ts, and according to the sign painted on the wall, it was "Open Day & Night." Soon, he was racing the *Redlands Special,* a Rajo-equipped Model T from Ascot up the coast to San Louis Obispo.

In 1933, Meyer moved his business to the thick of the action with a shop at 645 N. Robertson Blvd. in Los Angeles, but eventually, he relocated to a four-bay shop at 5280 Sunset Blvd. in Hollywood. He also got a chance in big-time racing when he took the wheel of the Muller Bros. No. 52 1932 roadster entered in the AAA-sanctioned road races of 1933 and 1934. Meyer drove at Mines Field (now LAX) but qualified 25 out of 27. Needless to say, the publicity was good for business.

After the war, by 1947, the program had heavier stock covers and four doubled-sided pages stapled together. It was much more professional. It now listed 400 racers, and there were eight advertisers.

In 1934, well-respected racer Eddie Meyer drove this roadster sponsored by the Muller brothers who operated a gas station at 6371 Sunset Blvd. in Hollywood. Miller qualified 25 out of 27, 11 seconds slower than pole-sitter Rex Mays.

Eddie and son Bud eventually dropped out of racing to concentrate on making high-quality parts, such as this crafty cylinder head that could be drilled for one or two spark plugs.

This is an Eddie Meyer twin-plug cast-aluminum cylinder head. According to an interview with Bud, the Meyers had 10:1 heads and an intake as early as 1938. They ran a Winfield cam, 108-octane fuel, and a manual advance.

Jay Kennedy of the Kennedy Brothers Bomb Factory in Pomona, California, adjusts the Stromberg 97s atop a finned Eddie Meyer dual intake. These were originally produced before World War II and were water heated.

Rare solid copper Federal Mogul heads had no water passages and relied upon Thermo Flow cooling. Bob McGee's roadster was originally fitted with a Bertrand cam, a Burns intake, and a pair of Strombergs.

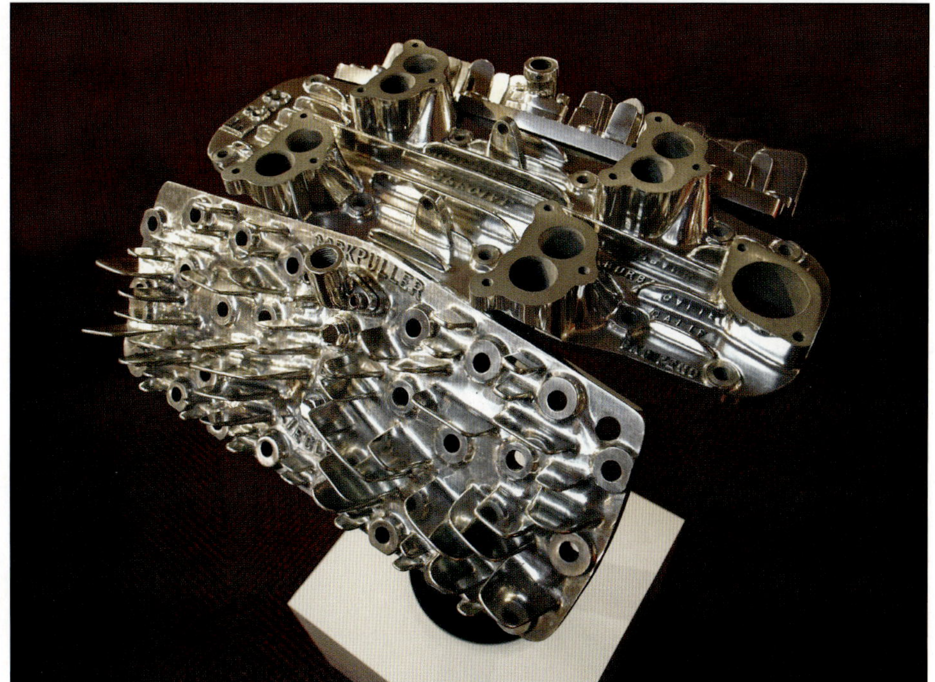

Similar to the Federal Mogul heads in that they have no water jackets, these Ziegler Corkpuller heads are cast aluminum with deep fins. The similarly styled intake is marked "Special Burbank Calif." (Photo Courtesy Scotty Gosson)

Meyer eventually gravitated toward boat racing in 1933. He helped develop the flattie for the 225-ci class while his son Edwin, known as Bud, handled the rest of the business. Later, around 1938, with $200 borrowed from Mrs. Thomas Ince, Eddie had patterns made for a dual intake for the Ford V-8. There's a good shot of him ripping across Rosamond on August 13, 1939, at 121.62 mph, except that it's generally regarded as being wrongly captioned and that it was son Bud rather than "Pappy" Meyer.

Federal Mogul

In 1899, J. Howard Muzzy and Edward F. Lyon founded what eventually became Federal Mogul in Detroit. The company began in the rubber business but soon gravitated to making Babbitt bearings, bushings, and other products for the auto industry.

In 1937, Federal Mogul produced some rare bronze heads for the 21-stud 1937 and 1938 Ford flathead. They also fit the early 1932–1936 21-stud engines. Besides their unusual bronze composition, the heads were unique because they were solid and contained no water jackets. Using Henry Ford's favored thermosyphon system, hot water exited at the top of the block and was directed back to the radiator. It was not a hugely successful design, but the heads looked cool when they were polished.

The most famous car to carry a set of Federal Mogul heads was Bob McGee's Deuce roadster that graced the cover of the October 1948 issue of *Hot Rod*. The car was restored by Pete Chapouris's So-Cal Speed Shop in the mid-1990s for collector Bruce Meyer.

Isky

No book about the history of American speed equipment would be

Like so many pre–World War II hot rodders who had little or no money, Isky started with a Model T. Eventually, he graduated to a V-8 to power his seminal hot rod that he still owns.

There are two significant things in this photograph: the winged skull radiator cap that Isky made in school shop class and the Ford V-8 with a Maxi OHV conversion, Edelbrock intake, and three Strombergs.

complete without the inclusion of Ed "Isky" Iskenderian, who as I write this has just passed 100 years of age and remains an active hero of the industry.

Isky was born to an Armenian immigrant farming family in Tulare, California, in the San Joaquin Valley, where his family had a vineyard. Unfortunately, a severe frost wiped out the crop, and the family moved south to Los Angeles, where his father opened a shoe store.

Isky attended the Polytechnic High School on the corner of Washington Boulevard and Flower Street, where he sucked up engineering like a sponge. While at school, Isky began tinkering with a Model T Ford roadster, learning the basics but also experimenting with exotic Maxi and Fronty heads.

After graduating, Isky apprenticed as a tool and die maker. In his spare time, he tinkered with radios and hot rods. Tired of Model Ts, he switched to Ford's V-8 and ran at Harper Dry Lake in 1939, where he clocked 97 mph.

His next project was started in 1940, and amazingly he still owns it more than 80 years later. He began with a 1932 Ford block bored to Mercury specifications, ported, and relieved and fitted with Maxi F heads that Isky reworked, even making his own copper head gaskets. He also made the one-piece valve covers engraved with his name *Iskenderian*. With a Winfield cam and an Edelbrock Slingshot intake, he ran 120 mph at a 1941 Western Timing Asso-

ciation meet at El Mirage as a member of the Idlers.

Unfortunately, Isky's tinkering was cut short by the outbreak of World War II. He enlisted in the Army Air Corps and served with the Air Transport Command in the Pacific Theater. Upon his return, Isky jumped into the performance business, having noticed the boom in lakes racing and the need for hot camshafts. Luckily, Isky had been befriended by Edward Winfield.

Winfield, who didn't open the door to many people, actually taught Isky his cam grinding secrets. Sensing a lucrative, unfulfilled market, Isky purchased a used cylindrical grinder and made his own cam grinding attachment. He installed the machine in a two-car garage behind his folks' apartment house.

Prior to 1959, Isky had been primarily selling cams on the East Coast, a fact that may have influenced "Big Daddy" Don Garlits, but Garlits's performance on the West Coast made Isky a national brand. (Photo Courtesy Dan Shannon)

Isky hawked his cams around the speed shops. They were a tough sell, but Lou Senter at Ansen and Karl Orr both took some. Isky's big break came in 1948 when his Model T graced the cover of the June issue of *Hot Rod* as "Hot Rod of the Month." He only got a page, but ink is ink. He also took out a small ad.

Advertising is everything, and Isky received a call from E&E Racing, an East Coast NASCAR team. It wanted two flathead cams—now! Remember, cams were in short supply, but Isky airmailed them asap. Within a year, he was selling five cams a day. Isky was also one of the first to offer a branded T-shirt.

Isky also formed a fast friendship with "Big Daddy" Don Garlits. In 1959, Tampa Don traveled west to compete in the Bakersfield Fuel & Gas Championships and lost out to the blown West Coast cars. At Isky's shop, they installed a Jimmy blower, and Garlits went on to put everybody on the trailer. Isky "the Camfather" has been doing it ever since.

Throttle Magazine

Europe had been embroiled in World War II since 1939. However, isolationist America was still racing. Jack Peters decided the time was right to launch a real hot rod magazine. The first issue of *Throttle* appeared in January 1941. It wasn't heavyweight at a mere eight pages, but it served as a necessary communication for the racer. Advertisers included Bell Auto Parts, Porter Mufflers, and Thickstun Manifolds.

Interestingly, in the second issue, Edelbrock, Jack Henry, Eddie Meyer, and Thickstun all advertised dual manifolds. It must have made each guy spin when he saw the competition advertising, especially Edelbrock and Henry, who were placed next to each other on the back cover. In May, Dave Burns joined the throng with his own Dual V-8 Manifold priced from $20.

Not all races were at the lakes, and in the February 1941 issue *Throttle* ran a full-page ad imploring people not to race on the street. Needless to say, the street saw plenty of

The world's first hot rod magazine, *Throttle*, appeared in January 1941. Published and edited by Jack Peters, it lasted just 12 issues and provided the fledgling speed industry with a place to peddle its wares.

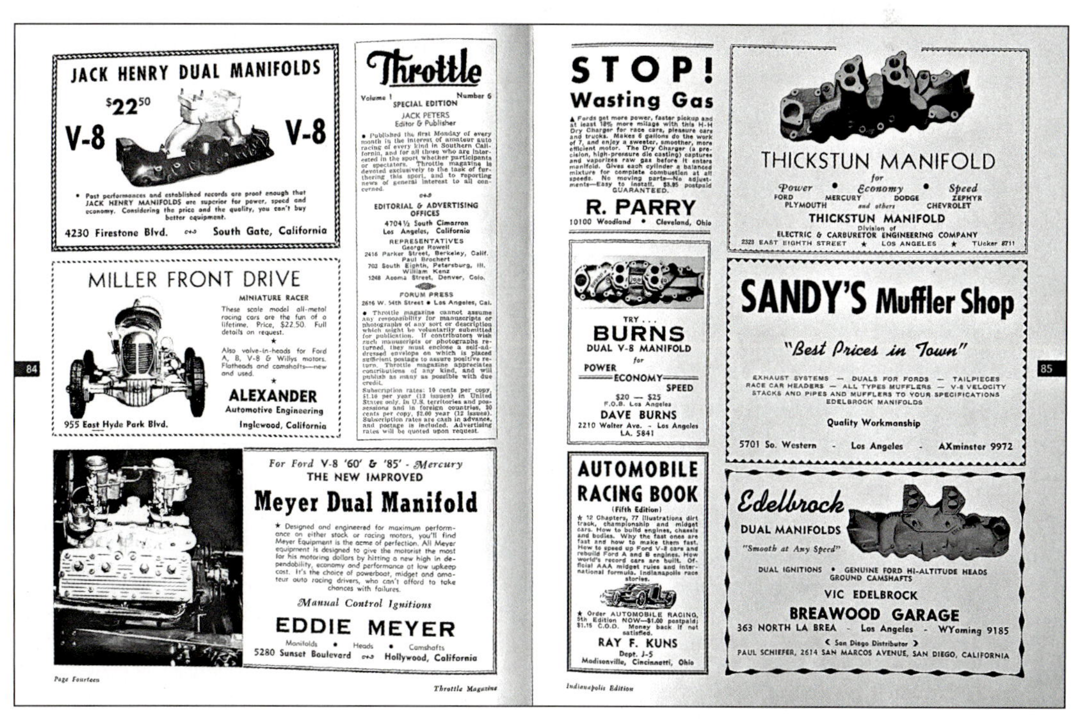

Can you imagine advertising your intake in the May 1941 edition of Throttle *and seeing that you are placed with all of your competitors: Jack Henry, Eddie Meyer, Dave Burns, Vic Edelbrock, and Tommy Thickstun?*

action because most of the race cars were not only weekend warriors but were also daily drivers.

Unfortunately, for Peters and his fellow racers, December 7, 1941, spelled the end. While *Throttle* never reappeared, Veda Orr, wife of speed shop owner Karl Orr, who had opened a speed shop in 1940 at 11140 Washington Pl. in Culver City, California, continued to publish the mimeographed *SCTA Racing News* to keep the troops informed about the scene back home. For now though, it was off to war.

One of the five intakes advertised in the May 1941 issue of Throttle *magazine was this dual unit from Jack Henry for both 85- and 95-hp Fords. He also made a similar intake for the Zephyr. (Photo Courtesy Old Crow Speed Shop)*

Phil Weiand: Say "Why-And"

The story of Phil Weiand could fill a book, but sadly we only have space for a brief overview. Weiand was born in 1913 in Los Angeles and went to school in Pasadena, where there was money and, consequently, a car scene. At age 14, he apparently bartered a mandolin for a 1922 Model T with a touring body that he soon discarded for a 1924 turtle deck.

In shop class, Weiand made his own intake, headers, and exhaust and tinkered with his Model T until he was ready to go race. By 1933, he had managed to assemble a hot Rajo-headed Model B with a Laurel cam, Stutz dual ignition, and a single downdraft carburetor atop his own intake.

Weiand's first trip to Muroc was in May 1933, when he ran a reasonable 91.90 mph. However, he was not satisfied. He swapped the Model T frame for a 1926 Chevy and fitted a pair of Winfield carburetors on another home-made intake. Eventually, he increased his speed to 116 mph.

Unfortunately, his life was about to change forever. On January 21, 1934, his car overturned on Lennox Boulevard in Inglewood, just east of what is now LAX. It wasn't really Weiand's fault; his frightened passenger had panicked and pulled on the emergency brake, throwing the car into a skid.

A further series of mishaps confined Weiand to a wheelchair for the rest of his life. However, *confined* is not a word that relates to Weiand. He and his wife, Joan, went on to build one of the industry's most respected and enduring brands.

As a result of his experimentation with induction, Weiand's first product was a high-rise intake fashioned after Jack Henry's manifold. Using $250 borrowed from his mother, Weiand had Hermann Husbey make

Lakes racer and Don Lee mechanic Mal Ord began making intakes before World War II to accept Winfield carburetors. But after the war, he adapted them to accept twin-choke carburetors. According to Dean Batchelor, fuel pooled in the log.

Ord also made cylinder heads and ignitions. They were installed on the famous Danny Sakai Modified. Sakai was killed in October 1941, but in June his car went 125.52 mph with a full Ord setup.

A polished Weiand high-rise intake in a 1934 sedan can be seen in this poor-quality but very early shot. Apparently, when Vic Edelbrock saw the pattern at Hermann Husbey's shop in 1941, he took a hammer to it, and Husbey had to start over.

Actor Robert Stack of the 1959 The Untouchables TV show was an avid lakes racer in this Cragar-equipped, Winfield-carbureted 1931 roadster with a truck grille. (Photo Courtesy Old Crow Speed Shop)

These high-compression 8:1 heads were made by Weiand to look like Canadian factory heads. Called cheater heads, the Weiand name was embossed under the water neck.

In 1951 at Bonneville, the Don Zabel–Bruce Robinson Deuce roadster entry featured a Howard's cam and a Weiand four-carburetor manifold. It ran 154.373 mph. Note the Weiand support truck in the background. (Photo Courtesy Old Crow Speed Shop)

In 1947, Weiand heads like these retailed for $76. Unlike most in the speed business, Phil Weiand decided to open his own foundry to better control costs and quality in 1951.

him some patterns for a dual-carburetor high-rise intake. There's a great story in Paul D. Smith's *Merchants of Speed* book about Vic Edelbrock seeing Weiand's patterns and smashing them with a hammer.

Notwithstanding Edelbrock's actions, Weiand went ahead and cast up 10 intakes that fellow rodder Barney Navarro machined in return for one of the castings. Weiand was in business, but World War II put things on hold.

Mercury Powered

In 1939, Ford had introduced its new 239-ci version of the flathead Ford V-8 with 24 (rather than 21) head studs. With a 3.1875 x 3.750 bore and stroke compared to the Ford's 3.0625 x 3.750 and 6.3:1 compression ratio, the Mercury produced a healthy 95 hp. It also benefitted from a beefier crank, rods, etc.

For the 1941 model year, Ford increased the compression ratio to 6.6:1 and the output increased to a magical 100 hp and was known as the 100-horse engine. By the time people got home from the war, they had access to a reasonably high-horsepower V-8 that had less overheating problems due to the fact that Ford engineers were finally able to relocate the water pumps to the block.

Most, but not all, engines had removable hardened valve seat inserts and could be had with aluminum pistons and heads. With millions produced, it was a hot rodder's dream come true. When looking back at con-

Doug Hartelt, a member of the Lancers, raced this B class Model T-based roadster. He was the high points leader in the 1947 season with a 1946 Mercury engine fitted with Navarro heads, a Smith cam, and Chuck Potvin's Izzy's ignition.

temporary race cars, notice that many were fitted with Mercury V-8s.

For 1946, the Mercury engine, now with a 6.75:1 compression ratio, was shared with Ford, and both brands proclaimed 100 hp. However, for 1949, they diverged once again. Ford stuck with the 239 while Mercury upped the anti to 255 ci (4.2L) with a 4-inch stroke and 6.8:1 compression ratio (Ford was the same). Maximum bhp for the Mercury was now declared as 110 hp with 200 ft-lbs of torque.

What became the hot ticket was a 4-inch Mercury stroker crank in a Ford block. In 1952, the compression ratio was raised to 7.2:1, although engines with a lower 6.8:1 compression ratio were still available.

The big news from Ford for 1939 was the introduction of the 239-ci Mercury with a 6.3:1 compression ratio rated at 95 hp. Then, in 1941, Mercury raised the compression ratio to 6.6:1 and rated it at 100 hp. Overnight, the Mercury was the way to go.

In 1949, Mercury engines were fitted with a 4-inch stroke crankshaft, and all cranks now had sludge traps. The $3^3/_8$-inch cranks had 3/8-inch sludge traps; 4-inch cranks had 5/8-inch traps (left). A 4-inch crank in a 221 resulted in 236 ci.

Stuart Hilborn

One young man who made an enduring name for himself at the dry lakes was Stuart Hilborn. A member of the Centuries Club, Hilborn began racing with a Model A roadster, first with a banger and then with a 1934 V-8.

According to Paul Smith in his book *Merchants of Speed*, Hilborn and his neighbor Eddie Miller Sr. "retained the engine's stock 239 ci displacement but added an aftermarket two-carburetor setup, filled and milled the cast iron heads, ported and relieved the ports, added a magneto, and installed a one-of-a-kind Miller camshaft." Note: A 1934 engine should have had factory aluminum heads but not always. Smith went on to say, "To ensure the engine was well lubricated, two stock oil pumps were modified and welded together."

According to the final issue of *Throttle* magazine, September 28, 1941, saw the fourth SCTA event at Muroc, where Hilborn wheeled his roadster through the dust to a reasonable 117.95 mph. Vic Edelbrock was the 1941 SCTA Points Champion. His speed at the event was 120 mph, but the fastest speed of the meet was set by Howard McKesson of the Walkers club in his modified V-8 with a Roots-type blower. Along with setting the fastest time of the day, McKesson ran 130.81 mph.

Hilborn's 239-ci 1934 flathead Ford V-8 had been fitted with a magneto and a special Miller intake with four downdraft carbs. It was an odd

Hilborn and Miller used three Stromberg E carburetors they already had and bought just one double-throat EE as used on Cadillacs and Duesenbergs, which made it basically a five-throat setup. (Photo Courtesy Jim Miller/ American Hot Rod Foundation)

At the July 17–18, 1948, Southern California Timing Association (SCTA) meet, driver Howard Wilson clocked 150.50 mph one way in the Hilborn streamliner. Notice the overhead traffic lights for starting. They were set to let a car go every 30 seconds.

A young Stuart Hilborn (left) collaborated with his older friend Eddie Miller on this quad-carburetor intake. Initially, it was for Hilborn's roadster, but here it is installed on his streamliner (without body) powered by a 1934 Ford flathead. (Photo Courtesy Jim Miller/American Hot Rod Foundation)

This may not be the very first Hilborn injection unit, but it is certainly an early steel (rather than cast) hand-fabricated piece. Despite its crudeness, it provided the template for production versions. (Photo Courtesy Scotty Gosson)

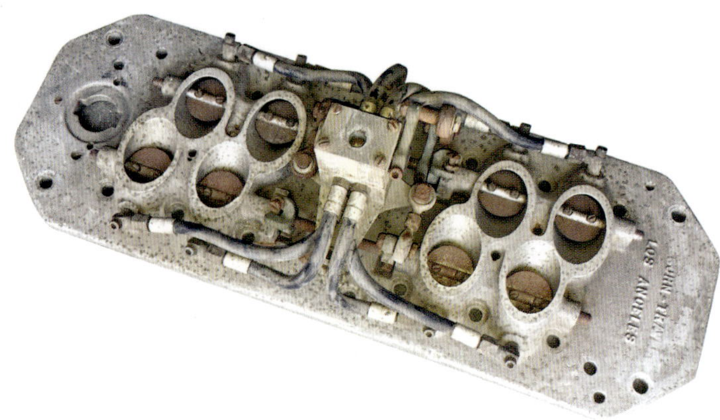

I found this early cast-aluminum injection unit at the Kennedy brothers' shop. It was embossed with the words "Hilborn-Travers Los Angeles," but Jim Travers soon departed.

Hilborn, of course, ignored all the naysayers who said constant-flow fuel injection would not work. He went on to develop a huge international business that supplied to almost every facet of motorsports.

Because they were just down Thunder Alley, Hilborn supplied Traco, which built engines for Lance Reventlow's Scarabs that were built by Troutman & Barnes using small-block Chevys. This is the LHD Mk I.

For many, the epitome of sports car racing came with the 1966-1974 SCCA Can-Am series dominated by Lola and McLaren. It was similarly a high point for Hilborn stack injection.

combination. They wanted four Stromberg dual-throat EE carbs, such as those fitted Cadillacs and other big cars, but they were too expensive. So, they settled for one junkyard EE and three Stromberg E carbs—essentially a 5-barrel intake.

Hilborn decided that his roadster was tapped out, so he purchased a streamliner from Bill Warth that ran in the 130-mph range with a Winfield Model A for power. Hilborn paid $75 for the streamliner without an engine, and his plan was to swap in the V-8 from his roadster. Despite an impressive record of 137.73 mph set on June 14, 1942, Hilborn felt that more could be done, but first, there was a war to fight. It would have to wait.

Sandy Belond

Like so many tales of hot rod lore, our story starts in those Depression days of the 1930s in Southern California. Named after his father, Jesse Sanford, "Sandy" Belond attended Manual Arts High School, South Vermont in Los Angeles. He graduated in 1937, which was the same year he joined the Idlers car club. At that time, he owned a natty, stock-appearing Model A roadster.

Although a member of the Idlers, Belond was far from idle. He opened his first business: Sandy's Muffler Shop on Figueroa at 41st Street. His business card offered, "All types of mufflers made and repaired." Also, "Twin Stacks for V8 or Model A, Mufflers and Pipes Complete: $8" or "Steel Wool Mufflers for Model A & V8 Fords. Complete with pipe [for] $4."

The swapping of flathead Ford V-8s into Model A Fords and many other marques as well as the sheer numbers of racing V-8s meant a lucrative business building headers for flatheads. (Photo Courtesy Belond family)

Contemporary photographs from Belond's extensive album show him, Joe Rethy, and Bruce Riggins working on Belond's mildly customized 1933 five-window with fender skirts, chrome rims, and whitewalls. Needless to say, it sported four exhaust pipes and Sandy's first dual-carburetor intake with a simple Y-shaped adapter for a brace of downdraft Winfields.

Deciding to go lakes racing, Belond joined the Road Rebels and also became a charter member of the Western Timing Association (WTA). The WTA held its first meet on May 5, 1939. Belond's album names Rebels members Jack Peters, Tiny Wilms, Ed Keer, Bob Lloyd, and Fritz working the timing stand and mostly wearing white coveralls with the words Road Rebels Los Angeles on the back.

A small image in the lower left corner of an album page depicts a Deuce roadster with nice chrome exhausts and the words "Smithy's Muffler Shop" painted on the hood. Porter Mufflers also ran its name on a pair of lakes roadsters. It paid to advertise.

No doubt this advertising ploy influenced Belond because by the next WTA meet, held at Rosamond on June 25, 1939, Belond had his own Deuce roadster, No. 23, sporting a full belly pan. It ran a credible 97.30 mph. Belond's photographs indicate he was

Here, at 5701 South Western in Los Angeles, Sandy Belond is working at the bench and Bob Headman, who went on to found Headman Hedders, appears to be welding up cans. (Photo Courtesy Belond Family)

Bob Rounthwaite entered this 1934 C/D Modified coupe in the 1951 Bonneville Nationals with support from Sandy Belond. The car had a 304-ci 1946 Mercury with Weiand heads, intake, and four Strombergs. (Photo Courtesy Belond Family)

probably running a rare Joe Davies intake that comprised two inverted Y tubes and a pair of Winfield carbs. Incidentally, Davies ran a Model A V-8 with full belly pan. Of course, the headers were Belond's own.

The year 1940 was another milestone for Belond, as he moved shop to 1231 W. Vernon Ave. in Los Angeles. Photos show his Model A V-8 now sans hood but sporting shiny intake stacks, exhaust, and headlights. One caption reads, "Drag Racing on Wilmington Avenue between Del Amo and Carson Street 1940."

Frank Kurtis

Frank Kurtis was born in Crested Butte, Colorado, on January 25, 1908. He developed his love for cars in his Croatian father's blacksmith shop in Pueblo, Colorado. The shop was doing both horse and buggy repairs as well as repairing new-fangled automobiles. In 1922, the Kurtis family moved to Los Angeles, where Frank found a job with Don Lee Cadillac. He soon rose to the position of foreman.

Donald Musgrave Lee had been selling Cadillacs since 1906, and in 1919, he became Cadillac's official West Coast dealer with a string of dealerships from San Francisco south to San Diego. That year, he also purchased the Earl Automobile Works

and rolled it into his Don Lee Coach & Body Works, creating the largest custom body builders in the nation.

With the acquisition of Earl's came Harley Earl, who went on to become the first head of GM Design in 1927. By the mid-1920s, Lee's coach building operations were turning out more than 300 custom bodies a year—that's almost one per day.

Perhaps the most famous of all Don Lee Cadillac dealerships is now more familiarly known as Casa De Cadillac. It was built in 1949 at the corner of Beverly Glen and Ventura Boulevard in Sherman Oaks, California. Lee died suddenly of a heart attack in 1934, and his son Tommy took over the business. Tommy, a racing enthusiast, could often been seen racing his imported European sports cars alongside the "gow" jobs. At the May 18, 1941, Russetta meet at El Mirage, Tommy took his Bugatti sedan to 112.41 mph.

Meanwhile, Frank Kurtis, who had been wrenching on Tommy Lee's midget cars, left Don Lee. In 1933,

Frank Kurtis dominated the midget car scene of the late 1940s and early 1950s. The design varied only slightly, but buyers could specify the powertrain. Here, in 1949, Shorty Landis takes the high side at Telford, Pennsylvania. (Photo Courtesy Dan Shannon)

Kurtis Kraft went on to dominate the "Big Car" circuit as well. Here is Portland's Len Sutton in #81 ahead of Bobby Grim at the 1960 110-mile national race at Sacramento. (Photo Courtesy Dan Shannon)

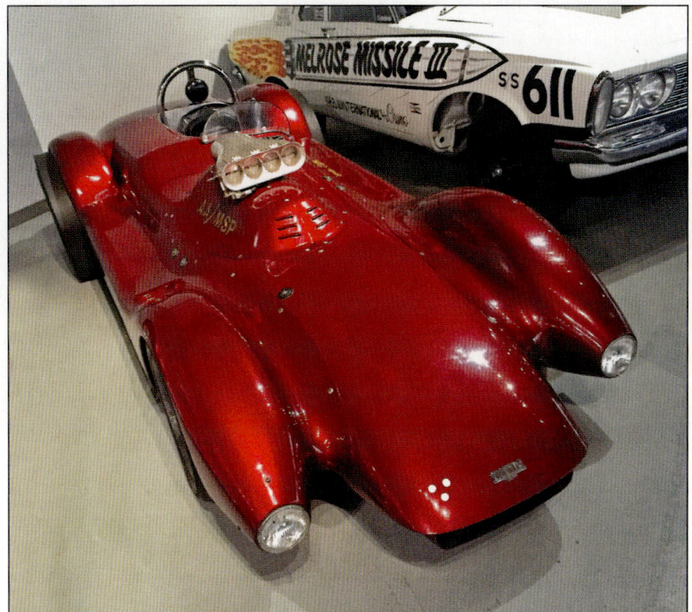

The last series 500 race car from Frank Kurtis was the City of Industry drag car campaigned by Sam Parriott, who took it to many a win. It now resides in the Wally Parks Museum.

Kurtis rented a spot in the Paramount Auto Top Shop, where he created some of his early customs, including a 1931 Ford roadster with a chopped and raked windshield and custom grille and a 1929 Oldsmobile sedan with a custom grille.

Using the experience gained working on Lee's midgets, Kurtis built a big car for the 1941 Indy 500. Sam Hanks drove the Offy-powered Tom Joyce 7-Up entry, qualifying second at 118.211 mph. Unfortunately, Hanks's rear wheel locked up on the southeast turn, causing the car to summersault. Hanks was knocked out but came to in an hour.

Under the hood was a supercharged, intercooled Winfield 181-ci V-8 that went on to be called the Novi V-8. Designed by Leo Goossen to Winfield's spec, the DOHC great 8 was originally developed for those mid-1940s front-wheel-drive Miller-Fords and therefore had the cam drives, the 10-inch centrifugal supercharger, and the three Winfield carburetors all mounted behind the block. The 2-cylinder banks were actually iron with integral hemi heads, and they were bolted to an aluminum crankcase.

Five years later, right after World War II in 1946, Kurtis fielded his Novi *Governor Special*. With Ralph Hepburn at the wheel, they qualified 19th with a speed of 133.944 mph—the fastest by more than 7 mph. They finished 14th after 121 laps and won $7,025, which was not an insignificant sum. However, the Winfield/Novi V-8 proved unreliable and was eventually superseded.

While Kurtis was never really in the speed equipment business, he was in the business of speed and as such one of the all-time great American race car builders.

In 1952, Kurtis introduced the 500-S that scared the sports car world with its "toothy grille." It could be had with any engine. Here, Ak Miller sits in his Kurtis-framed El Caballo II powered by a Hilborn-injected Chrysler Hemi.

CHAPTER 3

1945-1948
BOOM, BOOM, BOOM

The war was finally over, servicemen were returning home (many with fresh technical training), and an unprecedented boom in the automotive hobby was about to begin. With free time and ample skill, many creative entrepreneurs, or in many cases, simply enthusiasts, were about to embark on the journey of creating companies and speed equipment that is still relevant to this day.

So-Cal Speed Shop

On March 3, 1946, de-mobbed Army Air Corps serviceman Alex Xydias opened the So-Cal Speed Shop at 1806 N. Olive Ave. in Burbank, California, using $100 borrowed from his mother. Within a year, the shop front was vacated for a Sears prefab garage at 1104 S. Victory Blvd.

Although untrained, Xydias had an uncanny knack for promotion and knew instinctively that winning on Sunday meant that sales followed on Monday. His first foray into the world of speed was a V-8-60-powered belly tank from tank commander Bill Burke. The little tank that could did, and all too soon, Xydias and his crew were moving on up to a full-bodied streamliner.

With Dean Batchelor driving at the first-ever 1949 Bonneville Nationals, the streamliner went 193.540 mph and took the *Hot Rod* magazine trophy for the fastest one-way speed. It was a new standard for the hot rod community.

At the 1952 Bonneville Nationals, a new, now famously red-and-white scalloped tank with its flattened bottom clocked an amazing 197 mph, but times were a-changin'. Xydias's tank, just one of a fleet of So-Cal–sponsored race cars, was powered by a state-of-the-art Bobby Meeks–built Edelbrock-equipped Mercury running on nitro. Albeit unblown, it was as good as it got, but it wasn't good enough.

Xydias's friend Ray Brown and Brown's partner Mal Hooper had a Chrysler Hemi–powered tank. Brown purchased two engines that he downsized from 331 ci to 302 ci to put them in the same C class as Xydias. All week, the two teams battled back and forth, each one taking a short turn in the record books. When all was said and done, Xydias ran 197.17 mph, but Hooper took the gold with a speed of 197.88 mph. It was just 0.71 mph faster, but it was enough. It wasn't the end of the flathead (not by a long shot), but the game had changed.

Back to the Lakes

Stuart Hilborn came home from the war in 1946 after his stint as a weapons trainer for B-17 and B-29 gunners, eager to get back to racing the lakes. While waiting to be discharged, he began to think about fuel injection. According to Ron Kellogg, "The idea came to him while he was

Alex Xydias opened the very first So-Cal Speed Shop at 1806 N. Olive Ave. in Burbank, California, using $100 borrowed from his mother. Appearing (left to right) are Bill Faris, Ray Charbonneau, Dean Batchelor, and Keith Baldwin. (Photo Courtesy So-Cal Speed Shop)

The first SCTA event at El Mo was on April 28, 1946. The program entry says this is the Burke-Francisco Class C Modified roadster entry for May 6–7, 1950, but it may be a borrowed car powered by a 268-ci 1942 Mercury. (Photo Courtesy Dan Shannon)

In 1949, Xydias ran the streamliner with a V-8-60 and a bigger class C engine, both built by Edelbrock's Bobby Meeks. The V-8-60 set a record at 156.39 mph, but with the big motor, he set a record at 189.745 mph. (Photo Courtesy So-Cal Speed Shop)

After the streamliner had been wrecked at Daytona, Xydias and Clyde Sturdy assembled a new belly tank again powered by a Bobby Meeks–built, Edelbrock-equipped flathead with Edelbrock heads, intake, and four Stromberg 97s.

Xydias was a died-in-the wool flathead guy and did not relish the onslaught of the OHV engines, such as the Hemi with which friend Ray Brown beat him at Bonneville in 1952. Brown ran 197.88 mph to Alex's 197.17 mph. It was not much, but it was enough. (Photo Courtesy So-Cal Speed Shop)

In business in Pasadena since 1945, Don Blair was an industry pioneer. While he never made any product, he started the world's oldest, continually open speed shop now operated by Phil Lukens. (Photo Courtesy Dan Shannon)

Don Blair was quick off the mark and opened Blair's Speed and Power at 826 S. Arroyo Pkwy. in Pasadena. It remains the oldest, continuously operated speed shop in the world. Over in the San Fernando Valley, Alex Xydias opened So-Cal Speed Shop in Burbank on March 3, 1946.

Meanwhile, other racing enthusiasts began building parts to fill the speed shop shelves. Eight months after going to work for Eddie Meyer, toolmaker Louie Senter accumulated enough equipment of his own to open Senter Engineering with his brother Sol on Crocker St., Los Angeles.

With the backing of Edward "Ted" Tribolet, who was known as the Tomato King, Earl Evans was able to open a small aluminum foundry in El Monte that cast heads and intakes. There's a great shot of the Evans Products' corrugated iron building in Don Montgomery's book *Hot Rods in the Forties* that shows the names Evans & Tribolet on the sign. The building was located at 2214 Fawcett Ave. in South El Monte.

in the Air Force during the war. He borrowed time at a machine shop in Mississippi (where he was stationed at the time), tinkered with theory, and teased his mind." No doubt he had seen fuel injection on various military aircraft.

Lakes racing resumed on April 28, 1946, and business boomed. Returning service personnel had time and money to burn and a burning desire for excitement. They raced everything they could, and to feed the need, speed shops sprang up like weeds.

A dozen or so miles west in Los Angeles, Howard Johansen erected a building on South Main Street and started grinding cams on an old lathe. Down in Long Beach, Clay Smith had taken over Pete Bertrand's business when Bertrand died of pneumonia in 1942.

There were so many entries in the race to produce speed equipment that it's impossible to list them all, and all of this was in Southern California. Of course,

I doubt GOAT stood for "greatest of all time," but Don Blair's supercharged Goat was faster than most. His best time in 1946 was 141 mph with a 1946 Mercury that had Denver heads, a Weiand manifold, and a Harman cam. (Photo Courtesy Dan Shannon)

Ansen was formed in 1948 when Lou Senter partnered with engine builder Jack Andrews. They raced this Model A V-8 #104 fitted with Harrell cylinder heads. Senter and Andrews parted company in 1950. (Photo Courtesy Dan Shannon)

Ansen's Automotive Engineering, as it was called then, was first located at 3801 W. Jefferson Blvd. before it relocated to this neat facility at 6317 S. Normandie Ave. in Los Angeles.

Backed by "Tomato King" Ted Tribolet, Earl Evans opened an aluminum foundry in El Monte, California. The hiboys belonged to Nellie Taylor (black top) and Johnny Ryan, who worked for Evans before opening Taylor & Ryan Engines. (Photo Courtesy Dan Shannon)

things were happening in other parts of the country, but Southern California was the epicenter due to it being an aircraft manufacturing hub. The area had everything a burgeoning industry needed from foundries to machine and sheet metal shops to experienced craftsmen. There was also the agreeable weather and the proximity of a dry albeit dusty lake dyno.

The postwar lakes racers were an eclectic mix of cars left over from the prewar years, and they were driven by men who would figure large in the industry. There was Don Blair, a member of the Gophers club, in his Mercedes supercharged *Goat* that had belonged to the Spalding brothers. With Denver heads, a Weiand intake, and Harmon cam, it ran a staggering 141.06 in 1946.

Tony Capanna (Albata) was the Unlimited class record holder with a one-way speed of 145.39 mph, running a 16-cylinder Marmon engine. Speed shop owner

Karl Orr (Albata) was the SCTA points Champion from 1942 through 1946 with this 1940 Mercury-engined Modified. With a Bertrand cam and filled heads, he had the record at 133.03 mph.

Finally, there was Chuck Potvin (Lancers) with his 126-mph Deuce roadster powered by a 1940 Mercury engine equipped with Edelbrock heads, an Evans intake, and a Smith cam. All these men, and many more would go on to power an industry.

Meanwhile, Stu Hilborn and Eddie Meyer continued messing with Bill Warth's old streamliner, which was now painted black. According to the history section on HilbornInjection.com, "Having recognized the need for separate injectors to each cylinder, he then attacked the problems of getting equal flow from all injectors, at all speeds, by ingenious experimentation and burning of the midnight oil. He did a little grinding on the chamfer

Like many early manufacturers, Evans was racing to promote his product. He had great success with a belly tank that went 185 mph at Bonneville in 1951 with a Smith & Jones cam and a Potvin ignition.

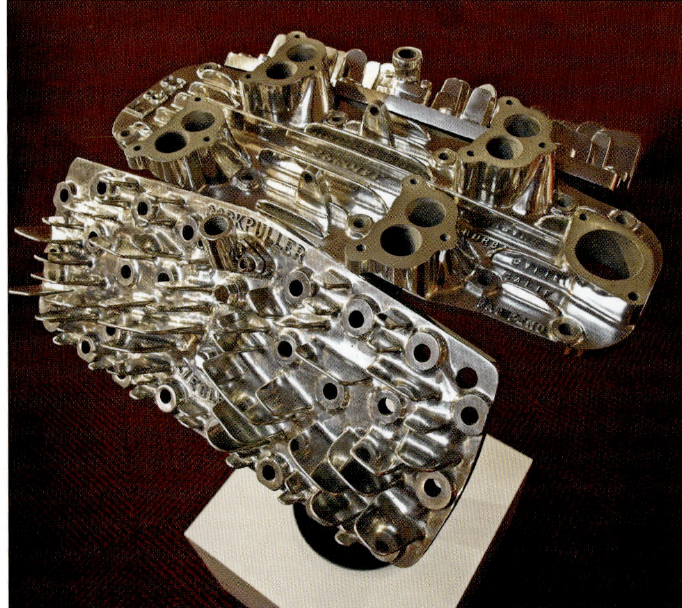

These Ziegler Corkpuller Heads are also similar to the Federal Mogul heads that had no water passages. However, rather than being cast in copper or bronze, they are heavily finned aluminum. (Photo Courtesy Scotty Gosson)

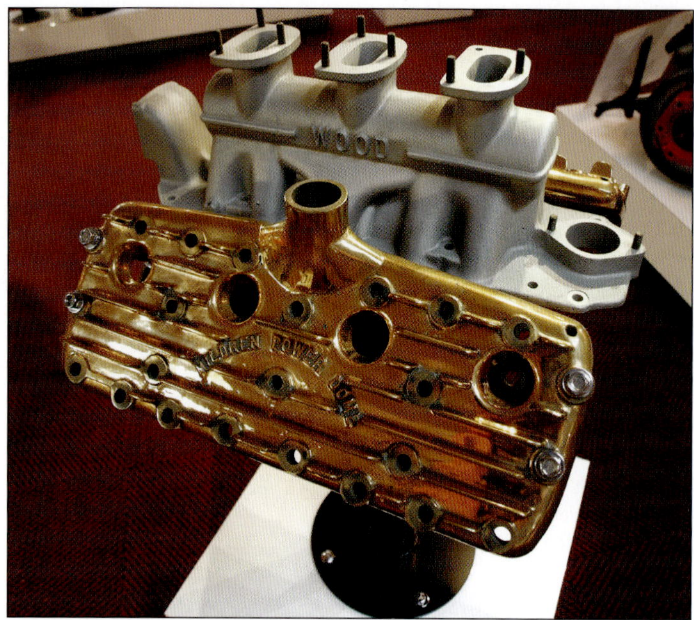

Very similar to the Federal Mogul heads, these Mildren Power Dome 24-stud heads are likewise probably bronze and made by Alex Mildren Racing in Australia. (Photo Courtesy Scotty Gosson)

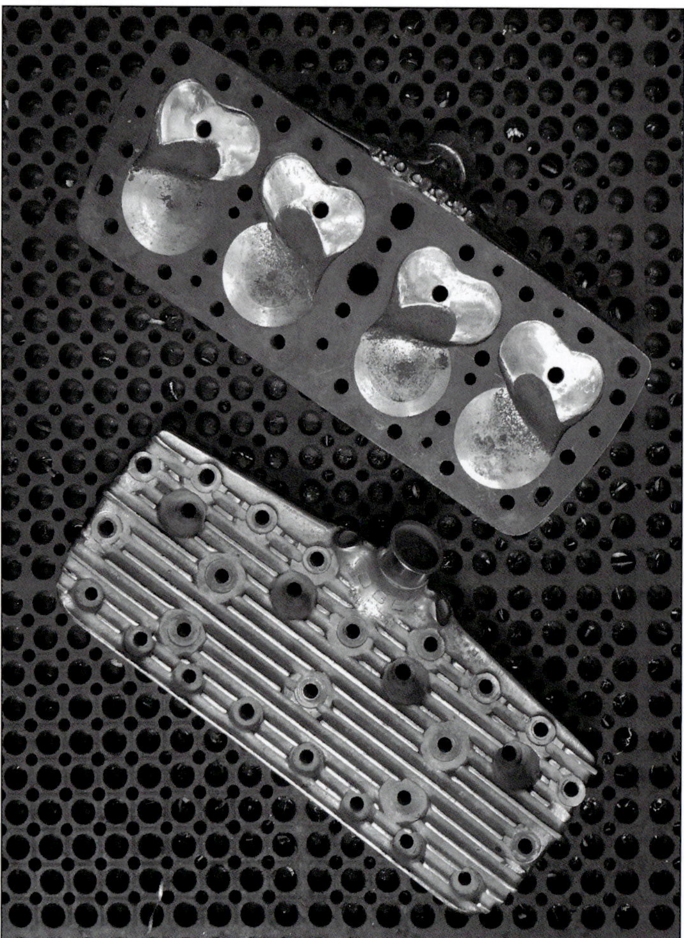

The first advertisement I found for Kogel was for aluminum circular turbulence heads in the March 1948 issue of Hot Rod. However, these Kogel heads are chrome plated, cast-iron Rocket heads with a 7.5 or 8.5:1 compression ratio.

Bill Von Esser of 2840 N. Kedzie Ave. in Chicago, Illinois, began advertising in the May 1948 issue of Hot Rod. *He had developed cast-iron and aluminum cylinder heads and aluminum intakes for the 21-stud flathead Ford. (Photo Courtesy Scotty Gosson)*

course, almost every car in the world would be fuel injected. Meanwhile, Hilborn's record-setting car went on to grace the cover of the April 1948 issue of *Hot Rod* as "Hot Rod of the Month."

On July 17, 1948, Howard Wilson took the black bomber across the El Mirage lakebed to an unprecedented 150.50 mph. The following day, he set the Class B Streamliner record at 146.47 mph—a photo of the fuel injection system was prominently featured.

According to HilbornInjection.com, in August, they ran an exhibition quarter-mile run at the August 28–29 SCTA El Mirage meet in 14.60 seconds at 123 mph. Reporting, Wally Parks said, "With this interesting exhibition, made on a loose and dusty course, SCTA members are looking forward to some official short-distance acceleration trials, plans for which are now in progress." Drag racing was obviously in Wally's thoughts.

One of Hilborn's first customers wanted fuel injectors on his 105-ci Offy midget engines, and its success led directly to a call from Lou Meyer and Dale Drake. They wanted Hilborn to test his injectors on their dyno. According to HilbornInjection.com, "At 6,000 rpm, carburetors gave 99 hp. The tests on the

at the inlet side of the fuel orifice, and Bingo! He found he could regulate the flow from each injector by custom shaping the chamfer to get more, or less, flow."

At his very first meet with his homemade injectors, he ran almost 140 mph. He was on to something.

Hilborn Wrecks

On August 10, 1947, Stu Hilborn was tanking his Class B streamliner across Harper dry lake when he hit a rough patch. According to Smith in *Merchants of Speed*, "A tire caught and snapped the wire spokes, collapsing the wheel and causing the car to flip end over end."

There was no roll cage, and Hilborn suffered severe damage to his back that kept him in a cast for three months. Undeterred, the streamliner was rebuilt by Eddie Miller but Hilborn turned over the driving chores to Howard Wilson, also a member of the Low Flyers.

In January 1948, Hilborn, who was still employed at the General Paint Company, exhibited at the Hot Rod Show to introduce his fuel injection system, now show chromed, to a skeptical audience. Eventually, of

After hitting a rough patch on August 10, 1947, a spoke of the stock 18-inch Ford wheel on Stu Hilborn's streamliner snapped. The wheel collapsed and caused the car to flip end over end. Hilborn never drove it again.

Rough around the edges, Barney Navarro's roadster had the center steering offset to the right. More importantly, under the hood was a de-stroked 176-ci flattie with four carburetors atop a Jimmy blower. (Photo Courtesy HandHFlatheads.com)

injectors gave 109 hp. Everyone was impressed. Meyer and Drake wanted injectors for their production engines, and they wanted to become dealers—right now! So, it was arranged."

The Hilborn streamliner ran again at the October 30–31 SCTA meet, but transmission problems slowed them to second place with a speed of 134.29 mph. With business booming, Hilborn put the streamliner up for sale in the classified ads section of the December issue of *Hot Rod*. The price was a sturdy $1,500. Apparently, the car was sold to Gerry Grant of Grant Piston Rings and may have appeared at an NHRA meet in Edna, Kansas, in 1954, but beyond that, it is lost.

Barney Navarro

As a founding father to hot rodding, Barney Navarro was an engineer whose way-out theories were very often put into practice with a great degree of success. His expertise in milling and machining parts resulted in flathead Ford V-8s that pushed the limits.

Navarro got his mechanical start while living in New York. His dad had purchased a Willys Knight for the drive home to Los Angeles, and Navarro was put to work, saying, "My dad rented space in a shop, and at the age of 10, I became a gofer, as I assisted in the engine overhaul."

Upon the family's return to Los Angeles, Navarro attended Eagle Rock High School and enrolled in evening machine shop classes at Glendale High. He was

quickly put to work by Bernard and Bob Weaver, who had a problem with their midget race car. They had a straight-8 Locomobile engine that was too big for their class, so they asked Navarro if he could cut it in half. He promptly did and recalled that it might not have been the fastest car at Gilmore, but it worked.

At age 16, Navarro had his first hot rod, a homely 1929 Hudson, which he fitted with twin carbs. He graduated in 1937 and went to work as a machinist at Heidrich Tool & Die. His heart, however, was in hot rods, and in 1940 he joined the Glendale Strokers Car Club along with the likes of Tom Beatty, George Hill, and Doane Spencer.

Navarro purchased a 1939 Tudor and quickly milled the heads and fitted a Weiand intake with twin carbs. It was the first intake Phil Weiand ever made, and it was paid for when Navarro machined Weiand's first batch of 10 castings.

The 1939 was not fast enough, so Navarro removed the 21-stud engine and installed it into a Modified roadster. In November 1941, it went 107 mph at the last Muroc meet before the war. Unfortunately, Uncle Sam

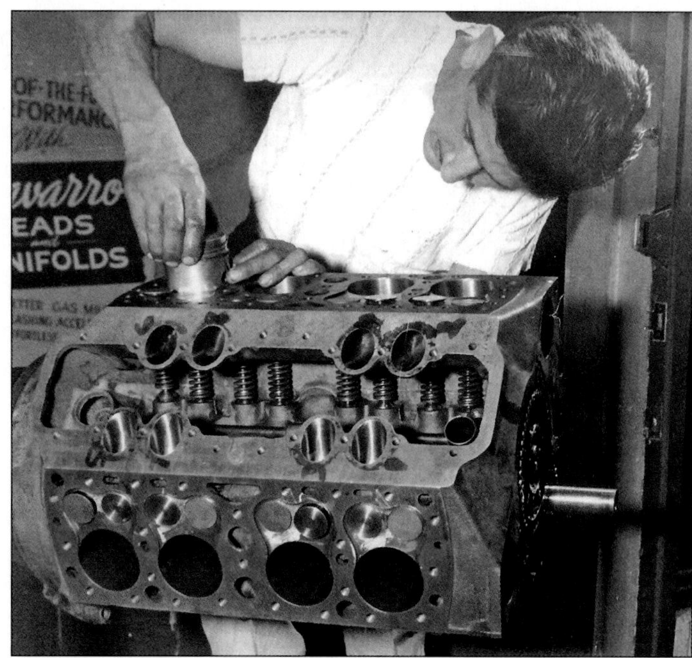

Seen here fitting pistons in a flathead Ford V-8, Navarro began working on engines for his father at age 10 and enrolled in evening machine shop classes at Glendale High in Southern California. (Photo Courtesy HandHFlatheads.com)

A leader not a follower, Navarro's heads and intakes were designed to improve performance. For example, his heads could be had with a 9.5:1 compression ratio. Navarro equipment is made in the same foundry today. (Photo Courtesy HandHFlatheads.com)

had designs on Navarro, and he entered the U.S. Army Air Corps where he trained as a navigator stationed at Fort Worth, Texas. However, he spent his spare time studying Ford's intake that led, eventually, to his own intakes and speed equipment business.

After the war, Navarro worked for Lockheed before returning to Heidrich, but what he really wanted was his own business. In 1947, with drawings he made while in the army, he had patterns made by Hermann Husbey before approaching Victor Caliva at Aircraft Foundry Company to cast them. What he didn't have was money. Nevertheless, Caliva cast the parts and later, when Navarro developed his own heads, he cast up a batch and told Navarro to pay for them as he sold them.

In 1948, Navarro advertised in the inaugural issue of *Hot Rod* and campaigned a lakes roadster powered by one of the first GMC-blown flatheads. The de-stroked 176-ci 1941 block was fitted with a Winfield cam, a Kurten ignition, and a 3-71 "Jimmy" driven by four V-belts. A fifth belt drove the water pump. By turning the Strombergs sideways and mounting them back-to-back, Navarro found he could cram four atop the blower.

The car, originally owned by Navarro employee Bob Trummel, was assembled in four days with the help of Tom Beatty. At the SCTA El Mirage meet on September 25–26, 1948, Navarro went 139.75 mph in his Class C roadster—up from 121.29 at the July meet.

More success came with Tom Beatty, who also ran a Navarro-blown 1927 that was tagged the *Rust Bucket*. The pair also teamed up on a belly tank project, and Navarro said, "Tom lived next door to my shop and had a covered car port where he could do the welding and assembly work."

The tank was powered by a 295-ci 1948 Mercury fitted with a 4-71 Jimmy that produced 10 pounds of boost. At the 1951 Bonneville Nationals, Beatty set a Class D Lakester record at 185.80 mph. The following year, despite destroying two engines, five pistons, and three cylinder heads, Beatty proved the naysayers wrong with a best one-way speed of 203 mph and a two-way record of 197.17 mph.

With the increase in popularity of the flathead Ford V-8, Navarro's business boomed for more than a decade, and he rightfully earned the nickname "Oldfield of the hot rod industry." From working out of his home and selling heads to speed shops out of the back of his truck, he moved to a commercial building at 718 Verdugo Rd. in Glendale, California. Unfortunately, the city forced him to move to 5142 San Fernando Rd.

As his interests expanded beyond the lakes and hot rods, he got involved in many different projects. One project was a Chrysler Hemi–powered boat for Henry Kaiser. That

Navarro's famous roadster was used as a test bed for Navarro's dual-carburetor intake. Notice the device on the carburetors was a water-injection assembly that Navarro experimented with. (Photo Courtesy HandHFlatheads.com)

led Navarro in an entirely different direction and the development of a heart-lung machine, which was used for 13 years at the Kaiser Hospital in Hollywood.

The Ardun

Victory over Japan (VJ) Day on August 15, 1945, signaled the end of hostilities for most but the end of prosperity for many supplying the military. Two such men were brothers Zora and Yura Arkus-Duntov of the Ardun Mechanical Corp. in New York. With their mainstay military contracts dwindling, Zora approached Ford about an OHV conversion for the flathead V-8 that was underpowered and overheated, especially in truck applications. Ford showed no interest at all, but Zora went ahead anyway, buying a couple of V-8s and designing his own heads with the help of engineer George Kudasch.

Rather than have the middle pair of exhaust ports asthmatically siamesed into one, the Ardun, a combination of *Arkus-Dun*tov, breathed better through four equally spaced ports. It was also compatible with the Ford block and valvetrain and used the stock cam but had hemispherical combustion chambers and large intake valves for improved performance.

"Build it and they will come" was Duntov's philosophy, and the Ardun was introduced in 1947. The conversion sold for a hefty $500, and installation took six skilled hours. Two thousand enquiries resulted from a feature in *Popular Mechanics,* but few sales materialized. It was too little, too late, too complicated, and too costly, and only about 200 to 250 sets were made. Ray Brock of *Hot Rod* called it, "a great hot water heater."

Despite minor success with an Ardun V-8-60, Duntov lost the Ardun Company, but he and Yura retained the name. Meanwhile, there were several other flattie OHV conversions including, Alexander, Cummings, Riley, and Stephens, but none were made in the quantities of the Ardun.

In 1951, Southern California hot rodders Don Clark and Clem TeBow of C-T Automotive in North Hollywood resolved some of the Ardun's problems. Their Ardun-powered 1932 roadster averaged 162 mph at Bonneville in 1951. In 1952, a similar engine was installed in Hill & Davis's *City of Burbank* streamliner and set a flying mile record of 229.77 mph. The following year, Charlie Scott drove the Scotty's Muffler Service belly tank and became the first to top 200 mph in an open-wheeled car with a speed of 201 mph.

No doubt one of the most famous proponents of the Ardun was Alex Xydias's So-Cal Speed Shop coupe that raced Bonneville and the drags with a front-blown Ardun. As Duntov had hoped, the Ardun was king but only for a day, as the GM overheads and Chrysler Hemis were about to dethrone it.

Late in 1949, Duntov went to England and convinced

The Ardun OHV conversion for flathead Fords is the stuff of legends. But when it was introduced by Zora Arkus-Duntov in 1947, it was too little and too late, and Ford was not interested. (Photo Courtesy HandHFlatheads.com)

An Ardun conversion for the Ford V-8-60 was also developed, no doubt due to the popularity of V-8-60s in midget racing and the engine's lack of power. Another version, the Emi Sul, was developed for Brazil. (Photo Courtesy Scotty Gosson)

Another OHV conversion for the flathead Ford V-8 was made by the Stephens-Frenzel Co. of Denver, Colorado. Unlike the Ardun, it had cast-iron cylinder heads. Only a handful of sets are thought to have been produced. (Photo Courtesy Scotty Gosson)

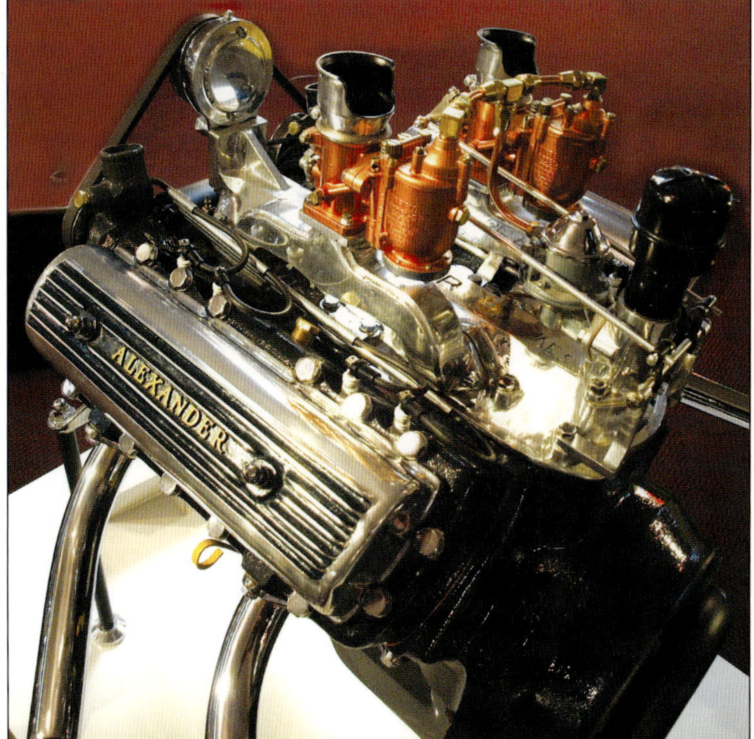

Designed prior to the Ardun during World War II, the Alexander conversion retained the stock intake port design but moved the exhaust port up into a new head and combined three exhaust ports into two. (Photo Courtesy Scotty Gosson)

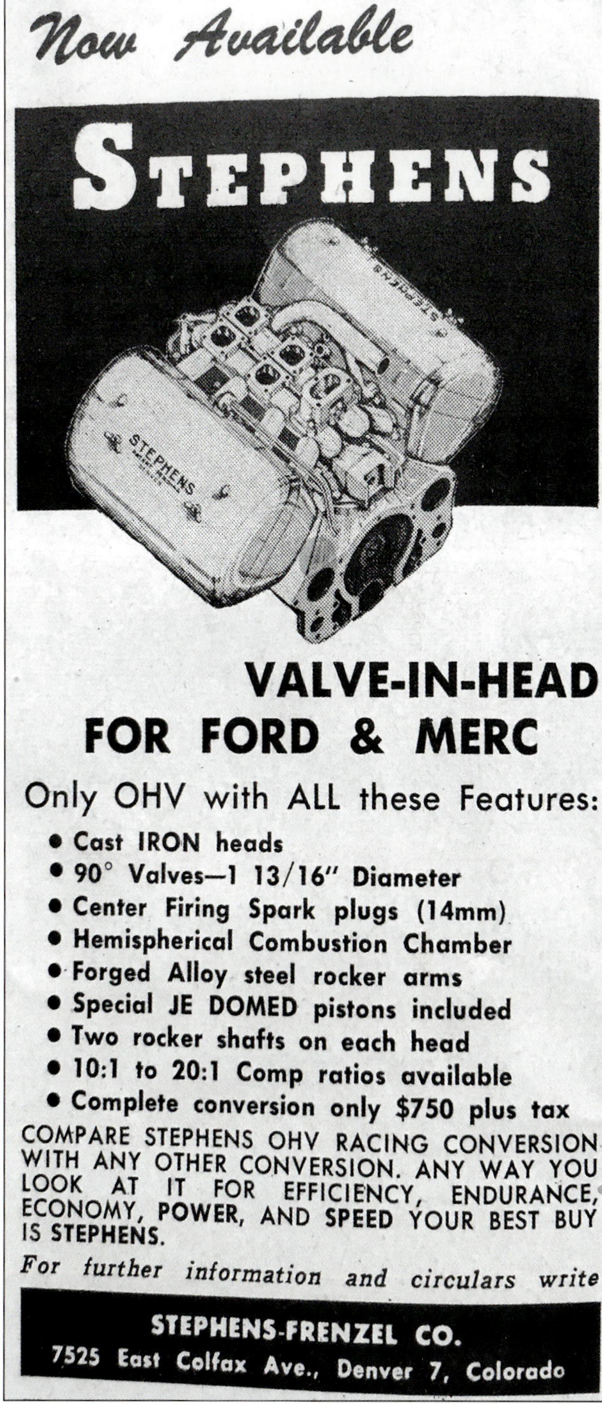

Stephens-Frenzel Co. of Denver advertised its "Valve-in-Head" conversion in Hot Rod magazine for $750. Note the JE pistons. Apparently, one ran at Pikes Peak but without success. (Photo Courtesy Scotty Gosson)

Arnold "Arnie" J. Birner was a pattern maker who tried his own OHV conversion in the 296-ci 1948 Mercury-powered belly tank run by Robert Allington at Bonneville in 1951. (Photo Courtesy Dan Shannon)

Arnold Birner's OHV conversion was extremely well done and attractive with cast-aluminum heads and oil pan. It also had individual port injection and a Harman & Collins magneto. (Photo Courtesy Scotty Gosson)

Early speed shop owner Lee Chapel developed the Tornado line of speed equipment that included this OHV conversion with cast-iron heads. It ran on a streamliner at Bonneville in 1951. (Photo Courtesy Scotty Gosson)

Sydney Allard to hire him. Postwar import restrictions necessitated shipping knock-down engines to be assembled in England at A.E.C. and Monaco Engineering. Allard was the sole customer of Arduns made in England, and a small brass plaque replaced the cast-in words "New York." Eventually, Allard took over all manufacturing and distribution rights. Duntov retained a royalty for every engine sold.

Charles "Kong" Jackson

Beginning in 1939, Charles "Kong" Jackson had been a prewar lakes racer who joined the Sidewinders and was elected to the SCTA board in 1939. In 1941, he was reported in *Throttle* as having run 101.68 and placed 15th in the WTA results for the May 25 event. By then, Kong was very active in the running of the events, including tech, start line, etc.

Kong realized that one of the several failings of the early Ford V-8s was the ignition system. Unfortunately, World War II got in the way of Kong's plans. As soon as hostilities ceased, Kong began making dual-coil, dual-points ignitions with a lot of help from his friend Ed Winfield.

Although the Ford had a dual-point distributor from day one, it had shortcomings, including point float that early racers counteracted with heavier springs. Besides, it just didn't have enough juice for high-speed applications. Kong had Winfield grind a larger cam with less lobe angle that coupled with properly sprung dual points, which elim-

Although he was lakes racing before, Charles "Kong" Jackson did not get his start in the speed business until after World War II. Then, with the help of Ed Winfield, he produced a better distributor than Ford. (Photo Courtesy Scotty Gosson)

Besides ignitions, Kong also made cast-aluminum cylinder heads and these versatile intake manifolds that could, by removing the top plate, hold two, three, or four carburetors.

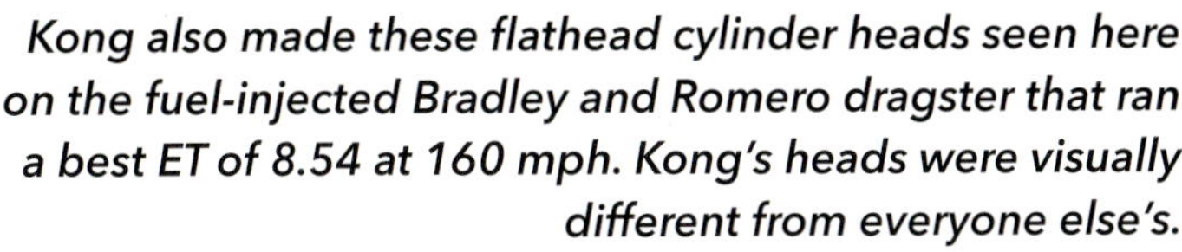

Kong also made these flathead cylinder heads seen here on the fuel-injected Bradley and Romero dragster that ran a best ET of 8.54 at 160 mph. Kong's heads were visually different from everyone else's.

Never mind the Fairy Tales..
HOW ABOUT THE FACTS?

KONG

...Is Still the Championship Ignition

OTHER OUTSTANDING PERFORMANCES USING KONG:

- Bonneville Champion '49 & '50—So-Cal Spl. Streamliner—Xydias & Batchelor
- Third Place overall (Sports Cars & Production Cars) '51 Mexican Road Race
- Car winning most awards at '52 Bonneville Meet—Sturdy & Xydias
- So-Cal Spl.—1st A-B-C Lakester A-B Record and Special Award from Proto Tool Co.
- Fastest 4 Cyl. Dragster—Cooper-Hays Twin Spark
- Famous (Spaghetti Benders) '34 Coupe
- 1st Place in the 100 Mile Championship NASCAR race at Langhorn, Pa. won by Jim Delaney driving an Osiecki equipped car.
- Plus many 1st Places and Records at El Mirage Dry Lake, Bonneville Salt Flats, Santa Ana, Saugus, San Diego and Pomona Drag Strips.

The "CHAMPIONSHIP" KONG complete (includes condensers and manual control cable).................................$63.50

Send for our complete, fully illustrated parts catalog—All the best in speed equipment—50c

A limited number of dealerships available
— WRITE ON YOUR LETTERHEAD —
KONG IGNITION DIVISION OF
SO-CAL SPEED SHOP
Dept. HR-6, 1104 So. Victory Blvd., Burbank, Calif.
Phone: CHarleston 0-4484

'50 S.C.T.A. Champions Stanford Brothers

'51 S.C.T.A. Champion Jim Lindsley

...and again in '52 the S.C.T.A. point champion used the KONG, and the 2nd place car also ran KONG.

Fox and Cobb New Record Every Meet

Clyde Sturdy So. Cal. Special

As can be seen in this Hot Rod *ad, Kong's friend Alex Xydias sold the ignitions through the Kong Ignition Division of So-Cal Speed Shop. Kong was too busy with the government.*

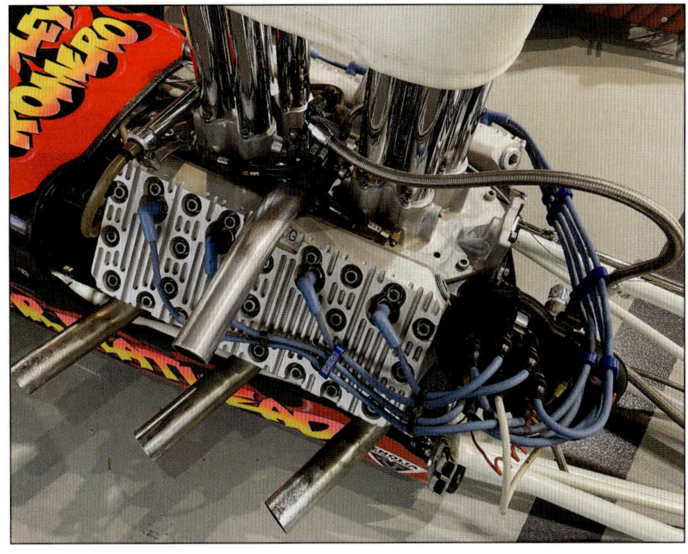

inated problems with point floating. The cam spun in ball bearings, and the unit came with an advance control cable that enabled the driver to adjust his ignition as needed.

Unfortunately, once again, Kong was called to do his duty, this time by the North Atlantic Treaty Organization (NATO), to teach aircraft maintenance to the Danish Air Force. Over the next decade, Kong worked on various defense projects, including the Polaris Guidance System. Nevertheless, by 1955, the Kong Rotofaze ignition was the hot setup. Not confined to ignitions, Kong also dabbled in making heads and intakes for the flathead Ford V-8.

Elco Twin-Plug Heads

On page 34 of Veda Orr's *Hot Rod Pictorial*, there are two photographs of Bert Letner's (Road Runners) #24 Class C track T roadster that ran 125 mph. Driven at the lakes by Art Lamey and on oval tracks by Troy Ruttman, it was powered by a 1940 Mercury fitted with Elco twin-plug heads. It made the cover of the May 1948 issue of *Hot Rod* magazine and was Hot Rod of the Month.

Letner, who owned a garage, and his buddy Ted Evans designed the unique, aircraft-derived heads and called them Elco (Evans and Letner Co.). To fire the 16 plugs, they use a converted 1 GK 400 Autolite ignition similar to those used on a Nash 6. I've never seen an ad for the heads, and they are rare, so I doubt they made many sets. In the late 1950s, Els Lohn launched the Eelco Co., while Elco with one "e" fell by the wayside.

Kong Jackson also produced some twin-plug heads, as did Eddie Meyer and Hogan in New Zealand, but they have never been very popular. Many years later, Don Orosco of Monterey Speed & Sport re-popped the Elco heads along with a Vertex-style angled-drive distributor that was also derived from the Nash Twin 8 distributor. Again, few sets appear to have been sold.

Speed Age

Before there was *Hot Rod* magazine, *Speed Age* appeared in May 1947. The magazine was initially published and edited by Don O'Reilly and Jimmy Quisenberry out of Hyattsville, Maryland. One of their main contributors was Roger Huntington, who wrote numerous technical articles for a number of magazines.

The first version of *Speed Age* ceased publication in December 1953. However, within a few months, the magazine had a new owner and was published through December 1959.

A rare pair of Elco twin-plug heads is used on this S.Co.T.-blown flathead being assembled at HandHFlatheads. Note how the plugs are spaced differently from the earlier Meyer heads.

The speed equipment industry needed magazines to spread the word nationwide, and before there was Hot Rod, *there was* Speed Age *that began publication in May 1947. Clark Gable and Barbara Stanwyck grace the cover.*

Hot on the heels of Speed Age *in June 1947 came* Road and Track, *which enjoyed a much longer shelf life dealing with American cars, foreign cars, and automobile racing.*

Road and Track

Just a month after the inaugural issue of *Speed Age* hit the newsstands, the first issue of *Road and Track* was published in June 1947 by two friends: Wilfred H. Brehaut Jr. and Joseph S. Fennessy of Hempstead, Long Island, New York. The first issue was 32 pages plus covers, and it was primarily aimed at the sports car enthusiast. The editor said each issue would be divided into three sections: American cars, foreign cars, and automobile racing.

There was only four pages of advertising in the first issue, and one half page was from Grancor of Chicago. Brehaut and Fennessy only published six issues of *Road and Track* between 1947 and 1949. By 1952, they had sold out to John Bond, and the name was modified to *Road & Track*. In its heyday, *Road and Track* rivaled *Hot Rod* as one of the world's most prestigious automotive magazines, selling more than one million copies per month.

Jack Engle

A member of the infamous Low Flyers car club, Jack Engle was a prewar lakes racer. He was born on June 16, 1920, in Regina, Saskatchewan, Canada, to American parents. His father Ed, a construction worker, moved the family to Santa Monica, California, where Engle attended Venice High School and then Santa Monica City College. At age 17, Engle bought his first car, a 1926 Chevy with an Oldsmobile 3-port head.

Engle worked as a machinist at North American Aviation, but in his spare time, he raced at the lakes. At the June 15, 1941, SCTA race at El Mirage, he went 91.27 mph in his Winfield-headed roadster. Unfortunately, as a result of Pearl Harbor, Engle was drafted into the U.S. Navy, where he did maintenance work on patrol torpedo (PT) boats in the Philippines. After the war, Engle opened a machine shop at the rear of his father Ed's Radio and TV store at 808 14th St. in Santa Monica, California.

An adept machinist, Engle purchased a Landis cam-grinding machine and set to work learning to grind cams rather than build engines. His first small advertisement appeared in the April 1948 issue of *Hot Rod* and advertised "Engle's Racing Cams, custom ground to your specifications and needs for all types of cars, we ship anywhere."

In the March 1949 advertisement, the company advertised custom grinds from $20 (4-cylinder) plus a core charge. That same year, Jack married Ona, and they eventually had two sons, Doug and Mark, who own Mark Engle Racing Engines.

Engle never did advertise much, and the company never received much in the way of magazine ink. How-

While Jack Engle did not advertise much, his company was well known for its involvement with John Peter's double-engine Freight Train *gas dragster, seen here at Lions with Bob Muravez at the helm. (Photo Courtesy Dan Shannon)*

ever, they developed a cool logo and an enviable reputation for quality and service. Writing in his book *The Business of Speed*, David N. Lucsko said, "Jack Engle . . . deliberately controlled his company's growth during the 1960s to remain flexible and custom-oriented."

When the Chevy 396 appeared in 1965, Engle was one of the first to figure out what cams would work best. A full-page ad in the October 1969 issue of *Car Craft* magazine touted "Mr. Super Stock" Wally Booth as having the "fastest 325 hp in the nation." Because if his shop's location, Engle attracted a lot of racing personalities, including "Freight Train" John Peters, who was the back-shop foreman. Engle died at age 88, and the company was sold in 2009.

Grancor

It's hard to imagine three boys of Italian descent growing up in Chicago and losing their mother when Vince was 8, Andy 12, and Joe 16, but the Granatelli brothers survived and indeed thrived. Their first job was to haul an old car battery around during cold Chicago winters and jump-start stalled cars for a dollar. They pooled their earnings and opened Andy's Super Service at 4506 N. Clarendon Ave., just off Lake Shore Drive. It proved successful.

Unfortunately, one night the shop was cleaned out by thieves. The brothers opened a new business at 5058 N. Broadway in Chicago, selling speed equipment from Edelbrock, Jahns, Winfield, etc. Meanwhile, they launched their own Grancor brand of flathead parts.

According to Ed Almquist in his book *Hot Rod Pioneers,* Joe said, "After we talked a relative into a $500 loan, we began making wooden patterns for high-compression cylinder heads and a dual intake for flathead Fords. From then on, the business took off like a bat out of hell." Almquist went on to say that they offered crate engines for $750 and installed engines for $1,200. "Twenty-two Grancor-Fords soon thundered through Chicago."

Helping drive the Grancor publicity machine was one of the old obsolete 1935 front-wheel-drive Miller-Ford Indy cars powered by a flathead they built themselves. It had their own heads and a three-port intake. Driven in 1946 in the first postwar Indy 500 by Danny Kladis, the Grancor entry lasted until the 52nd lap when it stalled.

The Granatellis returned in 1947 with Andy's entry under the Camco Motors banner, and now there were four carburetors. The driver, Pete Romcevich, was awarded 12th place after completing 167 laps. The Miller was parked, but the Granatellis were far from done with the Brickyard or the business of speed. According to Wm. R. LaDow, the brothers were doing $14 million in business by 1956. The following year, they walked away,

moved to California, and Andy and Joe purchased Paxton Products Corp. Three years later, they sold Paxton to the Studebaker Corp.

Ray Brown: Safety First

Ray Brown, another Eddie Meyer alumni, opened his own shop in 1939 at 5656 Santa Monica Blvd. in Los Angeles. Brown was a lakes racer, and in the immediate

A Grancor-equipped flathead mounted backward with four carburetors powered one of the old 1935 Miller-Fords to Indy in 1947 under the Granatelli banner. It placed 12th. (Photo Courtesy Dan Shannon)

With so much hungry industry in post–World War II United States, it was fairly easy to capitalize on a market opportunity. After having their shop cleaned out, the Granatelli brothers got into the speed equipment business.

Great friends Ray Brown (left) and Alex Xydias were rivals on the track. This is Ray's back-motor, Meyer-equipped V-8-60-powered 1927. In 1949, the car ran 134 mph. Note: Ray pioneered the use of safety helmets and belts. (Photo Courtesy Dan Shannon)

Unlike other lakes racers, Brown was concerned with safety and in 1946 installed some surplus seat belts. He was just a little ahead of his time because in the June 1948 issue of *California Timing News*, it was announced that "Crash helmets are a must now at any lake meet. The new law has been enforced by the county coroner after the recent mishaps at time trials. Safety belts are also required on all S.C.T.A. competition cars."

Compulsory seat belts may have resulted from an accident reported in the October 1947 issue of *California Timing News*: "Wally Henrich (Quarter Milers) is okay after his bouncing out of the Jack Cassell roadster as a result of Ed Korgan streamliner running into him on his record run."

Initially, Brown advocated belts for race cars only and was soon making them for fellow racers. However, he soon developed them for road cars and ran his first advertisement in *Hot Rod* in 1951. By 1952, he was running half-page ads for the "New Impact Saf-Tee Belt!" with the unsettling tag line "Death never takes a holiday!"

postwar period successfully raced a hot 1932 roadster that ran 123.87 mph in 1945. Brown's roadster sported a Meyer intake, a Clay Smith cam, Jahns pistons, and homemade headers.

Selling safety was not the easiest thing to do until it was mandated, nevertheless, drivers such as Art Chrisman adopted helmets. This one was lettered and striped by the infamous Von Dutch.

Decorated helmets have a long history, and this cute cartoon decorated the helmet of Gary "Red" Greth, driver of the famous Speed Sport Modified Fuel Roadster. The Lords was Red's car club.

Shirley Muldowney said aluminized-cotton fire suits "slowed the fire, but you still baked like a potato." Tom McEwen introduced the painter's mask breathers, and this is John Morton of the Surfers. (Photo Courtesy Dan Shannon)

Long before seat belts were mandated, Ray Brown pioneered their use. His 22,400–square foot factory in Pacoima employed 150 people working two shifts. They became the first supplier of seat belts and safety harnesses to the U.S. government. Meanwhile, people such as Frank Smith of Paterson, New Jersey, and Wal-Mar of Chicago advertised plastic crash helmets.

Weiand Cheater Heads

Over the years, a lot of mystique has grown up around the so-called Canadian Cheater heads. Many Canadian-built flatheads, including those of the Canadian Monarch version of the Mercury, came with alumi-num cylinder heads that had slightly higher compression ratios than the stock iron heads.

Because some stock car classes demanded stock heads, these stock Canadian heads became popular imports that could be milled to increase the compression ratio even more. Because he was running a 1927 roadster both at the lakes and on oval tracks, Phil Weiand knew all the tricks. He duplicated the smooth, finless Canadian head and made some bucks.

Jimmy

The story of GM's Detroit Diesel is long and convoluted. Suffice it to say that in the early 1930s General Motors began developing a two-stroke diesel for mass production that could be easily adapted to different applications. In 1934, the GM Diesel Engine Division was established. What became known as the Series 71 introduced in 1938 was available in 3-, 4-, and 6-cylinder variants. The model number 71 describes the amount of displacement per cylinder. Each engine was fitted with a scavenge pump designated 3-71, 4-71, and 6-71.

These engines helped power the war and were fitted to almost every D-Day landing craft. Of course, the military mechanics got to understand them. It didn't take long for hot rodders, such as Tom Beatty and Barney Navarro, to see the potential of pumping rather than scavenging.

Members of the Glendale Strokers since 1940, Beatty and Navarro began assembling their 1927 lakes roadster late in 1947. Between the Essex's rails, they lowered a Ford 59A block that was fitted with a Norden 180-degree crank, custom Winfield cam, Navarro's own heads, and a custom intake with a belt-driven 3-71 GMC Jimmy blower fed by four Strombergs. Stroked to just 176 ci, the screamer produced 270 hp at 6,500 rpm on the dyno.

In an interview with Henry Astor of the American Hot Rod Foundation, Navarro said, "I bought it from Kong Jackson for $60. I don't know where he got it. It was after the war, and I was working at the Hedreich Bros. die shop. So, I took the blower down there and made all the pieces for it there."

At the 1948 SCTA season opener at El Mirage, the Navarro roadster set a 136.77-mph record. By the end of the year, Navarro was running 146s, and at the first Bonneville Speed Trials in 1949, he went 147. It was the start of something.

Some stock car classes demanded a stock, factory head, so Phil Weiand manufactured these cheater heads. They looked like the stock Canadian factory heads but with higher compression ratios.

As we have seen, Barney Navarro (left) was a pioneer of the use of the GMC "Jimmy" Roots-type supercharger. Seen here is the 3-71 on his roadster. Notice the multiple V-belts. (Photo Courtesy HandHFlatheads.com)

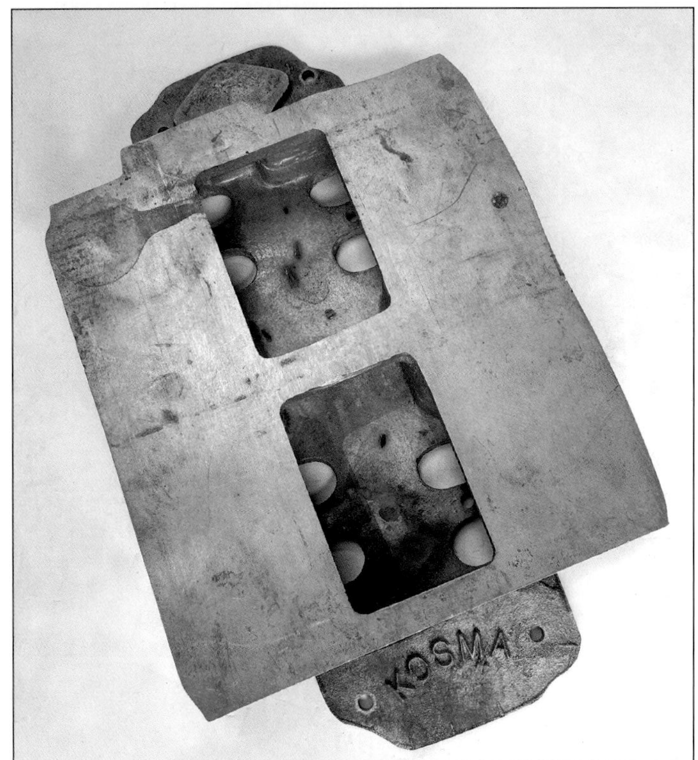

Fred Offenhauser

Fred Offenhauser's nephew was also named Fred, and he worked for his uncle with the understanding that one day all this would be his. Uncle Fred had other ideas, and while young Fred was away in the U.S. Navy in 1946, his uncle did the unthinkable. He sold the company lock, stock, and both barrels to Louis Meyer and Dale Drake. Meyer and Drake went on to continue the racing suc-

Fellow racer Tom Cobb was quick to follow Navarro's lead. Here is his roadster with a removable hardtop at Bonneville in 1951. Cobb used a 4-71, but like Navarro, he fed its thirst with four Strombergs. (Photo Courtesy Dan Shannon)

Besides making 4x2 intakes for flatheads, Paul Kosma also made a few of these blower manifolds. They were obviously designed to accept a Jimmy-size supercharger. It looks unfinished.

cess of the Offy engine from the original location at 2001 Gage Ave. in Los Angeles until 1967.

Fred Jr. returned from the service and found that the company he expected to inherit had been sold. Not one to let the grass grow, he teamed up with his friend Fran Hernandez, and in 1947, they formed Offenhauser Equipment Co.

Occupying some rented space at 8948 National Blvd. in Los Angeles, Offenhauser began making speed equipment, heads, and intakes for flathead Ford V-8s. Its first ad appeared in the October 1948 issue of *Hot Rod*. The use of the Offenhauser name quickly initiated a lawsuit from Meyer and Drake, but an understanding judge decided that both companies could use the name—a decision that led to some confusion.

Around that time, Hernandez and Offenhauser parted company: Offenhauser carried on with his brother Carl while Hernandez became one of the first hot rodders to experiment with nitro after joining Vic Edelbrock. In 1950, Offenhauser moved Offenhauser to Alhambra and its current location at 5300 Alhambra Ave. in Los Angeles.

According to Smith in his book *Merchants of Speed*, "By 1953 the Offenhauser catalog listed cylinder heads and manifolds for the V-8-85, V-8-60, Chevy 6 intakes and valve covers, Cadillac and Ford OHV 6 equipment." Offenhauser boomed along with the industry and at one

Not all blowers were mounted atop the engine, as evidenced by the "Skip" Higginbotham Farm's flip-body Model A roadster with a 6-71 front-blown Hemi. In May 1959, it set a Bakersfield record at 136.98 mph. (Photo Courtesy Dan Shannon)

Despite the confusion of two Fred Offenhausers and two companies, young Fred's Offenhauser Equipment Co. prospered. At last count, it had more than 900 patterns and remains a popular brand.

time boasted some 900 products. Fred died in 1992 and left the business to his two sons Jim and Tay.

Halibrand

There's nothing quite like winning the Indy 500 to propel your product to the fore, and that's exactly what happened to Henry Theodore "Ted" Halibrand when George Robson won the first postwar Brickyard in the Thorne Engineering entry.

Born in 1916 in Paterson, New Jersey, Halibrand moved just before World War II to Southern California where he worked at Douglas Aircraft as a service engineer. In his spare time, he raced an Offenhauser-powered Kurtis midget. Of course, the war put pause to the racing but immediately after the war in 1946, Halibrand opened shop at 5851 W. Washington Blvd. in Culver City, California, and the following year formed the Halibrand Engineering Co.

Amazingly quickly, Halibrand created a catalog of innovative racing products, such as magnesium quick-change differentials, safety locking fuel caps, steering boxes, torsion bars, and perhaps the first racing disc brakes. Despite the initial success, Halibrand's Mag wheels were not immediately accepted at the Brickyard. Racers felt that the old flexible Rudge Whitworth–type wire wheels had a little give, whereas the mags were rigid, tended to crack, and cer-

It's like stepping back in time, as nothing much has changed at Offenhauser since Fred set up shop in Alhambra, California, in 1950. No CNC machines here, but it still churns out product.

The shelves at Offenhauser are packed to the rafters with cool vintage speed equipment: everything from 59A flathead cylinder heads to multi-carburetor intakes for long obsolete vehicles.

It's one operation at a time, as drill presses are still used to tap threads. In this case, it's a dual-quad, low-profile cross-ram intake for a small-block Chevy.

tainly suffered some problems due to the different rate of expansion between the steel hub and the magnesium wheel.

Undaunted, Halibrand redesigned the entire wheel mounting system for 1950. In place of the splines, he keyed the wheel to the hub with six pins, and the pin-drive knock-off wheel became the industry standard. According to Drew Hardin writing for the Specialty Equipment Market Association (SEMA), "Every race car that won the Indy 500 between 1951 and 1967 was outfitted with Halibrand wheels."

While Halibrand did not invent the custom wheel, he certainly played a major role in their popularity. However, the company is equally well known for its quick-change rear axles.

Halibrand sold the company in 1979 to Harry Jackman (Wheels). Subsequently, the company was split and sold numerous times. Ted Halibrand died in 1991 of a heart attack.

As much as Frank Kurtis owned the oval track scene with his production-line race cars (big cars in this case), so did Ted Halibrand with his quick-change axles and wheels. (Photo Courtesy Dan Shannon)

1948-1951
AT LAST, THE 1948 SHOW

The year 1948 was a seminal point in the history of hot rodding. It began with the publication of *Hot Rod* magazine and continued with the invention of organized drag racing and the National Association for Stock Car Auto Racing (NASCAR). Nothing would be the same.

"Big" Bill France

On the eve of the great hot rod explosion on the West Coast, something happened on the other coast that was of equal importance: NASCAR.

"Big" Bill France was born in 1909 in Washington, D.C., where he grew up to become a mechanic and eventually owned his own auto repair shop. According to an interview conducted by Sylvia Wilkinson for her book *Dirt Tracks to Glory*, France often ditched school to go watch the board track races at Laurel, a high-banked track halfway between Washington and Baltimore. When he was 16 or 17, he took his father's Model T to Laurel and ran it up the 31-degree bank and said, "Dad complained about how his tires wore out so fast."

After two years in Central High School, France went to work in a garage. Meanwhile, he and Hugh Ostermeyer built a race car with an OHV Model T engine and a wooden body covered with canvass. He said it ran close to 90 mph at the half-mile dirt track at Pikesville, Maryland.

France's next car was another single seater built with Don and Babe Moore. It was powered by a 4-port Riley, and France ran it in as many races as he could. At the time, he was working in a gas station in the winter as a "cold-start" man, going out and starting people's cars. It was after marrying Annie in 1931 that he decided if he

Early NASCAR stock car racing at Daytona Beach was partly on the sand and partly on the highway. The north turn (shown here on February 10, 1951) got extremely tricky as the cars churned up the sand. (Photo Courtesy Dan Shannon)

was going to fix cars he might as well do it in warmth. He said, "When I saw Daytona Beach, I thought it was the prettiest place I'd ever seen."

After relocating to the beach in the fall of 1934, France got a job at Sax Lloyd's Buick-Pontiac-Cadillac garage. Just a few months later, he watched as Donald Campbell streaked across the sand at 276 mph in what was to be the last of the Daytona speed runs before the land speed action moved to Bonneville.

The city of Daytona needed a new attraction, and well-known racer Sig Haugdahl came up with the idea for a race that was part on the beach and part on a front-age road that ran parallel. The first race was in 1936, and France came in fifth, driving a 1935 Ford owned by Glenn Brooks. They won $300. In fact, the top five finishers were all Ford V-8s, and the winner was Milt Marion's Ford sponsored by Permatex Gasket Corp. The total purse was $5,000, and the city said it lost $22,000, but France could see that there was a whole lot more money in racing than wrenching.

The Elks Club promoted the 1937 race, and it too apparently lost money. It didn't look like there would be a 1938 race until the chamber of commerce asked France if he knew of anyone who might want to put on the race. France tried unsuccessfully to reach a local race promoter. When he couldn't, he told local businessman Charlie Reese about the situation. He said that he knew how to get the cars and drivers but had no money. Reese said, "I'll put up the money, and you can do the work." They were off to the races—literally.

In December 1947, a meeting was held, and Red Vogt suggested they call the organization NASCAR, and the association was officially incorporated on February 21, 1948. The first Strictly Stock race was held on June 19, 1949, at Charlotte Speedway. More than 13,000 fans saw Glenn Dunaway win the 200-lap race in a Ford, but he was disqualified for having illegal rear springs and the win was given to Jim Roper driving a Lincoln.

These were supposed to be stock cars. However, France conceded that they caught a few cheaters with high-compression heads or modified suspensions. Eventually, of course, the stock cars became far from stock, and the sport became a huge market for the aftermarket.

Hot Rod Magazine

The story of the founding of *Hot Rod* magazine has been told many times, particularly well in David N. Lucsko's book *The Business of Speed*. In Barstow, California, native Robert E. Petersen found himself unemployed after a stint at MGM studios. The 21-year-old Petersen joined Hollywood Publicity Associates (HPA) and soon found himself working on the promotion of the SCTA's First Annual Automotive Equipment Display and Hot Rod Exposition scheduled for January 23–25, 1948, at Los Angeles's National Guard Armory, Exposition Park.

According to Lucsko, Petersen soon discovered that there was no dedicated periodical in which to advertise this show beyond the *SCTA Racing News*. *Throttle* magazine ceased publication with its December 1941 issue and was never seen again.

Petersen formed a partnership with Robert Lindsay, and the pair quit HPA and used a loan of $1,000 to print 5,000 copies of their new *Hot Rod* magazine. The magazine was published to coincide with the SCTA show and with plenty of hard work selling it copy by copy, it was a hit.

Strangely, the first issue, which featured Regg Schlemmer's beautiful track roadster (Regg had a speed shop at Imperial Highway and Wright

Stock car racing always provided fans with a thrilling spectacle. Here, Bob Sampson scrambles to extricate himself after flipping at the Detroit 250-miler in 1952. (Photo Courtesy Dan Shannon)

The first issue of Hot Rod *magazine appeared in January 1948 in time for distribution at the Hot Rod Exposition sponsored by the SCTA. Instantly, Petersen realized he had a tiger by the tail.*

Although not an enthusiast, Petersen was not shy about coming forward and working to deliver the material for which Hot Rod *became known.*

Road in South Gate, California) carried only a one-page feature on the show. The March issue carried a one-page follow-up review. Petersen, no doubt had other ideas for his fledgling publishing empire.

There were a surprising number of advertisers in that inaugural issue of *Hot Rod,* starting with Navarro Racing Equipment, George Riley & Co., Regg Schlemmer, Smithy's Mufflers, Bell Auto Parts, Winfield, Blair's, Sharp, Weber, and Evans.

By the second edition, *Hot Rod* carried ads from Wayne Manufacturing, Ed Iskenderian, Kong, Howard's, Potvin, Lewie Shell, Smith & Jones, Ansen, Weiand, and Evans, etc. Business was booming, and *Hot Rod* had given the hobby, sport, and industry an international voice.

The March 1948 issue of *Hot Rod* carried just a one-page report on the Hot Rod Expo, which seems rather minimal for such a significant event. During the course of the show, Lou Baney and his team converted a dilapidated 1932 Ford into a sleek hot rod complete with every mechanical improvement.

On the back page of the April issue, Tattersfield & Baron introduced a new four-carburetor manifold for the flathead Ford V-8 plus new heads and "special pistons."

Open the very first issue of Hot Rod *and there's a quarter-page ad from Navarro Racing Equipment, advertising heads and this pair of intakes. Navarro was quick to understand the benefit of advertising.*

Parts With Appeal was always done in the best possible taste—well, it was 1949, but nevertheless, there was nothing smutty about the feature. Hot Rod *never even mentioned the brand unless it was there for all to see.*

Veda Orr, racer and wife of speed shop owner Karl Orr, published the monthly California Timing News, *which carried race results, photos, and, of course, news of both lakes and oval track racing.*

Parts With Appeal

The old adage that "sex sells" was true even in 1948 because that first issue of *Hot Rod* included a feature called "Parts with Appeal." Three quarters of a page was devoted to a photo of Jane Norred holding a fuel pump. In the second issue, Parts with Appeal became a full-page image of a young Norma Hammitt with a dual-carburetor intake. It was an odd piece of fluff because typically the manufacturer of the product was never mentioned despite a detailed description.

SCTA Hot Rod Show

The first annual Automotive Equipment Display and Hot Rod Exposition was announced to the racing public by Veda Orr in the December 1947 issue of *California Timing News*. Orr's published comments regarding the event can be summarized as a publicity exercise to avert adverse publicity regarding the hot rod movement.

With more than 55,000 tickets sold, the Expo was deemed a huge success and the SCTA even garnered a small profit. Such was the success that the SCTA hosted a second, weeklong event, again at the Armory from January 21–30, 1949. This time, more than 60,000 tickets were sold. Oddly, I could not find a single mention of the event in the preceding issues of *Hot Rod* magazine.

As there had been in 1948, there was a 35-cent program that listed all 60 show exhibitors that reads like a who's-who of hot rodding. Everyone from Ansen to Weiand advertised in the 28-page program that included a two-page "Speed Directory."

Meanwhile, other promoters saw the success of the Hot Rod Show and emulated the concept. In 1950, the Oakland Roadster Show was born, and that same year, Detroit hosted its first ever Hot Rod and Sports Car Show. The sports car tag was interesting because for 1950 the Los Angeles Hot Rod Show became the Hot Rod and Motorsports Show and was now sponsored by the Russetta Timing Association rather than the SCTA. Later that year, *Hot Rod* magazine sponsored a new event called the Motorama from November 16 to 19 at the Shrine Convention Hall.

Sponsored by the SCTA and presented by Hollywood Associates, the very first Hot Rod Show was held over three days at the Los Angeles National Guard Armory.

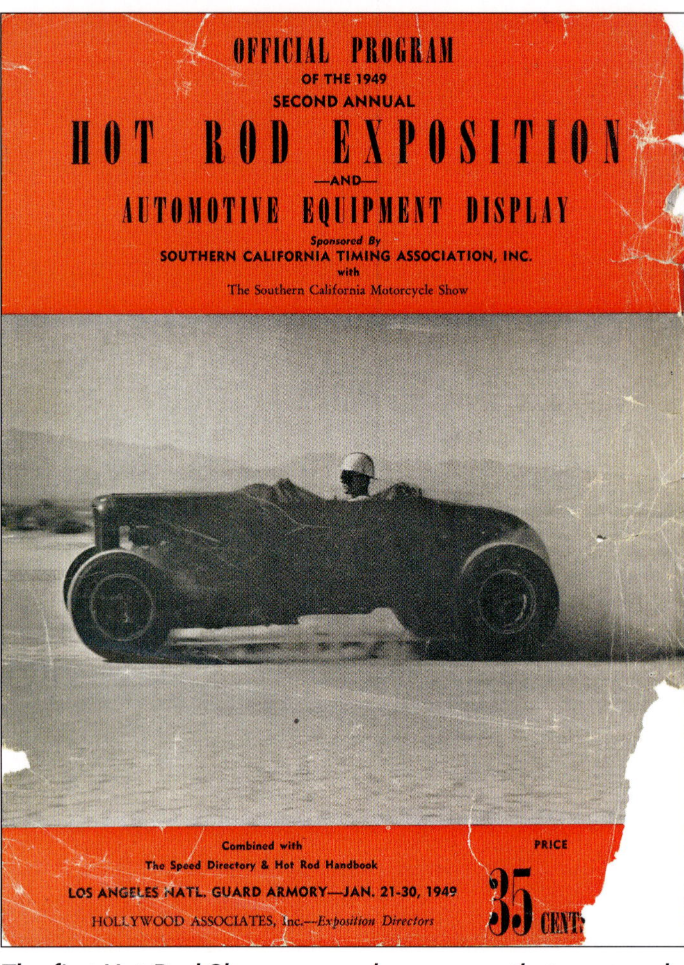

The first Hot Rod Show was such a success that a second show was scheduled for 1949 at the same venue with SCTA again as the sponsor. However, this time the Hollywood Associates name was written bigger.

More than a few people turned up, and the Hot Rod Show was a huge success. Even Ford had an exhibit proclaiming that 656 of 678 cars competing in the SCTA Speed Trails are powered by Ford or Mercury engines.

Al Sharp's Triplet

It's always questionable to make the statement that someone was first, but it's generally accepted that Al Sharp was the first to make and sell a Tri-Power setup for the flathead Ford V-8, which is often described by the abbreviation 3x2. Eddie Miller and Stu Hilborn had made a four-carburetor intake for Stu's streamliner, but it was never produced in numbers. There were triple carburetor intakes for Chevy sixes, but Al's Triplet, advertised in the February 1948 issue of *Hot Rod*, was the first production tri-carburetor intake for a V-8 engine to market.

After his family moved from Oklahoma, Sharp grew up in Los Angeles and went to George Washington High. Graduating in 1938, Sharp joined the Idlers car club and experimented with multi-carburetor setups on his Deuce roadster. Meanwhile, according to Paul Smith in *Merchants of Speed*, Sharp worked at Lumley's Auto Wrecking on Main Street in Los Angeles before moving on to train as a pattern maker in a local foundry.

By the time America entered the war, Sharp was working at the Long Beach naval yards. He was eventually called up and shipped to the South Pacific, where he applied his pattern-making skills for the navy as a foundry man's assistant.

Upon his demob, Sharp, along with Gordon Pilkington, started a company called SP Pattern Service (Sharp and Pilkington). According to Smith's book, Sharp said, "Gordy was a much better pattern maker than I ever was." The pair complimented each other, and the business prospered, making patterns for Braje, the Granatellis, Howard's, McGurk, and many others.

Toward the end of the 1940s, Sharp established Sharp Speed Equipment at 6225 Wilmington Ave. in Los Angeles. The company took a booth at the first Hot Rod Show and took a third of a page in *Hot Rod* to advertise its dual manifold. Also listed were high-compression heads, center-mount idler and generator brackets, and foot pedals (track or lakes).

Meanwhile, they were working on the "Triplet" that was advertised the following month—it was the pattern for the thousands of aftermarket and OEM Tri-Powers that followed. Interestingly, in that same issue of *Hot Rod*

Niekamp's roadster was no show queen, although it won America's Most Beautiful Roadster plus seven other awards. In 1952, Niekamp wheeled it to a speed of 142.50 mph at El Mirage.

was a new product release announcing some new cylinder heads that said, "The new job includes incorporated water manifold in the head, features greater thickness than heads used in the past on V-8s."

Again, according to Paul Smith, SP Pattern was sold to Lyle Knudsen. Knudsen was an early member of the Gear Grinders and a lakes racer who was actually mentioned in the final issue of *Throttle*, having made a run at 115.23 mph in his roadster. Knudsen also had a business with Red Wilson called KW Machine Co. that advertised "Racing Equipment for Ford '6' Engines" in the SCTA Program of October 19, 1947.

Sharp continued to make speed equipment and introduced a 4x2 intake in 1952. Some have argued that the 4x2 was unnecessary overkill, but in 1953, Al Sharp's friend Art Chrisman was the first to hit 140 mph in the Santa Ana quarter. Chrisman's dragster was powered by a Sharp-headed Mercury with a Sharp 4x2 intake.

As far as I can ascertain, Al Sharp was the first to market with his Triplet manifold, now known as a 3x2, but there was no room for a generator. His next product was some high-compression heads.

Chrisman's Sharp-equipped flattie was state of the art in its day. Note the Sharp heads, intake, and four Strombergs enabling him to hit 140 mph in the Santa Ana quarter. (Photo Courtesy Dan Shannon)

Flathead powered at the Pomona drags, the hood says Sharp Equipped, and the flattie was fitted with Sharp heads and the Sharp 4x2 intake. The Chrismans later switched to a Hemi.

Of course, Sharp was soon copied, and most manufacturers including Baron, Edelbrock, Schnell, etc., developed 4x2 intakes. This one is an Edelbrock with four Strombergs, but the Ford Speed Parts heads are interesting.

One of the most famous specials was **Old Yeller II** *built by Max Balchowsky of Hollywood Motors. It was restored by Jimmy Shine for Dr. Ernie Nagamatsu, who drives the heck out of it.*

Sharp Speed Equipment went on to be one of the more successful and enduring brands. The brand was purchased in 2012 by Mike Herman of H and H Flatheads, who continues to produce many of Sharp's products for the flathead Ford V-8.

Hot Rod Sports Cars

Soon after the end of World War II, European automakers began to export sports cars to the United States, where there were no indigenous examples. One of the first to create this type of hybrid was Brit Sydney Allard, who began modifying and souping up Ford V-8s as early as 1933.

One of the first American-built specials was the Baldwin-Payne Special built in 1947 by Willis Baldwin, who sold it to Phil Payne. The car, which still exists, had a 1932 frame that was shortened to a 103-inch wheelbase (from 106) while power came from a 268-ci Mercury engine with an Isky cam, Evans 9:1 heads, and dual carbs. More sports car than hot rod, it was very well executed and competes to this day in historic events.

According to Dean Batchelor in his book *The American Hot Rod*, "Many of this group were Ford based. The availability, adaptability, and low cost of the early Ford V-8 components appealed to the home builder who wanted to road race." Most of these cars, such as Max Balchowsky's channeled Deuce roadster built for Fred Vogel; Ak Miller's *El Caballo*, built for the 1953 Carrera Pan Americana; and Duffy Livingstone's *Eliminator*, were one-off specials not intended or destined for production.

Douglas Aircraft engineer C.E. "Chuck" Manning managed to develop a reproducible and therefore salable special, along with plans. It was based on a steel tube

Balchowsky was famous for Buick and Cadillac engine swaps. For **Old Yeller II**, *he chose a 401-ci Buick Nailhead fitted here with an Offenhauser intake and six Stromberg 97s, though at times it had 48s.*

Specials, particularly the American variety, usually had a copious engine bay that would take anything from a flathead to a Hemi. This builder chose an Oldsmobile Rocket fitted with an Edmunds 2x2.

frame and fiberglass body powered by a 296-ci Ford flattie with Edelbrock heads, Harman & Collins cam, and Spalding dual ignition. The second car was built by Sparks & Bonney for Jacques Bellesiles, and maybe a total of six were sold altogether. The *Manning Meteor* was well covered in the December 1952 issue of *Popular Science*.

The advent of fiberglass later gave rise to any number of specials that eventually became known as kit cars. They in turn became another booming segment of the aftermarket, especially when Bruce Meyers invented the dune buggy in 1964.

There were several magazines catering to the sports car clientele that included sports rods. As a consequence, the magazines such as *Car and Driver, Motorsport, Road and Track*, etc. enjoyed advertising from the likes of Almquist; Bell Auto Parts; Harmon & Collins; Isky; Liqui-Moly; Lee's Speed Shop; Midwest Racing Equipment of Cleveland, Ohio; Newhouse; Offenhauser; Speed-O-Motive; and Von Esser's of Chicago.

Oldsmobile Rocket 88

Big engines in small cars were nothing new to hot rodders. Heck, that formula was the essence of the genre, and Oldsmobile is generally regarded as the first factory to offer this muscle car combo. That said, in 1945, the Cadillac and Oldsmobile divisions of General Motors began separate but simultaneous development of OHV V-8 engines.

As the flagship division, Cadillac felt that it should get to introduce the new technology first. However, Oldsmobile persisted, and in 1949, using the existing 76 Futuramic B-Body platform, it dropped a healthy 303-ci engine with a 7.5:1 compression ratio and 135 hp into the lightweight Rocket 88, which may have been the first factory hot rod. Incidentally, the 88 was placed between the 76 and 98 and replaced the straight-6 engine 78—got that?

A relatively big engine in a relatively lightweight body rocketed Oldsmobile out of its staid reputation onto the NASCAR podium. According to various sources, Robert "Red" Byron won the NASCAR Strictly Stock class in 1949, and Oldsmobile went on to win 6 of the 9 NASCAR late-model division races in 1949, 10 of 19 in 1950, and 20 of 41 in 1952.

Indeed, the Rocket 88 was such a success it inspired Jackie Brenston to pen what is also regarded as the first rock-n-roll hit song "Rocket 88" recorded in Memphis in 1951. While Brenston is credited with writing the song, it is generally accepted that it was actually written by Ike Turner.

Oldsmobile's OHV Rocket proved popular with hot rodders. Engines began to appear in hot rods connected to what was usually a Ford transmission via a cast-aluminum adapter plate from companies such as Cragar or Wilcap. Of course, the same developments happened with the introduction of the OHV Cadillac engine.

When Oldsmobile introduced its Rocket 88, the automaker killed it on the NASCAR stock car circuits. You have to love those Rocket 88 illustrations as well as the chain holding the door closed. (Photo Courtesy Dan Shannon)

Darrel Greig's typical hot rod Oldsmobile Rocket V-8 was fitted with an Edmunds dual intake and a pair of stock GM Rochester AA 2-barrel carburetors. The intake cost $69.50 in 1951.

Gotha Automotive Specialists in Harvey, Illinois, made a number of products, including these neat valve covers and 6x2 intake for the Oldsmobile V-8. Note the SP Products carburetor tops made by Al Sharp and Gordon Pilkington. (Photo Courtesy Scotty Gosson)

However, it took time for these newfangled OHV engines to catch on, as had the Ford V-8.

A bone stock Rocket V-8 outperformed all but the best hopped-up flatheads, and although some diehards tried to hang on to the flathead, the writing was on the wall. The OHVs opened the floodgates for a whole new breed of speed equipment from companies such as Edmunds, which was quick to market with intakes, etc.

Goleta with a Splash of Nitro

Most people have never heard of Goleta, which is a small town about 11 miles up Highway 1 west of Santa Barbara, California. According to an account by Wally Parks in his book *Drag Racing Yesterday and Today* and Robert C. Post in his book *High Performance*, there was a paved road on the north side of the airport that ran east to west away from the mountains and toward the ocean.

Around 1948, members of the Motor Monarchs club from Ventura and engine builder Bob Joehnck of Santa Barbara, decided to approach the airport manager, Bill Swain, to see if they could use the property for legal drag races. Swain agreed but said they needed to get some insurance, which they did. Named the Santa Barbara Acceleration Association (SBAA), they started holding organized drag races every other Sunday in late 1948 or early 1949.

Contemporary photographs show a two-lane road with central markings probably about 25 feet wide. Cars ran east to west and, according to Parks, "Three-tenths of the distance was used for accelerating and the remaining two-tenths to get stopped."

Apparently, track length was limited by a locked gate at the top end. The finish line was a small, narrow bridge, and spectators could tell the winner by seeing which one bumped up over this bridge first. Timing was done with stopwatches. There were three classes: Roadsters, Fenderless Coupes, and Fendered Coupes. To raise money for trophies, they passed a hat and got a percentage from a chuck wagon that came out to sell burgers and hot dogs.

One weekend, two guys came up from Los Angeles to "drag it out." Fran Hernandez was in his stock-bodied 1932 three-window, and Tom Cobb was in a 1929 Model A roadster channeled over a 1934 frame. Hernandez was running a bored and stroked 296-ci Mercury with triple Strombergs. Cobb's roadster had a small Jimmy-blown 1934 Ford V-8.

Most would bet the blown car would win, but the strange-smelling coupe crossed the culvert a length ahead. Hernandez apparently quickly gathered his kit and got out of there, revealing to no one the secret of nitro.

According to Joehnck, racing at Goleta petered out when other better surfaces were found and when the SBAA got tired of all the work involved in putting on the races. Albeit short lived, Goleta was the site of the first organized drag races and probably the first use of nitro in a drag race.

It is generally accepted that the first drag races were held at Goleta, which is now Santa Barbara International Airport. They were organized by members of the Motor Monarchs club from Ventura. (Photo Courtesy Dan Shannon)

The car that everyone expected to win at Goleta because it was a fast blown roadster was Tom Cobb's, which is seen here at Bonneville in 1951 with its removable hardtop. (Photo Courtesy Dan Shannon)

Cobb, who operated a dyno shop with Stu Hilborn and Jack Engle, was an early fan of the GMC blower. At Bonneville in 1951, the roadster was powered by an Evans-equipped flattie and four carburetors atop the Jimmy. (Photo Courtesy Dan Shannon)

The winner of the infamous Cobb versus Hernandez race at Goleta was Fran Hernandez in his Edelbrock-equipped three-window coupe. What he failed to mention was the splash of nitro. (Photo Courtesy Greg Sharp)

Meanwhile, a few years later and east of the Rockies, the Memphis Rodders car club, established in 1947, staged events, eventually on a regular basis. Its events were held on an old airstrip at Halls, Tennessee, which is about 60 miles north of Memphis. In the late 1950s, *Hot Rod* covered its exploits quite extensively.

Drag racing was not the only auto sport that had a spiritual home at Goleta on what had been a Marine Corp. Air Station and eventually became Santa Barbara International Airport. Also racing at Goleta in 1949 was the California Sports Car Club, which organized trials in the summer of 1949 on the runways and roads of the former Marine base. Eventually, airport manager Swain organized the first annual Santa Barbara Road Race in September 1953. Two years later, actor James Dean raced his third and final race there on May 29, 1955, not long before he was killed in a road accident.

Edmunds to Fenton

Ed Almquist called Aaron J. Fenton a "born salesman." Fenton, whose real name was Finkelstein, grew up in Lincoln, Nebraska, where his father Ben owned Ben's Auto Parts on O Street. Eventually, young Finkelstein changed his name to Fenton, moved to California, and worked for speed equipment manufacturer Eddie Edmunds, who had likewise moved south to Los Angeles from Portland, Oregon.

According to Roy Pagnini's excellent website, eddie-edmunds.blogspot.com, Edward Edmunds was born on February 18, 1916. He eventually worked as a race car mechanic and got into the business of making heads and intakes in the 1930s. Apparently, he and his wife, Maryann, a graphic designer, moved to Los Angeles because it had better access to pattern makers and aluminum foundries (before World War II, Portland was still a lumber town).

After the war, Edmunds applied for and received a reconstruction finance loan to expand his business. He purchased a large warehouse at 2042 Stoner Ave. in West Los Angeles. Half the building was dedicated to manufacturing and the other half to installation. Edmunds's intention was to supply the government with hopped-up Cadillac engines for tanks,

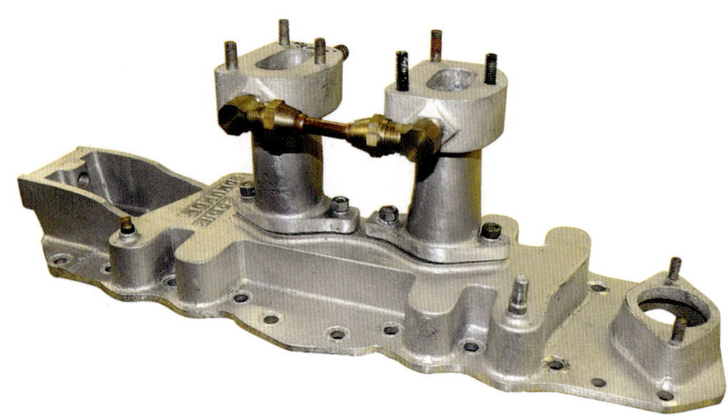

This is possibly a modern repop. Nevertheless, this dual shows the simplicity of early flathead intakes by Eddie Edmunds with simple sharp-angled runners and adapters for different carburetors.

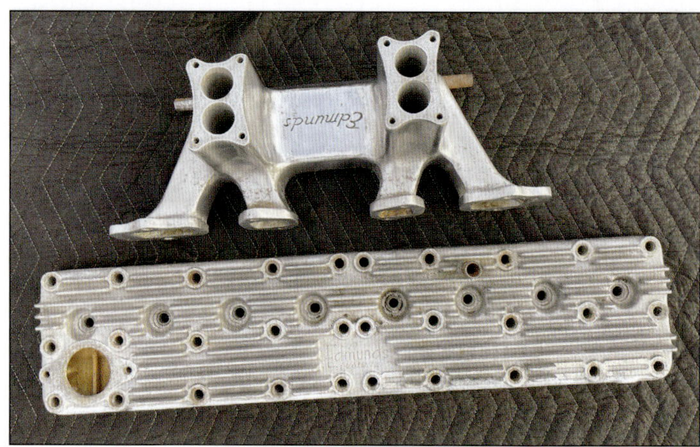

Edmunds was very quick to market with a wide range of parts for what we now think of as oddball engines, such as the Pontiac straight-8 or the 1937–1950 Hudson/Essex 8 for which this head and intake were designed.

but apparently, he was unable to deliver and subsequently went bankrupt. However, Edmunds did manufacture a vast selection of dual intakes for most American automobiles and cylinder heads for most flathead engines.

In a four-page brochure published in the spring of 1952 with prices effective March 1, Edmunds listed 37 different cylinder heads and 55 different intakes for Buicks through Studebakers. Also listed are a bunch of custom accessories, from Cadillac exhaust headers to custom oil-bath air cleaners. The brochure also carried a rather fancy coat of arms, which was quite normal in the 1950s because the Italian coachbuilders all had a coat of arms.

Edmunds was the subject of a 2½-page story in the September 1952 issue of *Popular Mechanics* that told of the Keikhaefer Aeromarine Motors's Chrysler Saratoga entry in that year's Mexican road race. The vehicle was fitted with the Edmunds dual-intake manifold "that set a new speed record with amazing sprints of 112 mph." The article went on to say: "Nearly a third of the cars in that race carried Edmunds equipment."

Unfortunately, Edmunds struggled to stay on top of his game, and Fenton eventually took over the production and sales of Edmunds's line of cast-aluminum heads and intakes for the flathead Ford V-8 under the name of Standard Automotive Mfg. While those cast parts bore his name, it was his cast-iron exhaust manifolds for flathead Fords as well as Oldsmobile V-8 models and Ford

Edmunds, who was less concerned with performance than drivability, failed to secure a government contract for high-performance Cadillac engines but found a ready market with racers. (Photo Courtesy Dan Shannon)

Aaron Fenton (Finkelstein) took over the Edmunds brand and continued to develop new products, such as this flathead intake designed to accept a Carter 4-barrel carburetor. Other manufacturers made similar intakes.

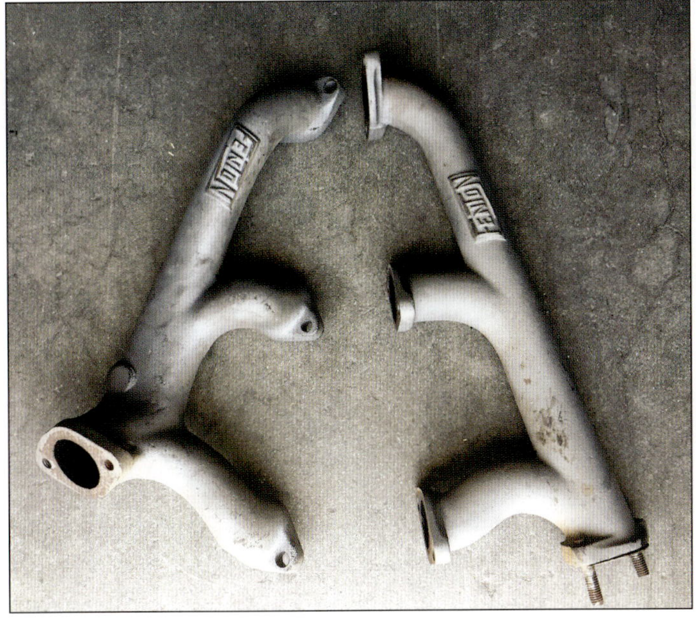

Fenton came out with cast-iron headers in the very early 1950s not only for the flathead Ford V-8 as shown but also for 1937–1951 Chevrolet six as well as for 1935–1952 Plymouth Dodge applications.

There's a lot going on here with twin Stromberg 97s atop a S.Co.T. blower and Fenton finned aluminum cylinder heads on a 24-stud flathead Ford V-8. In 1953, these heads would have retailed for $74.

Santa Ana Drags

sixes that really put the Fenton brand on the map. In 1952, Fenton, located at 3401 East Pico Blvd. in Los Angeles, introduced a dual-triple intake for the straight-6 Chevy.

Fenton kept his prices low and pursued the mass merchandisers, such as Montgomery Ward, rather than the small speed shops. That philosophy did not endear him to many in the industry. Nevertheless, Fenton built a huge brand that eventually gravitated by the late 1960s into the one-piece cast-aluminum wheel business. Sadly, his health deteriorated along with his company. However, many of his parts are still produced.

With hot rodders racing just about anywhere they could, it was inevitable that some enterprising Americans would commercialize the activity. Those guys were Cloyce Roller Hart, known as C.J. "Pappy" Hart; Creighton Hunter, who delivered oil and spark plugs; and Frank Stilwell, a used car and motorcycle dealer.

Hart was already 39 in 1950 and was known as "Pappy." He operated a gas station and used car lot on Bolsa Avenue not far from a small airport north of Newport Bay, California. That airport, a training base for U.S. Air Force pilots, is now John Wayne International Airport.

Compared to other impromptu strips, Santa Ana was organized. Using an abandoned taxiway, the initial entry fee was 50 cents, there was insurance using Stilwell's motorcycle racing connections, there was an ambulance, and there was timing equipment for top speed at the end of the quarter. The navy got 10 percent of the gate.

The first event was July 2, 1950, and there were 55 entries. There was no prize money; instead, Pappy handed out trophies that could be sold back to Pappy for

C.J. "Pappy" Hart's wife, Peggy, was quite the woman, as can be seen in this shot from 1953 of her behind the wheel of her Cadillac-powered rail wearing safety shorts and a sweater. The Cadillac looks stock. (Photo Courtesy Dan Shannon)

One of Pappy's partners was Creighton Hunter, who raced several cars, including this 1924 T roadster known as the Hunter Oil Special. It was sponsored by Mooneyes, and supposedly it had the first use of the Mooneyes logo. (Photo Courtesy Dan Shannon)

Seen many times and duplicated more than once, Dick Kraft's The Bug *was a Mercury-powered rail job with finned heads and three Strombergs. It regularly raced at Santa Ana in the early days, eventually hitting 113.92 mph. (Photo Courtesy Dan Shannon)*

Another regular at the early Santa Ana drags was Don Blair in his radically channeled T bucket. It had a similarly equipped flattie with finned heads and triple Strombergs. (Photo Courtesy Dan Shannon)

Whether flat or vertical, the Frenzel centrifugal supercharger is an impressive-looking piece of kit. Unfortunately, it never delivered the promised goods in terms of boost. (Photo Courtesy Scotty Gosson)

the wholesale cost of $7. In his book *High Performance*, author Robert C. Post said, "Hart had designed a timing system with a pair of photoelectric cells that activated a clocking device set up in an old hearse parked at the finish line."

According to Dean Batchelor in *The American Hot Rod*, "The Santa Ana strip started out with top speed timing at the end of the quarter mile because most rodders were accustomed to seeking the highest speed. It soon became obvious that the car that recorded the highest speed wasn't necessarily the first car to reach the end of the quarter mile."

The fastest time recorded by an automobile in 1950 was 120 mph set by brothers Harold and Don Nicholson, who operated Nick's Speed Shop in Pasadena.

As he was often quick to point out, Pappy Hart did not invent drag racing, but he and his partners sure made a safe business out of a dangerous pastime. Seeing the potential, other strips soon opened at Kingdon, Saugus, Paradise Mesa, and indeed across the nation and eventually the world.

Centrifugal Frenzel

In 1932, Duesenberg offered a centrifugal supercharger on its Model SJ. Mounted horizontally above the engine and driven by a vertical shaft, the supercharger only produced 5 pounds of boost. Nevertheless, the SJ claimed a top speed of 129 mph and 0–100 mph in 17 seconds—all from a car weighing 2.5 tons.

Two years later, the development work having been done, the brothers Joseph, Robert, and Ray Graham of the Graham-Paige automobile company offered a centrifugal supercharger in their Custom Eight. The supercharger was very similar to the Duesenberg design with a large aluminum impeller and housing mounted horizontally just under the carburetor. It looked like a frying pan with a lid.

At least one of these Graham superchargers found its way onto a race car. The evidence of Ted Cannon's McDowell-Model A lakes racer was pictured in Dean Batchelor's book *The American Hot Rod*.

Since Stanley Chavik assembled this 21-stud with Eddie Meyer heads, he has completely changed the spec. This is a reproduction Frenzel supercharger with a pair of Stromberg 97s.

Obviously, these shaft-driven superchargers did not lend themselves to an aftermarket bolt-on application, hence the McCulloch. In turn, other belt-driven systems, such as the S&S, led to the distinctive, vertically mounted Frenzel. It was an odd but nonetheless impressive assembly, especially when polished.

Introduced late in 1949 and featured on the October 1952 cover of *Hot Rod* and the November 1950 issue of *Road and Track*, the Frenzel was the work of John Frenzel of Frenzel Engineering, 634 S. Franklin St. in Denver, Colorado. The story goes that Frenzel produced 12 kits plus the prototype. The night before he was due to ship them to dealer Warren Fraser's Custom Engine Parts on Washington Boulevard in Culver City, someone broke into his shop and stole three along with the prototype.

The Frenzel was fairly expensive (around $175) and produced only about 3.5 pounds of boost. Frenzel never made more than the original baker's dozen. That said, Aaron Loveless of Loveless Performance is putting them back into limited production.

Italmeccanica and S.Co.T.

In postwar Europe, Italy and other countries were trying to get back to work, but materials and markets were in short supply. Nevertheless, in Turin (Torino), Italy, circa 1950, the Italmeccanica Co. (IT) was formed

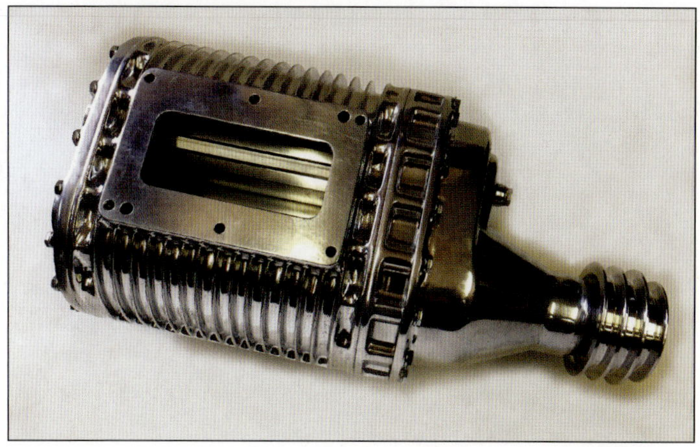

Still desired 70 years on, the S.Co.T. blower is faithfully reproduced in Southern California and available from HandHFlatheads.com, however, it does have updated internals.

to build automobiles powered by supercharged Ford V-8 engines. The car was a failure, but the blower was somewhat more successful.

According to Jay Fitzhugh in *The Rodder's Journal #29*, IT produced nine different blowers with capacities ranging from 500 cc to 4,000 cc for the Ford and Mercury. Supercharger kits were imported by Italmeccanica in New York and distributed by Antonio Pompeo of Hi-Power in New York and John Edgar in Los Angeles.

Unfortunately, those early IT kits were made of poor materials, were held together by an odd assortment of mismatched European fasteners, and had crude instructions. Consequently, IT was dissolved only to reemerge as Societa Compressori Torino. In due course, the company announced a new and improved blower to be marketed as S.Co.T. for $424.50. The problem was that many inferior IT blowers were dumped on the U.S. market for as little as $262.50 with a second carburetor thrown in for free. Eventually, Hi-Power of New York dumped its remaining Ford kits for $85.

Duff & Roy's Glasspack

Frank "Duffy" Livingstone gave the performance industry so much but is unfortunately barely remembered. Born in Springfield, Illinois, in 1925, Livingstone's folks moved west the following year and settled in Pasadena, California. In March 1942, at 17 years and 2 months old, he enlisted in the U.S. Navy and served until 1946, flying in Panama and the Southwest Pacific.

When he was discharged, Livingstone returned to Pasadena and immediately bought a hot rod from Dave Mitchell at Mitchell's Roadster Shop at 1709 Colorado Blvd. in Eagle Rock, California. He then went to work for Mitchell's, where he learned to weld.

Made in Turin, Italy, the Italmeccanica/S.Co.T. superchargers came in a range of sizes: 500, 750, 1100, 1500, 2000, 4000, and 4500 cc crank-driven assembly. The 4000-cc unit was recommended for Ford/Mercury applications.

Frank "Duffy" Stanley Livingstone (on the left) and Art Ingels lift the cowl on Duffy's Deuce roadster. It is being mocked up here with a 337-ci flathead Cadillac. Livingstone, of course, went on to develop the go-kart that Ingels invented. (Photo Courtesy Dan Shannon)

Livingstone also purchased a Deuce roadster from Mitchell. He pushed a flathead Caddy V-8 with a home-made dual intake and a LaSalle transmission. In an interview with Tom Medley, Livingstone remembered the car ran about 113 mph at El Mirage.

Meanwhile, Mitchell's Roadster Shop became Mitchell's Mufflers, and the shop was relocated. It moved to 803 E. Colorado Blvd. in Pasadena, which had previously been the location of the Al Hawkins Speed Shop. It was while working for Mitchell that Duffy built the very first glasspack muffler. Prior to that, mufflers were packed with steel wool.

In 1953, Livingstone partnered with his old high school friend Roy Desbrow, whose channeled yellow 1932 Ford pickup had been on the cover of the January 1952 issue of *Hot Rod* and had been Hot Rod of the Month. It went on to become one of the "75 Most Significant 1932 Ford Hot Rods." Meanwhile, the friends opened Duff & Roy's Muffler Shop behind a gas station in Pasadena at 152 E. Huntington Dr.

Within three years, Duff & Roy's had three locations, and the glasspack mufflers were selling well under the glasspack (GP Mufflers) brand. They also sold steel wool–packed mufflers as steel-pack (SP Mufflers) brand. Apparently, they bought the casings, cores, and the end caps from Porter Mufflers in Los Angeles, and put the glass in the mufflers. According to Dick Martin, "The first glass-pack mufflers didn't work so great, as the resin melted or the material would blow out the back of the muffler."

In his interview with Tom Medley, Livingstone said, "We built a 40x20 building out of muffler tubing, but in the muffler business, it was 'get big or get out,' so we got out." Livingstone's and Desbrow's contribution to the muffler business was far overshadowed by their even bigger contribution of what we now call "karting" but was called "go karting" back then. However, that's another story.

Norden 180-degree Crank

Charlie Braden's Norden Machine Works was located at 5853 W. Washington Blvd. in Culver City. According to Scotty Gosson, Barney Navarro turned to Braden to assist with construction of a 180-degree "flat plane" manganese-molybdenum crank for a Ford flathead V-8.

The 180-degree concept had been tried about 30 years previously by Ed Winfield in his Model T. The stock Model T had a firing order of 1-2-4-3, causing cylinders 2 and 3 to draw off of the same carburetor after the preceding cylinder in line had already gotten a full shot. Winfield correctly felt that these cylinders were not getting as much fuel as cylinders 1 and 4, which was robbing power from the engine. To correct this, he reconfigured both the crankshaft and camshaft to change the firing order to 1-3-2-4, ensuring that each cylinder got a full shot.

Navarro felt the same about the flathead V-8. He consulted with Winfield and had Braden make the crank. The flathead suffers breathing problems with a 1-5-4-8-6-3-7-2 firing order, wherein cylinder 1 follows cylinder 2 but also, with the center cylinders sharing an exhaust port, there is the problem of dilution of the intake stroke from the adjoining cylinder's exhaust. The solution was to use a "flat" crankshaft that changed the firing order to 1-8-3-6-4-5-2-7, ensuring a healthy intake charge to each cylinder.

Also, in 1948, Norden announced its "Hypertension Carburetors" in the April 1948 issue of *Hot Rod*. These pressurized carburetors were able to be used in updraft, downdraft and sidedraft applications. Four were used to some effect on the 1955 Jado Special at Bonneville, but they didn't appear to catch on.

Ed Winfield, seen here with goggles (third from left), at Hanford, California, on July 4, 1921, experimented with a 180-degree, flat-plane crank to increase power in his Model T. In theory, he was correct, but in an understatement said, "It had a little vibration." (Photo Courtesy Old Crow Speed Shop)

Paint in a Can

According to the National Aerosol Association, "The first use of an aerosol arose during World War II." Scientists from the U.S. Department of Agriculture developed the idea of pressurized insect spray to help protect soldiers from malaria-carrying mosquitoes in the South Pacific during World War II.

The invention of paint in a can may be traced back to 1924, when scientists explored the idea of using liquefied gas to atomize drops of liquid. In 1949, at the suggestion of his wife, Bonnie, Edward H. Seymour of Sycamore, Illinois, added paint to existing spray-can technology to demonstrate an aluminum paint he developed for painting steam radiators. Meanwhile, Robert Abplanalp, founder of Precision Valve Corp., invented the first mass-produced aerosol valve.

Seymour's patent was awarded in 1951 and Abplanalp's was awarded in 1953. From that point forward, the industry exploded. Seymour of Sycamore became a major player in the aerosol paint industry, and in the mid-1960s launched its automotive division.

As America prepared for its first shot at the moon, the word "coatings" entered our vocabulary and a hitherto unknown company Sperex, located at 2239 Pontius Ave. in Los Angeles (the company eventually moved to Gardena), began advertising very high temperature (VHT) flameproof coatings. The paint revolutionized the industry, and everyone and his or her uncle began to paint everything in sight from blocks to headers.

According to a release at the time, "NASA technology contributed to development of the paint. Sperex was provided a technical support package detailing the research of Goddard Space Flight Center on long-life inorganic coatings. The information helped Sperex perfect its own formulations."

In 1989, Sperex, which also developed VHT Track-Bite, was acquired by P.J. Harvey's PJH Brands, a Scottsdale, Arizona, performance chemical company that was founded in 1972. With all that said, the VHT brand is now a division of Dupli-Color, a Sherwin-Williams company.

Cadillac was probably the first to use a flat-plane crank starting in 1915. It was followed by other manufacturers that now include the C8 Corvette, Mustang GT350, and several European cars.

The first paint in a can that many of us remember using might have been Sperex Very High Temperature (VHT).

CHAPTER 5

1951-1955

THE CHRYSLER HEMI SPELLS THE DEATH OF THE FLATHEAD FORD

Mickey Thompson's Bantam coupe from 1952 pretty much said it all, as the big Chrysler Hemi pushed the tiny flathead aside. Prior to the Hemi, Thompson ran two Mercurys in the Auto-Moly Special with Gene Cole driving at Bonneville in 1952. The coupe ran an impressive 194.34 mph.

The following year, Thompson replaced the back motor with the $40 junkyard Hemi, a 4-71 blower that cost just $10, and five carburetors. Thompson said the following in Tom Madigan's book *Mickey Thompson: The Lost Story of the Original Speed King in His Own Words*: "However, I did learn one important fact—the blown Chrysler on fuel was the answer. The question was, how to make it run."

The swap from one four-letter word (Merc) to another (Hemi) said it all.

The Chrysler Hemi

It goes without saying that World War II propelled engineering development, as speed and power became all-important. Chrysler worked with Continental on the development of a giant 1,792-ci V-12 that was used in the Patton tank. It produced 810 hp and 1,560 ft-lbs of torque and enabled Chrysler's engineers to gather some valuable information that they put to good use in their postwar automobiles.

In 1948, Chrysler engineers John Platner, a graduate of the Chrysler Institute of Engineering, and William Drinkard, manager of the engine development department, worked to downsize that tank engine for use in an automobile. What they came up with was a 90-degree, 330-ci, cast-iron V-8 engine with hemi heads. Code-named A-182, the Hemi was not quite ready for production. A lot of valvetrain development still needed to be done along with some ignition and crankshaft work.

Nevertheless, Chrysler debuted the Hemi V-8 for the 1951 model year as standard in the Imperial and New Yorker models and optional in the Saratoga. The "Fire Power" capacity was 331 ci due to an oversquare 3.81-inch bore and 3.63-inch stroke. With a 7:1 compression ratio,

Introduced for the 1951 model year, Chrysler's Fire Power Hemi kissed the flathead Ford V-8 goodbye. It is a tight fit in a Model 40, but with four Stromberg 97s atop a Weiand intake, it's just enough.

In 1952, Mickey Thompson's 196-mph Bantam was powered by two Evans-headed flathead Ford V-8s. For 1953, he replaced one flattie with a $40 Junk Hemi to which he added a $10 junk Jimmy.

In 1953, Dodge introduced its small 241-ci Red Ram that, like its big brother, initiated plenty of speed equipment, such as this Offenhauser intake with three 94s. (Photo Courtesy Scotty Gosson)

By the time the Chrismans got to Great Bend, Kansas, for the first Nationals in 1955, the Sharp-headed flattie had been replaced with a massive Hilborn-injected Hemi that broke transmissions. (Photo Courtesy Dan Shannon)

it produced 180 hp and 312 ft-lbs of torque but weighed a whopping 745 pounds. One head alone weighed almost 120 pounds, and a belt better be worn when lifting one.

Chrysler's DeSoto division came out with its smaller 276-ci Fire Dome version in 1952, and Dodge followed suit with its smaller still 241-ci Red Ram in 1953. Although all three engines differed in detail, they shared the same basic architecture. Despite their weight, the Hemis were gold, and the aftermarket soon glommed onto them as the next step to the top of the podium.

Obviously, it took time for the industry to tool up for the new engine, and some never did, but in the April 1951 issue of *Hot Rod,* Don Francisco began to explore the possibilities. The industry followed suit.

This was a tight race in the early 1950s between Ak Miller in the Deuce roadster and Wally Parks in his Model A roadster. Notice the 356 Porsche ready to run behind them. (Photo Courtesy Greg Sharp)

The Pomona Drags

Long before the Winternationals (1961) and the World Finals (1984), drag races took place at Pomona by the Choppers car club and members of the Pomona Valley Timing Association (PVTA). Looking for a safe, off-highway place to race, the club first tried Fontana, a few miles east. Eventually, the club got the ear of Pomona Police Patrolman Bud Coons, local Chief of Police Ralph Parker, and the Pomona city council, which allowed the use of the Los Angeles County Fairgrounds. It is now called the Fairplex Pomona.

Pomona was no stranger to auto racing, though. The first half-mile dirt oval was built at the fairgrounds in 1934. In 1949, the L.A. County Fair debuted an auto-racing program, and in the 1950s, JC Agajanian promoted stock car races on the dirt oval. Sports car races were also held there in the 1960s.

According to Robert C. Post in his book *High Performance*, the first Pomona drag race in 1951 featured a showdown involving Joaquin Arnett of the Bean Bandits and Bob Rounthwaite's five-carb'd, 326-ci GMC-powered *Thingie*. *Thingie* won, but Arnett set a new strip record at 129.88 mph.

That same year, over at the legendary 5959 Hollywood Blvd. in Los Angeles, *Hot Rod* magazine editor Wally Parks had his eye on the quarter mile.

Parks had been involved in the Southern California motorsports scene since the mid-1930s, and as a member of the Road Runners, he participated in the 1937 formation of the SCTA. Parks had raced at the lakes but saw the bigger potential of organized quarter-mile drag racing that negated the need for a hot, dusty dry lake bed as a venue.

Drag races could be held all over the country on unused airfields. Besides, the lakes were getting roughed up from all the abuse. Heck, it was already happening, it just needed organizing, and if nothing else, Parks was an organizer. He wrote in *Hot Rod*, "The Pomona meet had shown what could be done in all parts of the country for eager and willing hot rodders."

With the blessing of *Hot Rod* publisher Robert E. Petersen, Parks founded the National Hot Rod Association (NHRA) in 1951. He continued to grow both the publication and the fledgling association, officially launching the NHRA in 1953. Small ads ran in *Hot Rod* offering memberships for just $2.

Parks worked diligently for the sport, and I remember once asking him if he was tired.

The #25 car was not the only race car in the Chrisman stable. This is his 1929 Model A Tudor. In 1954, Jack Chrisman turned 114.64 mph with a mild 75-percent nitro mix and a flattie. With a Hemi, he turned 125 mph. (Photo Courtesy Dan Shannon)

By the mid-1960s, Pomona held two national events: the Winternationals and the World Finals. It was firmly established on the drag racing scene because of good weather and the sheer volume of local race cars. (Photo Courtesy Dan Shannon)

"I've been tired all my life," Parks replied.

The NHRA's first sanctioned event, the Southern California Championship Drags was staged at Pomona in April of that year.

"We had seats for 200, and we drew 15,000," said Parks.

Parks finally departed Petersen Publishing in 1963, having attained the position of editorial director for all publications. He took the NHRA with him.

So-Cal Slicks

When the So-Cal belly tank lakester topped out at 198.34 mph at Bonneville in 1952, Alex Xydias knew he had to do something that would get people's attention. Drag racing was the next big thing, and he operated the So-Cal Speed Shop, so he had to move with the times. Always the canny operator and seat-of-the-pants marketer, Xydias wanted a car that he could run at the drags but occasionally at the lakes and at Bonneville.

As it happened, the Russell Langthorne and Jim Gray three-window Class C Modified coupe with a 1945 292-ci Jimmy 6 that ran 153.061 mph at Bonneville in 1951

was for sale. Out of Oxnard, California, the car was chopped (though not as chopped at the time as the Pierson brothers coupe) and had a nice sprint car nose formed by Frank Kurtis.

Xydias purchased the coupe and cut a million holes in the chassis.

"That was a lot of work to very little benefit," Xydias said.

While Xydias was hole-sawing, Buddy Fox and Tom Cobb suggested that they run the car for the 1953 season. They would use their 258-ci flathead fitted with a front-mounted GMC blower, four Stromberg 48s, and a Scintilla mag. At the 1953 Bonneville Speed Week, the so-called *Double-Threat Coupe* set the Class C record at 179.749 mph.

According to Xydias, quoted in the *So-Cal Speed Shop* book by Mark Christensen, "Then one day, a guy came into the So-Cal Speed Shop with a pair of brand-new Ardun heads."

Xydias quickly made a deal and pushed them under the counter for the future. Fox & Cobb parted company, so Fox put his motor in the coupe, and he and Xydias went drag racing. They set the Class B record at the Pomona drags at 121.16 mph.

This is the only color shot I have ever seen of the So-Cal Speed Shop coupe running at Pomona with recap slicks from Bill Krech at Inglewood Tire Service. Soon, purpose-built slicks dominated the sport. (Photo Courtesy SO-CAL Speed Shop)

Pretty soon, the recaps were replaced by purpose-made slicks from companies such as M&H Racemaster, which had seen the need and the potential market. Its first slick came in 1957. (Photo Courtesy Dan Shannon)

In time for Bonneville, Xydias hammered the top a little harder, as hard as the Pierson brothers coupe, and built up a new front-blown Ardun with another Scintilla mag from Joe Hunt and four carburetors in line rather than a quadrant. They were not quite prepared enough, Xydias remembered, and the car did not do well. However, back on the strip with 10-percent juice, they bumped their record by 8 mph to 132.79 mph. What also gave them a boost beside the nitro was the use of some grippy slicks.

Writing in his book *High Performance,* Post said, "Alex Xydias, proprietor of the So-Cal Speed Shop in Burbank, began marketing special 'asphalt slicks' in 1953, recaps with seven inches of tread and purportedly yielding 'four times the traction of a regular tire.'"

According to Xydias, the recaps were from Bill Krech at Inglewood Tire Service, which was located at 1105 E. Redondo Blvd. in Inglewood, California. Incidentally, Krech rented out the front of his shop to race driver, cam grinder, and hot rod builder Frank "Wildman" McGurk and was a charter member of SEMA.

Among other venues, Xydias advertised the So-Cal "Slicks" Special Drag Race Tire in the October 1953 issue of *Hop Up*. Sizes available ranged from 5x16 at $13 to 8.00–8.20x15 at $21.50. However, the small print said, "Prices listed are to cap your tires (for exchange). We can sell 'Slicks' outright on a guaranteed casing for an additional $3.50 each."

At the time, there were only a few producers of slicks besides Inglewood: Bill Casler located at 1004 W. Brooks St. in Ontario, California, who was famous for his

Cheater Slicks; Bill Moxley located at 1527 E. Van Buren St. in Phoenix, Arizona; and Bruce Alexander of Bruce's Recaps in Oakland, California, whose slogan was "Bite by Bruce."

Hot Rod ran a story in the February 1958 issue titled, "Answers to Your Racing Tire Problems." The story said, "Bruce has re-capped over 10,000 tires for racing purposes over the period of the last 12 years," indicating he started around 1946.

Alexander built tires for such luminaries as Hershel McGriff, Lee Petty, and Marshall Teague. He went on to help Firestone develop its first stock car racing tire introduced in 1956.

There was also Russell Tire Co., located at 2101 San Fernando Rd. in Los Angeles, that advertised in the January 1948 issue of *Hot Rod*. At that time, the majority of racing slicks for both dirt and asphalt were recaps.

4-Barrels Are Better than 2

The first 4-barrel carburetors were introduced in 1952 at the same time by Carter (WCFB) and Rochester (4GC) on the 1952 Cadillac Series 62 as the company celebrated

As we have seen in the business of speed, if two is good, four must be better. The introduction of the Carter WCBF 4-barrel carburetor in 1952 revolutionized the industry. A bunch of 97s was no longer the only answer.

GM's Rochester Division had its own 4-barrel: the 4GC. It was a pair of 2Gs stuck together, looking very similar to its Carter counterpoint. That said, it could flow significantly more than three 97s.

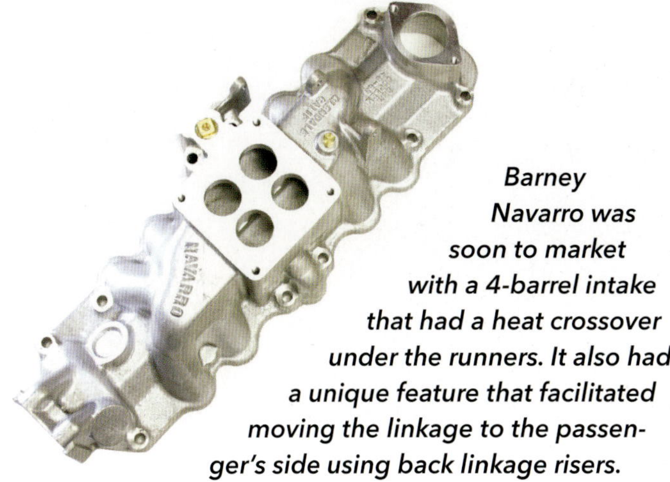

Barney Navarro was soon to market with a 4-barrel intake that had a heat crossover under the runners. It also had a unique feature that facilitated moving the linkage to the passenger's side using back linkage risers.

Quick to market, Weiand was advertising its new 4-barrel intake for flathead Ford V-8s in the April 1953 issue of Hot Rod *magazine. It boasted a 180-degree firing order, was exhaust heated, and had a chrome-like polish, all for just $46.*

its 50th anniversary. With two primary and two secondary bores, the 4-barrel carburetors were also available on the Oldsmobile 98, the Olds Super 88, and the Buick Roadmaster.

Although weighing a hefty 18 pounds, the Carter WCFB (which stood for Will Carter Four Barrel) enabled manufacturers (and in turn hot rodders) the ability to dramatically increase performance. Indeed, the 1962 Cadillac boasted 190 hp at 4,000 rpm, the highest rating in the industry at the time.

The Rochester, which was nothing more than a pair of 2Gs joined at the hip, was produced with 486-, 553-, and a whopping 692-cfm ratings. In comparison, three Stromberg 97s flow 486 cfm (3 x 162 cfm each). As soon as these carburetors appeared in showrooms, the speed merchants were on them. Companies, such as Edelbrock, Edmunds, Navarro, Offenhauser, and Weiand, were quick to develop 4-barrel intakes for the Ford flathead.

Interestingly, in a *Hot Rod* magazine test, Marlan Davis wrote, "The single-quad intakes weren't up to the best 'ancient' multi-carburetor Stromberg 97 intakes."

That said, if one 4-barrel carburetor was good, two must be better, but we're getting ahead of ourselves. That setup wouldn't appear for a couple years.

Studebaker

The August 1952 issue of *Hot Rod* published a story titled "The Studebaker V-8 Engine." The subhead said, "Reasons for a new engine, choice of design, problems encountered in development, and performance characteristics," as presented by Studebaker Corporation engineers: E.J. Hardig, T.A. Schreger, and S.W. Sparrow.

The story was almost nine pages long and gave a detailed analysis of Studebaker's 232-ci V-8. With five main bearings and solid lifters, it made 120 hp at 4,000 rpm and 190 ft-lbs of torque at 2,000 rpm. It was thrifty

The late Jim Ewing, founder of Super Bell/Bell Tech, epitomized the 1953 Commander mystique when he drove his Stupidbaker to Bonneville and went 226 mph with a Donovan Olds motor.

too, not that many cared. In the 1951 Mobilgas Economy Run, a Studebaker Commander with overdrive took first place, having achieved 28 mpg on the 840-mile route from Los Angeles to the Grand Canyon.

The engine, which was eventually punched out to 289 ci, was a hit with the aftermarket. Quick to market was John McKusick's Precision Tool & Mfg. in Los Angeles with a Stu-V intake for dual stock carbs. *Hot Rod*'s September 1952 issue carried a six-page feature on McKusick's Studebaker conversions and road tests.

For the 1953 model year, Studebaker introduced the distinctive and some say polarizing Commander. Designed or at least credited to renowned French-born industrial designer Raymond Loewy, credited designer of the Greyhound Scenicruiser and of Coca-Cola stuff, the 1953 Studebaker was certainly a departure. Some say it referenced the French Citroen DS. However, the Citroen was not introduced until 1955, so the influence was possibly in the other direction. In fact, Bob Bourke, an employee at Loewy's South Bend, Idaho, studio, designed the 1953.

Nevertheless, *Motor Trend* magazine described the all-new 1953 Studebaker as "The most refreshing, stimulating and progressively styled car to emerge from a stock car manufacturer since the days of the Lincoln Continental and the coffin-nosed Cord."

With that said, it was polarizing and despite its peppy engine, customers stayed away in droves. Studebaker

These days, Studebaker V-8s are not the popular choice, but Diana Branch powers her 1932 Tudor with a 299-ci version fitted with an R3 factory cam, Mallory ignition, and a rare Edmunds intake with twin Studebaker Strombergs.

Diana's husband, Tom, has a similar setup in his roadster. However, the engine is a 1963 again with a factory R3 cam and Mallory ignition. However, his intake is a rare Spencer with four Strombergs with backdraft tops.

only sold 151,576 units in 1953, half of which were Commanders and only 19,236 were Starliner coupes. Bonneville racers did like it, though.

I've never been able to find any definitive aerodynamics test results, but the car looked slippery, and salt racers quickly embraced it. Indeed, Frank Morgan of Marysville, California, ran one at the 1953 Bonneville Nationals in B-Coupe as did Grand E. Hayes of Salt Lake City. Since that day, Loewy Studebakers have been a stalwart of the salt but rarely with the stock engine.

Although Studebaker eventually ceased to build automobiles, in March 1966, the parent company had thrived for more than a decade as a closed investment company, a conglomerate corporation with numerous non-automotive divisions. In 1961 alone, the company enjoyed more than $100 million in sales.

STP

No doubt one of the most iconic logos of all time has to be that of STP. It was first introduced in 1954 as a product of Chemical Compounds Inc. in St. Joseph, Missouri. An abbreviation for Scientifically Treated Petroleum, STP was started with $3,000 by Charles Dwight (Doc) Liggett, Jim Hill, and Robert DeHart. The men packaged STP oil treatment in a backyard garage at night and sold it from the trunks of their cars during their business and pleasure trips.

There are bare knuckles on this Knucklehead. Al Keyes's safety gear included loafers and a T-shirt as he hunkered down on Chet Herbert's Beast that propelled Herbert into the cam business. (Photo Courtesy Dan Shannon)

In 1961, STP was purchased by the Studebaker-Packard Corp., and in 1963, Andy Granatelli was appointed CEO. He began to increase the brand's marketing efforts through auto and boat racing promotions. Within three years, annual sales had reached $43 million.

Chet "the Beast" Herbert

One of the first speed equipment manufacturers to explore the Chrysler Hemi was Chet Herbert. Herbert, who graduated from Santa Ana High School in 1945, began his career with a 1936 Ford coupe and then a 1939 Mercury coupe. In 1946, he shifted gears to race motorcycles. Sadly, his own riding career was short lived due to contracting polio in 1948. Nevertheless, he remained an industry force albeit from the confines of a wheelchair.

The first *Beast* was a stripped down, nitro-burning, 80-ci 1948 Harley knucklehead that at the second-ever Santa Ana Drags on July 16, 1950, made an incredible 103-mph pass. Rider Al Keyes took home Top Eliminator, and eventually the *Beast* hit 135 mph.

Capitalizing on his bike's success, Herbert got into the cam business. Renting some space in Ernie Backman's Quonset hut at 2049 S. Main St. in Santa Ana, he fashioned his own cam grinder from a Sears Roebuck lathe.

Herbert's innovation was to adapt the Harley roller cams for performance automotive use. At first, this development was derided by others, but according to Ed Almquist in his book *Hot Rod Pioneers*, "By the mid-1950s, most Bonneville speed records [that were] running with overhead-valve engines had roller-tappet cams."

Herbert was soon in production and advertising cams for Cadillac, Oldsmobile, Chrysler, De Soto, Chevy, GMC,

The STP logo, introduced in 1954, has to be one of the most iconic in the industry.

A young Chet Herbert, confined to a wheelchair because of polio but unconfined in every other way, consults on the back-motored Cal-Loui roadster—the first in 1954 to a two-way average of 200 mph. (Photo Courtesy Greg Sharp)

Dean Moon and Moon Discs

Dean Moon grew up south of Los Angeles in Santa Fe Springs, California, a booming oil town where his father "Pop" Moon operated a café complete with a go-kart track named Moonza after the Italian track Monza. While attending Whittier High School, Moon worked in the café and also at Urich-Gibbs Lincoln-Mercury in nearby Whittier, where he learned basic auto mechanics. His first product was a fuel distribution block that he made in shop class.

After graduating high school, toward the end of World War II, Moon joined the Merchant Marines and toured the Pacific. Returning from duty, he teamed up with his brother and officially started Moon Automotive.

In 1951, Moon was racing a 1932 Tudor that was part sponsored by Urich-Gibbs, and it made the cover of the

and oddly MG. Featured in one of his December 1952 *Hot Rod* ads was the *Beast III*, which was known as the fastest single-engine car in America. Powered by a 1951 Chrysler V-8 that was equipped with Herbert's roller tappets, the *Beast III* averaged 235.99 mph. The logo on the front wheel covering was a giant rendering of a cam lobe and a roller tappet.

The Cal-Loui roadster was powered by a Chrysler Hemi fitted with an axial flow supercharger introduced in 1956 by Norman Latham. This is a modern version installed on a Lincoln V-12 by Troy Ladd's Hollywood Hot Rods.

Built in 1952, Chet Herbert's Beast III (background) was powered by a 1951 Chrysler Imperial Hemi fitted with Hilborn fuel injection and a Vertex magneto. Art Chrisman drove it to a one-way best of 238.095 mph.

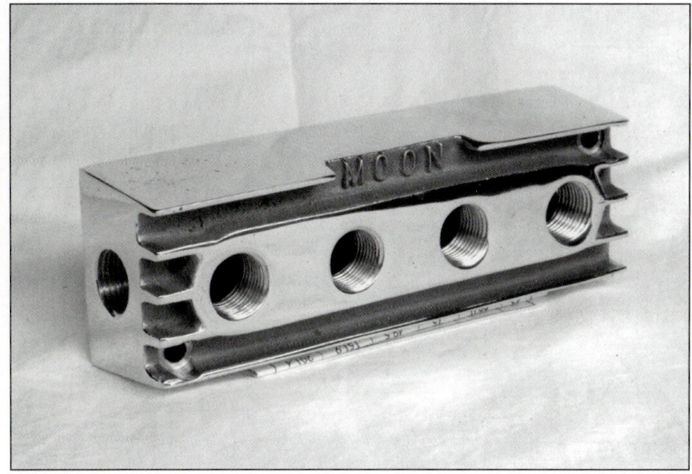

Dean Moon's first ever product was made in school shop class. Eventually, Moon developed this cast-aluminum fuel distribution block for distributing fuel to a multi-carburetor assembly. (Photo Courtesy Mooneyes)

Chet Herbert's Beast III *was restored by Dave Crouse of Custom Auto for Mark Brinker, who later donated it to the Wally Parks Motorsports Museum. It proudly displays the distinctive roller cam logo.*

Moon's home run came in 1951 with his seminal, spun aluminum Moon Discs. He'd first seen the aluminum discs on Ak Miller's needle-nose, #15 Modified 1927 roadster at Bonneville. Moon Discs are spun in the same way today as they were in 1951. (Photo Courtesy Mooneyes)

December 1951 issue of *Hop Up* magazine. Running it at a Russetta meet, the brothers hit a credible 141 mph (12 mph faster than they had run at the previous meet) and placed third in the B Sedan class.

That same year, Moon spotted the aluminum wheel discs on Ak Miller's 1927 roadster that ran at Bonneville in 1951. Apparently, Moon borrowed Ak's tooling to make his own. However, Uncle Sam had other ideas, and Moon was drafted into the U.S. Air Force and sent to Korea. The discs would have to wait.

Luckily, if you can call being drafted lucky, Moon was trained as an aerial photographer. This put him in great stead when he returned and began marketing Moon Equipment that, of course, included his spin on the now iconic wheel discs.

With a few dollars in his pocket, Moon purchased a lot at 10820 S. Norwalk Blvd. in Santa Fe Springs, literally just down the block from Moon's Café. There, he built Mooneyes USA, the company that continues to this day. He later became one of the founders of SEMA as well.

Dean Moon was one of the founders of the Specialty Equipment Market Association (SEMA) in 1963 and became president in 1964. Manning the Moon booth at a SEMA Show is John Stark and a sleepy-eyed young lady. (Photo Courtesy Mooneyes)

Harvey Crane Cams

Sensing a growing industry, apprentice machinist Harvey Crane Jr. founded Crane Cams in a corner of his father's machine shop in Hallandale, Florida, on January 1, 1953. His work began after purchasing a second West Coast cam for his Deuce hot rod and finding it not the same as his first purchase. Crane figured he could do better, and according to Ed Almquist, "Crane purchased a Storm-Vulcan cam grinder for $600 per month," which

In his youth, Harvey J. Crane gained a reputation for building hot flathead Fords. On January 1, 1953, he opened Crane Engineering. In 1966, he began refunding the cost of a Crane cam and kit to each Nationals class winner. (Photo Courtesy Dan Shannon)

was a lot of money in 1953.

As were many others, Crane was called up and sent to Korea. Business was put on hold until he returned. Soon after that return, Crane stepped up his game, purchased even better Van Norman equipment, and moved into a 3,500–square foot facility.

Crane, like his cams, enjoyed a bumpy ride in advertising battles with those West Coast grinders, particularly Isky, and with his own company. He was expelled from Crane Cams on January 24, 1989. It was indeed a bumpy ride.

B&M

Established in 1953 by high school friends Bob Spar and Mort Schuman, B&M Automotive Products began as a general automotive repair shop. In 1955, Bob's brother Don went to work for B&M, and in April 1959, Don bought out Schuman.

In the late 1950s, Bob and Don began tinkering with GM's Turbo Hydra-matic 4-speed transmission that had been introduced in 1939 for the 1940-model-year Oldsmobiles. The transmission was continually being developed by General Motors to keep up with the competition. However, for 1956, it was substantially revamped as the Controlled-Coupling Hydra-matic.

The Controlled-Coupling Hydra-matic incorporated a secondary fluid coupling and a pair of sprag clutches in place of the former friction clutch and brake bands. Now, shifting was done in part by alternately draining and filling the secondary coupling. The dual-range feature allowed the driver to hold the transmission in third gear until the maximum allowable upshift points, which improved performance in traffic or in mountain driving.

The Hydra-matic was a good, tough box for drag racing, but the Spars correctly surmised it could be better, especially if they could find a way to make the transmission stay in low gear until the driver wanted to shift. Toward the end of 1958, after almost two years of experimentation, they figured out how to disable the safety

Soon after B&M transmissions burst upon the market in 1953, it seemed that there wasn't a race car that didn't carry its logo, including K.S. Pittman, who is wheels up at Lions Drag Strip. (Photo Courtesy Dan Shannon)

override and modify the vanes on the fluid coupling to allow higher RPM. Looking for a good name for their invention, they combined "Hydra-matic" and "stick shift" to form "Hydro-Stick."

What made the Hydro-Stick slick was the fact that upshifts and downshifts during normal driving remained automatic. However, the shift lever could be used to override the auto shifting. In 1960, the Hydro-Stick was the subject of a six-page article by Don Francisco in the February issue of *Hot Rod*. In 1961, the Hydro-Stick became the only patented 4-speed automatic racing transmission in history.

B&M went on to become a major force in the performance aftermarket. In 1963, it was one of the 13 founding companies of SEMA.

In 1969, B&M teamed with Andy Granatelli and Plymouth on a program to develop the only automatic transmission for Indy/United States Automobile Club (USAC) racing.

Corvette

If *Car and Driver*, *Motor Trend*, and *Road and Track* could be believed, the American market for European sports cars was vast. There appeared to be Alfa Romeos, Allards, Ferraris, Jaguars, MGs, and the like on every corner. If not on every corner, they were on every track, and

Basically, a B&M Clutch-Flite had the bellhousing removed and the torque converter replaced with a clutch and flywheel. The idea was that drivers could leave hard like a stick car but have the consistency and speed of an automatic.

B&M was founded in 1953 by Bob Spar and Mort Schuman, but soon Schuman was replaced by Spar's brother Don. Little did anyone realize that B&M would initiate the drag racing shift to automatic transmissions. (Photo Courtesy Dan Shannon)

Located at 1200 Whiteside St. in Los Angeles, Harry Weber began grinding cams and making flywheels in 1946 after apprenticing in his father's machine shop since the age of 10. Love the cast-in names.

Schiefer Manufacturing was started by Paul Schiefer in La Mesa, California, in the 1940s. The stamped 500 indicated this cast-aluminum flywheel is for 1949-1953 Cadillacs or Oldsmobiles. (Photo Courtesy Scotty Gosson)

From a styling point of view and from the innovative use of fiberglass, the 1953 Corvette was revolutionary, but from the technical and driving side, it was a truck in sheep's clothing.

GM's Harley Earl initiated the 1956 Corvette-based SR-2 when he heard his son Jerry was going to buy and race a Ferrari. The first SR-2 was not competitive, but Bill Mitchell made a lightweight race car out of it.

the domestic brands were nowhere to be seen. Detroit's Big Three didn't have a sports car between them or anything like it.

Chevrolet had a slump in sales, and as a consequence, GM styling guru Harley Earl initiated his Special Projects group to start working on a sports car in 1951. EX-122, code named Project Opel, was part truck and part sports car—well, kind of.

Unlike the aluminum-bodied, high-revving, twin-cam, swing-axle European sports cars, the Corvette was a low-tech build out of the parts bin. The chassis and suspension was that of the 1949 passenger car complete with a solid rear axle. Power came from the existing 235-ci Stovebolt straight-6 Blue Flame engine, albeit with three Carter sidedrafts, a high-compression head, and a high-lift cam. But there was no suitable manual transmission available, so the 2-speed Powerglide was used, figuring no one wanted a manual box. It was a sports car in shape only. It did, however, have a revolutionary reinforced fiberglass body.

Project Opel, named after GM's European arm that was purchased in 1931, was a hurried introduction. The first dream car was unveiled on January 17, 1953, at the Motorama at New York's Waldorf Astoria to a ho-hum reception. The first production car rolled off the Flint, Michigan, assembly line five months later on June 30. By December, Chevy had the 1954 Corvette in production at St. Louis, Missouri.

Despite the Corvette's lukewarm reception, Chevrolet persevered. The automaker has since used the Corvette to introduce new developments, including the 1955 introduction of its first V-8 since 1919.

Blue Flame Special or Wayne and the Stovebolts

Henry Ford once famously said, "I've got no use for a motor that has more spark plugs than a cow has teats."

Eventually though, he had to eat those words after Chevrolet introduced its straight-6 in 1929. He said in 1930, "We're going from a four to an eight, because Chevrolet is going to a six."

One drawback to the Stovebolt (so called because the bolts holding it together resembled bolts used in stoves) was that it had three small intake ports and four exhaust ports all on the same side of the head. It was not a performance head, and in the opinion of Lockheed engineer Wayne F. Horning, that meant that what was needed was a new, crossflow head. That was to come in 1939, and unfortunately, World War II got in the way.

After his stint in the navy, Horning returned to Lockheed and teamed up with his old friend Jim Borger to form the Western Mechanical Development Co. Its first product was a cast-iron, 12-port head for the Chevy 6-cylinder based loosely on Ed Winfield's rocker-arm design for a Ford.

Chevrolet's venerable old Stovebolt straight-6 began life in 1929. In 1941, it was bumped out to 235.5 ci, and in 1953, it became the Corvette's Blue Flame Special with a hot cam and three side drafts.

A Wayne-headed GMC powered the Kelly-Junkin Class C Modified roadster to 155.54 mph at the Bonneville Nationals in 1952. The straight-6 was also equipped with a Howard intake and Scintilla magneto. (Photo Courtesy Dan Shannon)

This crossflow head had six large exhaust ports on the driver's side and six oval intakes on the passenger's side. The head had cutdown Cadillac valves, Buick rocker arms, and stock Chevy inner valve springs and keepers. New to the head were tubular pushrods, new inner valve springs, and new retainers. Meanwhile, Frank Venolia helped with the bottom end that used a stock Chevy crank, GMC truck rods, and pistons cast in 142 TS aluminum.

The head proved itself in boats, on oval tracks, and at the lakes in Johnny Hartman's dual-purpose roadster that turned 142.24 mph as a Class B Lakester. Meanwhile, Jim Borger moved on and was replaced by Harry Warner. Late in 1947 or early 1948, the company was renamed Wayne Manufacturing Co., located at 3206 Fletcher Dr. in Los Angeles.

The company enjoyed some short-lived notoriety when the engine was chosen to power Marvin Lee's Pasadena Roadster Club streamliner that appeared on the cover of the very first 1949 Bonneville Speed Trails program. At the time, the open-wheel car driven by Bob Denny held the Class B Streamliner record at 153.545 mph, but Denny qualified with a speed of 160.42 mph.

The engine was a 248-ci Wayne-headed 1942 Chevy block with GMC rods, a Bill Spalding cam, and Tom Spalding ignition. However, various induction systems were tried, including multiple carburetors and Hilborn-Travers fuel injection.

As partnerships often do, Horning and Warner decided to go their separate ways. Warner purchased all the patterns and fixtures for the 12-port heads, as well as the company name, and moved lock stock and head to

7153 Encinal Ave. in La Crescenta, California. The separation caused endless confusion because Horning stayed put at the original address under the name Wyane F. Horning and continued to offer Chevy and GMC racing engines but (for now) not heads.

Of course, Horning was working on a new head, specifically for the GMC six, that was written up in the May 1951 issue of *Hot Rod*. Meanwhile, a Wayne-headed GMC was installed in Marvin Lee's bright yellow rebodied and renamed *City of Pasadena II* streamliner that unfortunately crashed at the 1950 Bonneville Speed Trials with C.L. "Puffy" Puffer driving. The car was destroyed, but thankfully, Puffy and the Jimmy were okay. Despite the accident, the speed (over 200 mph) was impressive, and the Wayne GMC head gained an enviable reputation.

No doubt looking for new markets to conquer, the salvaged engine was installed in a car for the 1952 Indianapolis 500, again with Puffy Puffer driving. Unfortunately, the car failed to qualify. It was the only GMC-engined entry among a field of Offys and the odd Ferrari.

Disheartened, Horning sold the business to speed merchants Frank McGurk, who purchased the patterns for the new pistons and intake manifolds, and Bill Fisher, sometimes known as "California" Bill, who purchased the patterns and the molds for two-piece aluminum valve covers and inventory. Horning returned to the aerospace industry.

Meanwhile, when the Corvette powered by a 235-ci Blue Flame straight-6 appeared in 1953, it looked

"California" Bill Fisher purchased the Horning 12-port GMC head and went on to publish "California" Bill's Chevrolet GMC & Buick Speed Manual. The book is still in print today. This Jimmy has Hilborn injection and a Ronco Vertex magneto. (Photo Courtesy Scotty Gosson)

Another Wayne-headed GMC is equipped with five single-throat Carter carburetors on a McGurk intake, Mallory magneto, a Nicson aluminum valve cover, and wet-sump oiling system. (Photo Courtesy Scotty Gosson)

A composite poster shows Nick Arias II at Bonneville in 1953 with the Wayne-headed Arias-Toros 1937 Chevy coupe and the Howard's 12-port aluminum head (in the foreground) that Arias was promoting. (Photo Courtesy Nick Arias III)

quite racy with three gold iridized single-throat sidedraft Carters with chrome stacks. However, it was still not a crossflow design and produced only 150 hp. The Corvette was a sheep in wolf's clothing with nowhere near the bite of the Wayne head.

Harry Warner, who continued to make 12-port heads for Chevys, decided to do the same for GMC. Like Horning, Warner decided Indy was the venue. In 1951, Bill Johnson's car sported a 12-port Chevy but failed to qualify. Warner returned in 1953 with the Wayne Manufacturing Special, actually the same car but with new driver Jorge Daponte who came all the way from Buenos Aires but did not qualify.

Despite the disappointments, Warner continued to produce heads for both Chevy and GMC. He moved the business to 432. S. Victory Blvd., Burbank, California, just down the street from Alex Xydias's So-Cal Speed Shop at 1104 S. Victory Blvd.

While there, Wayne developed a new DOHC head and had plans for a 24-valve version. Apparently, 3 of the 12-valve heads were produced, but their whereabouts are unknown. The 24-valve head was apparently never produced. Why? Because Chevrolet's 1955 introduction of the OHV small-block signaled the demise of the Stovebolt. Sure, there were stalwarts who would carry the "six" flag, and still do, but it would never outpace the V-8.

Of course, Wayne was not the only manufacturer of speed equipment targeting the Chevy/GMC six. Howard, for example, made a manifold to take five Stromberg 97s. There were also Scintilla mags and breathers from Stelling.

One company that did have a strong following in the Chevy six world was Nicson. It was operated by Nick and his son Chuck Glaviano, hence "Nic-son," at 4546 E. Washington Blvd. in Los Angeles. There, they made dual and triple manifolds for Chevy and GMC sixes. Nicson's *Hot Rod* ad of September 1952 also advertised cams, pistons, ignitions, and "heavy cast aluminum valve and push rod covers."

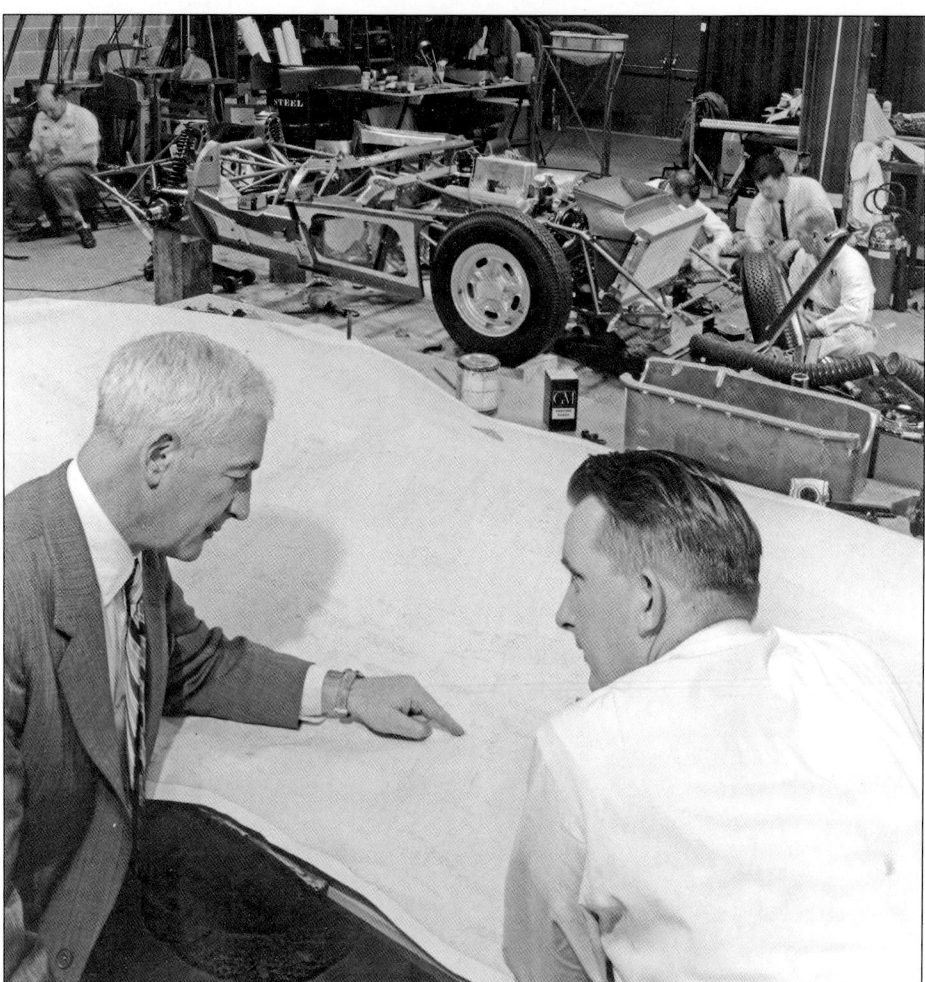

Building on the experience gained with the SR-2, Zora Arkus-Duntov (left) began working on the SS. Power came from a 265 punched out to 283 ci and fitted with new aluminum heads and redesigned fuel injection. (Photo Courtesy General Motors)

The Letter

On December 16, 1953, Zachary "Zora" Arkus-Duntov, father of the Ardun conversion for the flathead Ford, penned a memo to Maurice Olley, Chevrolet Motor Division's director of research and development. The subject: "Thoughts Pertaining to Youth, Hot Rodders and Chevrolet."

Duntov had joined General Motors on May 1 after seeing the new Corvette on display at New York's Waldorf Astoria. Like many, he was impressed with its styling but, like most observers, was less impressed with its mechanical specifications. Consequently, he wrote to Ed Cole, Chevrolet's chief engineer, and told him what he thought. He was hired as an assistant staff engineer but obviously had ideas above his pay grade.

The first paragraph of his memo to Olley states: "The hot rod movement and interest in things connected with hop-up and speed is still growing. As an indication: the publications devoted to hot rodding and hop-upping, of which some half-dozen have a very large circulation and are distributed nationally, did not exist some six years ago. From cover to cover, they are full of Fords. This is not surprising then that the majority of hot-rodders are

eating, sleeping, and dreaming [of] modified Fords. They know Ford parts from stem to stern better than the Ford people themselves."

The memo was prophetic, and Duntov was off to the races, literally. On September 9, 1955, he took a heavily camouflaged 265-powered Turbo-Fire '56 Chevy sedan to Pikes Peak. According to the movie made of the run, Duntov slashed more than 2 minutes off the class record, completing the 12½ miles in 17 minutes. Impressed, he told Ed Cole that he thought he could run a Vette up to 150 mph at Daytona Beach.

Duntov prepared three Corvettes for the February 1956 Daytona Speed Week. He drove his 1955 mule fitted with 1956 body panels. Betty Skelton and Jon Fitch drove 1956 Corvettes with 265-ci engines each fitted with a special high-lift Duntov cam. Fitch placed first in the Production Sports Car class with a speed of 145.33 mph, while Betty came second with a speed of 137.773. Duntov did apparently hit 156 mph on one run but was unable to back it up.

Touted by General Motors, which was observing the racing ban, as a "research project," the Corvette SS ran at Laguna Seca circa 1987 with John Fitch behind the wheel and Duntov riding shotgun.

Despite not officially hitting 150 mph (the headwinds were against them) and despite the AAA racing ban, Duntov's efforts were going a long way toward establishing the small-block Chevy as the racing engine. Interestingly, after the standing mile in which Duntov hit 92.142 mph, a teardown revealed an over-bored block. He was subsequently disqualified and switched to the Modified Sports Car class, which he won with a speed of 147.30 mph. Duntov wasn't done yet, though.

Y-Block

Introduced in March 1932, the Ford flathead V-8 was revolutionary, but by 1953, it was decidedly archaic, outmoded, and outperformed by all the new OHVs hitting the highways. The Y-block got its name because of its deep skirts that gave the engine a Y cross-section when viewed from the front. It was a sturdy and heavy engine at 625 pounds that initially had a capacity of 239 ci (Ford) and produced 130 hp (some 20 hp more than the final 1953 flathead). The Mercury version had 256 ci and produced 161 hp. Capacity gradually increased to 312 ci in 1956 with output at 285 hp for the 8V racing special or 300 for the Paxton supercharged version.

Unfortunately for Ford, the 1955 introduction of

Introduced in 1952, Ford's deep-skirted Y-block was the company's first OHV engine. The aftermarket was quick to embrace it, including Offenhauser with valve covers and that triple-carburetor intake. (Photo Courtesy HandHFlatheads.com)

Remembered for building one of the seminal Deuce roadster post–World War II hot rods, Doane Spencer (left) looks at installing a trans adapter to this Y-block. It was never installed in the car. (Photo Courtesy Greg Sharp)

Perhaps the ultimate Y-block, this conversion by the UK-based Weslake company featured aluminum heads and Lucas fuel injection. (Photo Courtesy Scotty Gosson)

the small-block Chevy was hot on its heels. While not very powerful to begin with, the Chevy soon overtook the Y-block. Nevertheless, Vic Edelbrock Sr. and his employees Don Towle and Bobby Meeks quickly began to develop parts, including a 3x2 intake. They used a 1955 Thunderbird that Vic had purchased and went drag racing, but they couldn't beat a supercharged T-Bird that was owned and raced by Dick Jones.

Small-Block, Big Heart

Over the years, several V-8s have revolutionized the industry. They include the Ford flathead V-8 of 1932, the Chrysler Hemi of 1951, the small-block Chevy of 1955, and more recently, the Chevrolet LS introduced in 1997.

To signify the new V-8 engine, the V of the Corvette emblem was made larger and colored gold. The block itself was of thin-wall casting, meaning that it was lightweight as well as compact. Nevertheless, it enjoyed 4.4-inch bore spacing and offered the ability to overbore it far beyond the stock 3.75 inches. With a 3-inch stroke, the initial displacement was 265 ci (4.3L). However, the factory limit was a staggering 400 ci.

Not surprisingly, *Hot Rod* magazine got the inside story and ran the article "Analyzing the Chevrolet V8" in its January 1955 issue. Ironically, it showed where the performance aftermarket was still at. The magazine ran a flathead "Head Hunting" story in the following February 1955 issue.

The article listed all the usual suspects, including Edelbrock, Edmunds, Evans, Grancor, Navarro, Sharp, Weiand, etc., as well as some little-known brands, such as Fisher and Hickey. However, the writing was on the wall, well, actually on the cover of the February 1956 issue with the tag line: "Snap up your car with a '55 Chevrolet V8 Engine." It was the first of many, many engine swap stories that inspired thousands of enthusiasts to yank out that tired flattie in favor of a small-block Chevy.

Within months, ads started to appear for adapters and conversion kits. Shell Motors, for example, advertised Chev 8-to-Ford adapter bargains for a mere $26.95. In the same February 1957 issue of *Hot Rod*, the story "From Stock to Hot" proclaimed that "speed equipment

When it was introduced, the '55 Chevy (seen here as a pace car for the Indianapolis 500) and its OHV small-block revolutionized the hot rod business. Suddenly, the flathead was obsolete.

Introduced for the 1955 model year, Chevy's small-block revolutionized motorsports, just as the flathead Ford and the Chrysler Hemi had before it. The industry was quick to tool up. (Photo Courtesy Scotty Gosson)

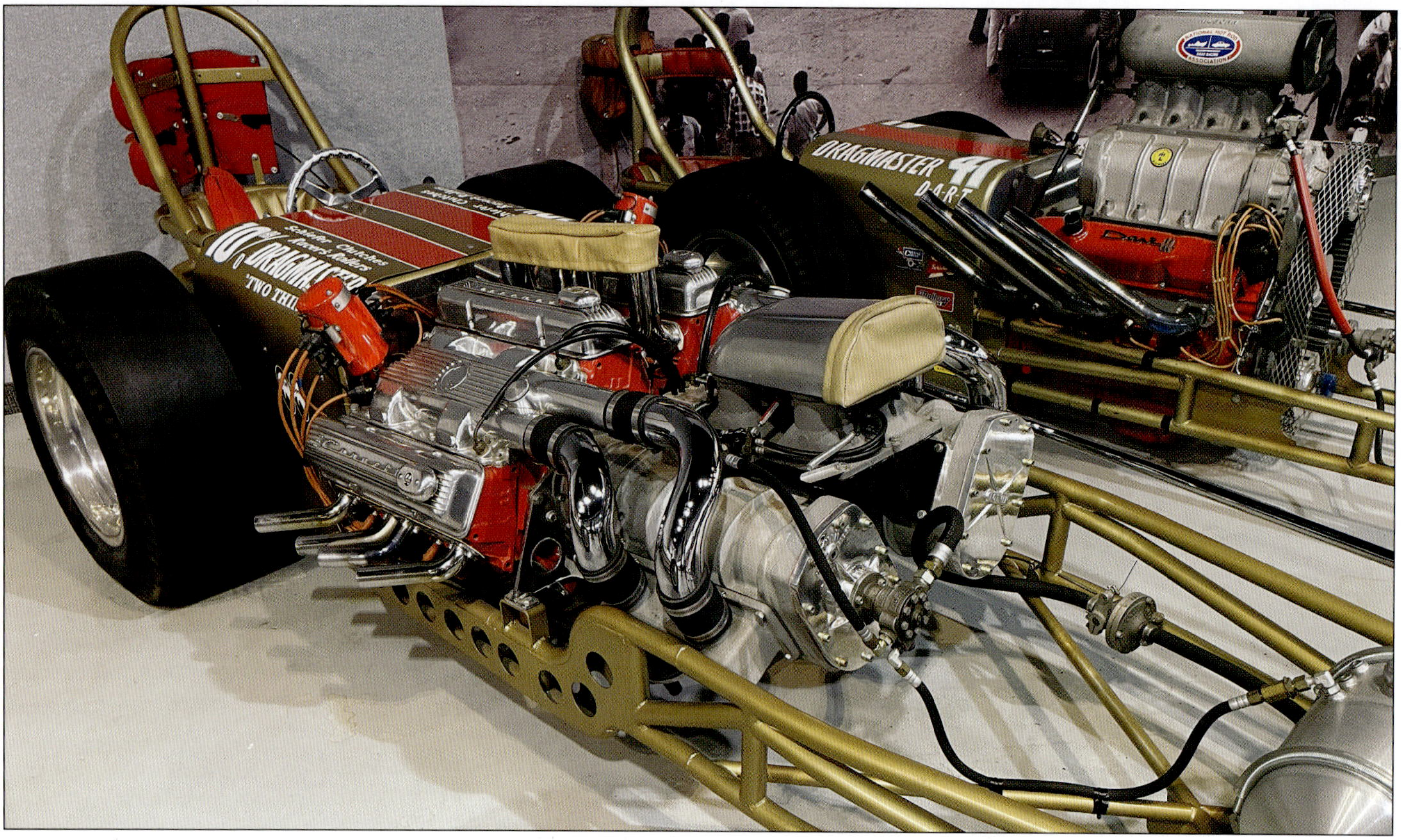

Dode Martin and Jim Nelson's Dragmaster Co. developed a kit for anyone to go drag racing. Their Two Thing *was the pinnacle with a pair of front-blown Chevys that in 1961 went 174.92 mph.*

manufacturers are quick to meet the hot rodder's demands for modern horsepower–early chassis combinations. You'd be surprised what fits what!"

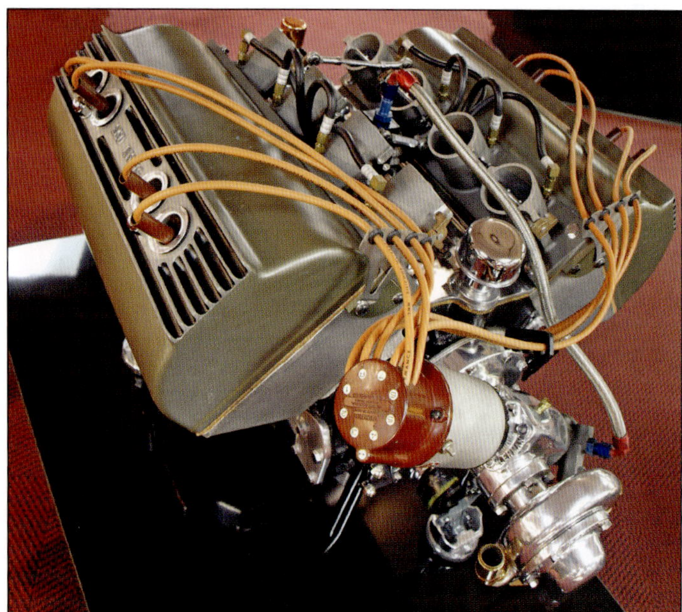

Few and far between, this Ardun-inspired hemi-head conversion for the small-block Chevy was made by Leo Lyons of Riverside, California. It was mainly used for drag racing and some circle track racing. (Photo Courtesy Scotty Gosson)

The story went on to list cast-aluminum adapters from Cragar, Cyclone, Hildebrandt, and Hurst for adapting almost any OHV engines. This included adapting early Ford or Cadillac engines into Oldsmobile chassis or 1954–1957 Chrysler and Dodge engines to GM's Hydra-matic. The ingenuity, the ability, and the agility of the aftermarket knew no bounds. Just as the Ford flathead offered the industry unbound potential, it was perhaps nothing compared to that of the small-block Chevy.

Naturally, engine-to-transmission adapters were only one product. The speed equipment business quickly tooled up to make every item imaginable from engine mounts to tube headers to cast-aluminum intakes. The small-block Chevy had "gold mine" written all over it.

Death at the Track

Unfortunately, 1955 was a sad year for motorsports. On May 26, World Champion Alberto Ascari died at Monza. A week later, American Billy Vukovich was killed while leading the Indy 500 on Memorial Day weekend. The sign does say, "Motor Racing is Dangerous," and deaths are unfortunately part of the action, but nothing prepared people for what was to come next.

Over in France at the 1955 24 Hours of Le Mans endurance sports car race, Pierre Levegh was driving a

The continuing death toll on the world's racetracks eventually caused the American Automobile Manufacturers Association (AMA) to dissolve its competition board and agree to withdraw from motorsports of any kind. (Photo Courtesy Dan Shannon)

Mercedes SLR at an estimated 150 mph when it exploded and crashed into the crowd, killing more than 80 spectators and injuring almost 200 more. Safety equipment was minimal and seat belts, harnesses, and roll cages were not required.

The horrific accident at Circuit de le Sarthe had far-reaching effects. In 1957, the American Automobile Manufacturers Association (AMA) dissolved its competition board and agreed to withdraw from motorsports of any kind. It was a gentleman's agreement, and pretty soon the agreement was ignored. Manufacturers were soon back on the track, either through the front or the back gate. The USAC was formed to sanction auto racing. It was a tragic end to a year that had shown so much promise.

1 Hp per Inch

In 1955, Chrysler claimed a dual 4-barrel Carter version was the first production car to produce 300 hp. The displacement was increased in 1956 to 354 ci. The engine now produced as much as 355 hp and became the first American engine to produce 1 horsepower per cubic inch.

Two years later, the infamous 392-ci version was introduced, and it was almost square, having a 4-inch bore and a 3.906-inch stroke. It had a taller, raised deck compared to previous engines. However, the heads were cast with wider ports so that earlier manifolds could be used with the new heads on the new block. The following year, a single-carburetor version with a 9.25:1

The Day & Nite *rail out of Washington State circa 1960 at the Bakersfield Fuel & Gas Championships had an early Chrysler Hemi. Note the lack of chrome and flame-painted valve cover and scoop. (Photo Courtesy Dan Shannon)*

compression ratio was rated at 345 hp while a dual-carburetor version offered 375 hp.

The 392 is significant because it became the drag racer's engine of choice, especially in the fuel ranks: Top Fuel, Funny Car, and Fuel Altered. The engine was tough, and all kinds of power-enhancing devices could be thrown at it from blowers to nitro, and it thrived.

Rebel, Rebel

James Dean died before his second movie, *Rebel Without a Cause*, was released on October 27, 1955. In fact, Dean was hardly known at the time but because of his untimely death in a horrific auto accident on his way to a race in Salinas, California, he has achieved cult status. He was a car guy, and for that we cherish him all the more, not least of all because he was killed by Donald Turnupseed at just 24 while driving his new Porsche 550 Spyder.

Of course, the movie *Rebel* endeared us to Dean because his character, Jim Stark, chicken races a 1946 Ford coupe against Buzz Gunderson's 1941 Chevy—both of which were stolen for the race. Gunderson gets his sleeve caught on the door handle and it's all over.

No speed equipment was used in the making of this movie, but we all know what was going on. It set us up for George Lucas's *American Graffiti*. Of course, *Rebel* was only one of dozens of exploitation flicks that Hollywood

churned out in the heyday of the 1950s and 1960s. Most were dross, but Orson Welles managed to slide some greasy hot rod hoodlums into his 1958 masterpiece *Touch of Evil*. It's arguably one of the best noir movies of all time, but it certainly doesn't present hot rodders in a good light. Dean, meanwhile, went from *East of Eden* to *Giant,* but all the time he was just a rebel without a cause.

Lions, aka The Beach

On page 4 of the volume one, number one issue of *Drag News* on March 4, 1955, there was a small, almost insignificant announcement: "LAD's Strip Under Way. Secretary Bob Jerauld announces start of construction on their new strip within the next few days."

Jerauld was secretary of a group of 11 Long Beach–area Lions clubs that banded together to build perhaps the most infamous of all drag strips: Lions. To give it its correct name, Lions Associated Drag Strip or, as it was generally known, "the Beach."

The strip, on land leased from the Los Angeles Harbor Commission, was located between Santa Fe and Alameda streets, about a mile north of Willow in Wilmington/Long Beach. Police Officer Gordon Browning, who was at the time secretary of the NHRA, was instrumental in finding the location.

In the August 19 issue of *Drag News,* it was announced that Mickey Thompson had been selected to be the new manager. Operations were expected to begin in September. The big news, of course, was the intention of using red, yellow, and green lights operated by a hand-held switch. This, it was hoped, would eliminate anticipated flagman starts. Car classifications would be in accordance with the NHRA except for the addition of a Dragster class.

Lions finally opened on October 9, 1955, a few weeks after the opening of another purpose-built strip: San Fernando. *Drag News* described it as, "Probably one of the greatest auto racing spectacles in local history."

The place was packed. The pit gates had to be closed, officials had to limit the number of runs, and the parking overflowed into the surrounding streets. Mickey announced he would double the number of bleachers.

A lot of drivers had problems with the lights, so starter Ralph Helm resorted to the flags. Nevertheless,

While working two jobs in 1955, Mickey Thompson found time to build and manage Lions Drag Strip. Here, early in 1958, he smokes the tires of his twin-Chrysler rail that turned a best ET of 9.72 at 158 mph. (Photo Courtesy C. Strutt/ Dan Shannon Collection)

C.J. "Pappy" Hart, one of the founders of organized drag racing with Santa Ana, became the manager of Lions Drag Strip in 1965, succeeding Mickey Thompson. He later became a consultant to many other tracks. (Photo Courtesy Dan Shannon)

some impressive times and speeds were recorded. Fritz Voigt was Top Eliminator with a speed of 131.38 mph. Top speed went to Ed Losinski, who ran an impressive 151.26 mph. Low ET was 10.54 set by Lloyd Scott driving the Howard and Weiand Special *Bustle Bomb*.

The Last Drag Race was the weekend of December 1–2, 1972, but Lions Drag Strip lives on in the hearts and minds of drag racers the world over whether they raced there or not.

The famed Winged Express ran at Lions circa 1964. Note the door says Harrell, Borsch, and Muse because the car was owned and the engine built by Harrell Engines of speed shop and flathead fame. (Photo Courtesy C. Strutt/ Dan Shannon Collection)

CHAPTER 6

1955-1962
GLORY DAYS

In 1954, Oakland drag racing innovator Al "Romeo" Palamides of Palamides Racing Equipment Co. teamed up with Jim O. Ellison, a San Francisco machine shop owner. They designed and crafted cutting-edge, high strength-to-weight ratio magnesium racing wheels for dragsters.

American Racing Wheels

Eventually, Palamides and Ellison met up with the forward-thinking Tom Griffith, an engineer who was ahead of his time, and American Racing Equipment (ARE) was incorporated in 1956. ARE ran small advertisements for 15x3.5-inch 12-spoke front wheels and two widths of 15-inch rear slotted mags. The fronts weighed just 10½ pounds, while the rears began at 15 pounds. The wheels were a huge innovation for drag rac-

Romeo Palamides's famous canopied dragster from 1958 was restored by driver Pete Ogden and sits in the Justice Brothers Museum. Unfortunately, the wheels are not original Moon discs.

ers looking to reduce weight.

By luck or design, Palamides's injected Hemi-powered slingshot graced the cover of the November 1956 issue of *Hot Rod* magazine. It was great publicity for the fledgling brand. Interestingly, the slingshot featured ARE wheels on the rear but not on the front where there were steelies with Moon discs.

As with many race-derived products, there was a trickle-down effect to the street, as enthusiasts wanted to emulate their racing heroes. As a consequence, ARE was soon in the

The old, steel wheels and Moon discs on Art Chrisman's Hustler, *meets the new, American Racing Equipment slots and spokes on Tony Waters's stretched Model T roadster. Chrisman went on to win. (Photo Courtesy Greg Sharp)*

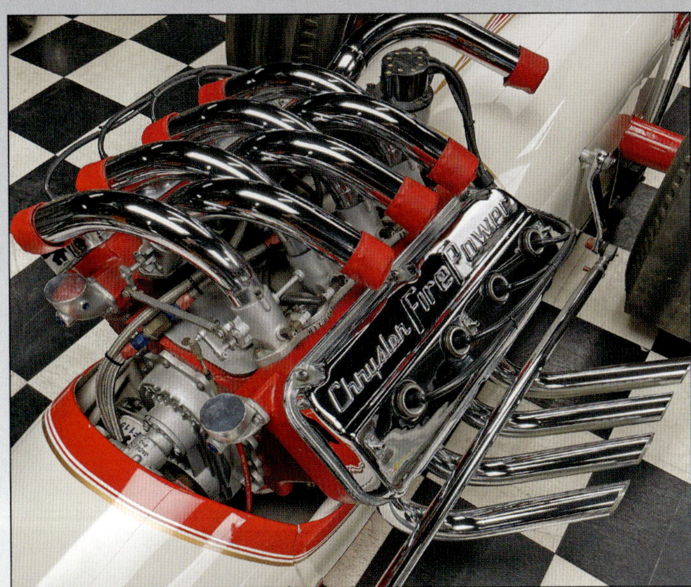

Palamides's rail was powered by a 1958 392-ci Chrysler Hemi, seen here in restored condition with Hilborn cross-ram injection, Thompson front cover, Jackson fuel pump, and Vertex mag.

Initially, Romeo Palamides's ARE wheels were only available in magnesium for racing purposes, for example, these 12-spoke fronts ($52 each) and Torq Thrust rears ($65 each). Note: Prices have increased.

It's rare for aluminum or magnesium rims to go rusty. However, magnesium oxidizes before your very eyes no matter how much you polish. Pretty soon, ARE had to be in the aluminum wheel business.

In 1963, American Racing introduced the most iconic wheel design ever produced: the Torq Thrust.

business of making aluminum street wheels. In 1963, ARE introduced what has been described as the most iconic wheel ever: the Torq Thrust. It literally changed the look of automobiles forever.

Two Engines for the Price of One

Rochester Coil Co. had been founded in New York in 1908, the year General Motors was formed, by brothers Edward and Joseph Halbleib principally as a supplier of automotive electrical components. The company was reorganized in 1909 as the North East Electric Co. It was soon selling electric lighting and starting components to the Galt Motor Co. In keeping with its plans to acquire suppliers, General Motors purchased North East in 1929 and renamed it Delco Appliance.

Delco produced more than 120 products ranging from instruments to shocks and, despite the Depression, was so successful that General Motors reorganized it into the Rochester Products Division in 1939. Rochester's venture into carburetors came at the end of World War II in 1945 when it licensed a design that evolved into the AA 2-barrel that appeared on the 1949 Oldsmobile Rocket engine and was nicknamed the Turtle Back.

In 1952, Rochester introduced the 4G 4-barrel carburetor that was also known as the 4-Jet and the Quadrajet. This nomenclature has caused a great deal of confusion among younger enthusiasts who know the Quadrajet as the 4M (spread bore) that was introduced in 1965.

The engineers at Oldsmobile must have been miffed when Pete Estes took the 3x2 Tri-Power with him to Pontiac in 1956. This is an original 1957 version of the J2.

Speed equipment manufacturers, such as Edelbrock, were presold on the Tri-Power concept when the OEMs adopted it as a cost-effective option. It was therefore relatively easy to tool up for the new OHVs.

After World War II, GM's Rochester Division licensed a carburetor design that became the AA 2-barrel. It was fitted to the 1949 Oldsmobile and nicknamed, for obvious reasons, the Turtle Back. It is seen here on an Edmunds intake.

As we have seen before, if two is good and three is better, then four must be optimum. Weiand introduced its WC4D for the 283-ci small-block Chevy and either Stromberg 97s or Holley/Ford 94s.

Rochester documentation refers to both 4G and 4M as Quadrajets.

Three years later, in 1955, Rochester introduced the 2G, a manual-choke 2-barrel carburetor that flowed from 285 cfm to 450 cfm. Commonly known as the 2 Jet, it was used on more than 125 applications and was eventually developed into the 2GC with an automatic choke and the 2GV with automatic choke with vacuum activation. Interestingly, the 2G formed the basis for several factory tri-power assemblies, including Oldsmobile's 1957 J2 option and, of course, Pontiac's Tri-Power.

Interestingly, the Oldsmobile's W code J2 Tri-Power option actually appeared two weeks prior to Pontiac's similar setup. It appears that Pete Estes, who originated the 3x2 in 1956 while at Oldsmobile, was elevated to chief engineer at sister division Pontiac. He brought the Tri-Power with him, and it became part of Pontiac's youthful direction. I'll bet the guys at Oldsmobile were less than happy.

The 2G was a simple, effective, inexpensive, and virtually bulletproof design. Compared to fuel injection that was just beginning to make its presence felt in the mainstream auto industry, the 2G was a no-brainer. For once, the speed merchants had shown the way—heck, they had been building tri-power intakes since Al Sharp introduced the first for a flathead Ford V-8 in 1948.

Ford was a little slow to the table with its tri-power system. It wasn't introduced until 1961 with the launch of its 390-ci engine. That said, the one-year-only 1958 Mercury Super Marauder 430 was available with three 2300 Holley 2-barrel carburetors producing 400 hp. It was the first factory car to do so. Apparently, few were made, maybe 250 at most, but it was also an option on the 1958–1959 Lincoln. By 1964, Rochester was producing 15,000 carburetors a day.

As an aside, Lynn Wineland, editor of *Rod and Custom* at the time, designed an extremely rare finned air cleaner assembly that was probably cast with the help of Wineland's friend Dean Moon. Ford, meanwhile, was quicker to the dual-quad party.

While Ford introduced a dealer-installed dual-quad for the 312 in 1956, it didn't introduce a Tri-Power until 1961 for the new 390. Bored for 1962 to 406 ci, it produced 405 hp.

Of course, Edelbrock was not the only manufacturer to see the potential market. Offenhauser advertised three-carburetor as well as a dual-quad manifolds in the July 1961 issue of Hot Rod *magazine.*

Weiand's corresponding ad from the September 1957 issue of Hot Rod *magazine showed both 3x2 and 4x2 intakes for a small-block Chevy. Again, they were designed for various carburetors.*

Chrysler and the Dual-Quads

Chrysler jumped to the lead in the horsepower wars when it introduced the 331-ci Hemi in 1951. The automaker did it again in 1955 with the introduction of the Chrysler C-300 coupe. The coupe is considered by many to be America's first high-performance production car— the first of the so-called "letter" cars.

Though it was a two-door coupe, and a big one at that (it was 218.8 inches long), it outperformed both the Corvette and the Ford Thunderbird. It won its first NASCAR race and went on to win 37 NASCAR and AAA races that were more than 100 miles long. At NASCAR races, it was decorated to say "world's fastest stock car."

Under the hood, a 331-ci FirePower Hemi fitted with a high-performance cam, solid lifters, and dual-quads. It produced 300 hp and was said to have exceeded 127 mph and set the production-car flying-mile record at Daytona. The following year, the 300B could be had with a 354-ci engine rated at 355 hp and was touted as the first American car to produce 1 horsepower per cubic inch. The top speed was now quoted as 140 mph.

In 1957, the 300C was fitted with the venerable 392 that produced 375 hp. A limited edition was offered for 390 hp, but apparently only 18 of those were built.

Meanwhile, on Grand Avenue in Detroit where Chevrolet was regarded as the performance division of General Motors, Cadillac often benefited from technical advancements first. For example, Cadillac was the first division to get a 4-barrel carburetor on the 1952 Series 62, and in 1955, the Eldorado was the first to get dual-quads.

The Series 62 Eldorado's engine was a regular 331 ci with a 9:1 compression ratio and bore and stroke of 3.8125 x 3.625. It was rated at 270 hp at 4,800 rpm and 345 ft-lbs of torque at 3,200 rpm. The carburetors were a pair of Rochester 4GCs. The dual-quad engine was available as an option on other models. For 1956, the 331 was bored out to an even 4 inches to result in 365 ci while output rose to 305 hp.

Interestingly, the aftermarket began advertising. For example, Howard's Racing Cams were advertising 270 hp at 4,500 from as early as 1952 in the December issue of *Hot Rod*. Down in the small print, the ad mentioned a dual carburetor manifold, and that is what was shown on the engine dyno in the ad.

Meanwhile, a Cadillac V-8 built and fitted with speed equipment from Cal Connell's Detroit Racing Equipment (DRE) powered an Allard JR and was entered in the 1953 Carrera Pan Americana. Located at 20181 Conant Ave. in Detroit, DRE supplied a dual-quad intake and a pair of

Introduced in 1955, Chrysler's C-300 was fitted with the 392 Hemi. In 1958, Norm Thatcher took this manual 300D to Bonneville and set a record at 156.387 mph in E Class Coupe and Sedan. (Photo Courtesy Dan Shannon)

Rochester carbs, but its main business appears to have been the sale of complete crate engines.

Connell, whose father owned the oldest Cadillac dealership in Michigan, built engines for Johnny Fedrick's Indy entry and for band leader Guy Lombardo's racing boat *Miss Tempo*. Incidentally, Eddie Edmunds also listed a dual intake for the 1949–1952 Cadillac V-8 for $69.50.

Farther east on Detroit's Grand Avenue, the venerable old Packard Motor Co. came to the table too late

In 1952, Detroit's Bill Waddill raced a Crosley that was powered by a 1950 Cadillac engine (with upside-down valve covers) and a Detroit Racing Equipment intake and dual four-throat Carters. It went 150.50 mph. (Photo Courtesy Dan Shannon)

Frank Burrell was a Cadillac engineer at General Motors who worked on the Chaffee tank engine and designed these dual intakes with Carter WCDs for Cadillacs in 1947. Burrell is now produced by HandHFlatheads.com.

There's very little info about Cal Connell's Detroit Racing Equipment, but here's a rare ad for his Cadillac intakes designed by Frank Burrell. Connell's real business was supplying complete Cadillac engines.

Imagine opening the hood of your 1960-1961 Chrysler 383 to 413 and seeing this wild snake pit of an intake with a pair of Carter 2903s. These long aluminum intakes are now fairly rare.

with too little. By 1955, it was almost out of business, but it had one last hurrah in the shape of an all-new OHV engine. It came in three sizes: 320, 352, and 374 ci, and the bore center was fully 5 inches for a potential of 500 ci. In 1956, Packard offered a dual-quad Rochester 4GC assembly on the 374 Caribbean rated at 310 hp, making it one of the year's most powerful production cars.

Federal Highway Act of 1956

Unlike Nazi Germany's Autobahn system, the United States did not really have an integrated, nationwide road system. In the late 1930s, as a result of the Great Depression, President Franklin D. Roosevelt began to express interest in a network of highways: three north to south and three east to west. Congress decided to explore the concept, and in 1938, the Federal Highway Act directed the Bureau of Public Roads to initiate a feasibility study. On April 27, 1939, Roosevelt recommended that Congress consider action.

Government moves in slow and mysterious ways, and it wasn't until January 26, 1956, that the Federal Highway Act provided for a 40,000-mile network of interstate and defense highways to be built over 13 years. To pay for it, gas tax was raised from 2 to 3 cents a gallon when prices at the pump averaged 30 cents per gallon (an equivalent of $2.92 in 2021).

In 1908, about 200,000 vehicles were on American roads. By 1932, that number jumped to 21 million. By the start of World War II, there were almost 30 million, but by 1956, there were more than 54 million. By the advent of the muscle car in 1964, there were 72 million. By 1973 and Gas Crisis time, there were well over 100 million, and the number just keeps growing.

Carter AFB

One would think that the letters AFB stood for something more technically interesting than "aluminum four barrel," but that's it. William Carter, the founder of Carter Carburetor, was born in 1884 in Union City, Tennessee, and received only five years of formal education. At age 17, he opened a bicycle and general repair shop but soon realized that Union City was too small to make a living. He consequently moved to St. Louis, Missouri, where more than 600,000 people resided in 1909.

Despite a small automotive population, it was growing due in large part to the 1908 introduction of the Ford Model T. Carter began to tinker with carburetor design, and by 1910, he had patented his first product. It was unique in that it used a manifold vacuum to suck fuel from the tank to a reservoir above the carburetor.

In Detroit in 1956, the Walter P. Chrysler Freeway is busy, and there are more than 54 million cars on the road. By 1964, that number increased to 72 million. (Photo Courtesy Dan Shannon)

While Buick was never really regarded as the performance leader within the GM group, it did get the new William Carter 4-barrel (WCFB) before other divisions in 1952.

Perched atop a stock Chrysler Hemi intake, here's a Carter WCFB. You can clearly see the cast-iron base and zinc body that together weighed a hefty 18 pounds, and that's without the additional float bowl.

Unfortunately, by 1916, Carter found himself in financial trouble, and by 1922 he had lost his company to the American Car and Foundry Company that became ACF Industries. In 1925, the company began selling to Chevrolet and in 1928 added Chrysler to its customer base.

Around this time, ACF purchased the Ball and Ball carburetor that had been produced by the Penberthy Injector Co. After World War II, ACF introduced a new series of Ball and Ball (BB) carburetors, the single barrel (BBS), and the dual barrel (BBD). The company's big break came in 1954 with the introduction of the 2-barrel BBD with a water-heated integral choke on the 276-ci De Soto Firedome.

The next milestone came with the introduction of the world's first 4-barrel carburetor creatively named the William Carter Four Barrel (WCFB). It was first installed on the 1952 Buick straight-8. With a cast-iron base and zinc body, the WCFB weighed a hefty 18 pounds. It allowed manufacturers to extract the horsepower trapped in the emerging 8-cylinder engines.

In 1957, Carter introduced the "square bore" 400-cfm AFB first fitted to the 1957 Ford 312, which could also come equipped with a Holley or an Autolite equivalent. Because of its 4¼-inch bolt pattern, most of these 4-barrels were interchangeable. What made them popular was the fact that they were relatively easy to work on, as the carburetor did not need to be removed from the manifold to change jets, floats, or metering rods. Pretty soon, pairs of the popular AFBs (that eventually were available up to 950 cfm) were finding themselves perched atop dual-quad intakes.

As fuel injection began to dominate fuel delivery, the Carter plant was closed in 1984. The following year, ACF shuttered the entire Carter operation. However, Edelbrock Corp. continued to wave the AFB flag, selling them as Edelbrock Performers. They were actually made by Weber USA, whose parent company was Magneti-Marelli in Italy. Beginning in 1988, Weber continued to make Carter AFB carburetors under the Edelbrock name and calibrated to match Edelbrock intakes.

This is a hot-rodded Gen I 331-ci Cadillac engine fitted with Hildebrandt valve covers, a DRE intake, and a pair of GM factory WCFB carburetors circa 1959–1963. (Photo Courtesy Dan Shannon)

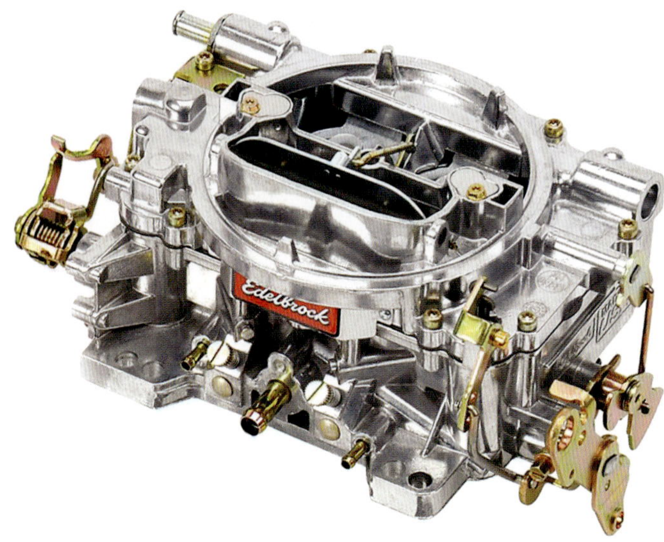

The contemporary 750-cfm Edelbrock Performer #1407 with manual choke can trace its lineage all the way back to the original Carter WCFB introduced in 1952. (Photo Courtesy Edelbrock Corp.)

A recent hot rod build featured two Carter WCFBs that came from a single-application 327 or 348. Set up by Jimmy Bridges, they reside atop Mike William's small-block built by Phil Lukens at Blair's Speed Shop.

Fuelie Vette

For the 1957 model year, Chevrolet upped the ante in the horsepower race by adding Rochester fuel injection to the new 283 engine. "Fuelie" became (and indeed remains) a buzzword in the realm of Corvette collectors and aficionados.

Developed by GM's Rochester division, the Ramjet fuel injection was touted as producing 1 hp per ci of engine displacement, as did the Chrysler 300B of 1956 with the 354-ci/355-hp option. Unfortunately, we did not have the benefit of computerized electronic control in 1957, and the Ramjet was an entirely mechanically operated, continuous-flow, port-injection system.

Basically, an air meter measured airflow into the assembly and signaled the fuel meter that controlled fuel delivery. Unfortunately for Fuelie owners, the system had its problems, particularly during cold start. Obviously,

Under the hood of Bill Mitchell's 1956 SR-2 resided a fuelie 283-ci small-block built by Smokey Yunick and fitted with a high-lift Duntov cam. The engine dynoed at 310 hp. It came just in time for the AMA racing ban.

Duntov's 1957 Corvette SS was fitted with fuel injection with the air intake on the end of the plenum chamber, as it was on the CERV I shown here. The stock version was on the side. (Photo Courtesy General Motors)

The first production Rochester fuel injection unit was this flat-top version introduced in 1961, offering 275 hp (RPO353) or 315 hp (RPO354). However, the dual carburetor 245-hp 283 was also available. (Photo Courtesy FavCars.com)

For 1963, the top engine option on the Corvette was the fuel-injected 327 (RPO L84) rated at 360 hp. It was a hot-looking assembly with a lot of drive-in cache, but to this day, people struggle with them.

For a while, swapping fuel-injected Corvette engines into anything and everything was popular, but for many, getting them running and maintaining optimum performance was difficult. (Photo Courtesy Dan Shannon)

Duncan Pittaway's Cheetah has a Bill Thomas-developed Corvette-based induction system with two throttle bodies on top. Apparently, Thomas's setup gave 68 more hp and 72 ft-lbs of torque compared to a stock Corvette assembly.

Rochester continued development of the system but never quite worked out the bugs, and it was phased out by 1965. While they look cool and continue to enjoy that Fuelie cache, they are not the most reliable way to deliver fuel to an engine.

What the factory fuel injection system did more than work was actually put the words and notion into the vocabulary. The systems got everybody used to the term so that eventually, when the time and technology was right, the public would embrace it.

Tunnel Ram

I would hazard a guess that most enthusiasts would credit one of the aftermarket speed merchants as the inventor of the tunnel-ram intake, but look closely at the intake of the 1955 Cadillac El Dorado. There were a few Rochester-type 4GC 4-barrel carburetors or Carters atop a cast intake—the only way forward was up.

Toward the end of the decade, a group of possibly 21 Chrysler engineers calling themselves the Ram Chargers (later contracted to Ramchargers) decided to go racing. Their first foray was an atypical 1949 Plymouth business coupe powered by a 354-ci Hemi fitted with the better-breathing 392 heads and a 300C cam.

Atop the engine, which was already level with the hood line, they mounted a very unusual intake fabricated from angle iron, steel plate, and a nest of eight rubber hoses. Atop the plenum was a pair of Carter carburetors and a similarly fabricated scoop. As ungainly as the contraption looked, it performed well, and the car ran mid- to high-12s with a best of 117 mph. In 1960, they swapped the 354 for a 392.

Meanwhile, according to Tom Madigan's book *Edelbrock: Made in USA,* "Record holder and Street Eliminator champion Carroll Caudle of Carroll's Automotive Service in Amarillo, Texas, had taken a late-1950s Chevy fuel injection manifold, cut the top off, fabricated a flange, and mounted two four barrels in a row—not opposed like the Edelbrock dual-quad log ram. The manifold made horsepower at the top and bottom ends of the power band."

At the end of the racing season, Caudle shipped the manifold to Edelbrock, where Bobby Meeks and Murray Jensen tinkered with the design. They ultimately developed a large plenum chamber feeding individual runners to each port. On top, they installed a pair of Holley 600-cfm carburetors mounted in-line. With a new cast base, the Edelbrock TR-1 was born, and it revolutionized the racing world.

Campaigned in 1959–1960 by Chrysler engineers that became the Ramchargers, the High & Mighty *1949 Plymouth was a racing test bed that ran high 11s in the quarter mile with a top speed of 117 mph. (Photo Courtesy Marc Rozman)*

Powered by a 354-ci Chrysler Hemi fitted with 392 heads (392 block in 1960), the High & Mighty was visible for miles because of the super high-rise intake fabricated by Pete McNichols, who also made the exhaust. (Photo Courtesy Marc Rozman)

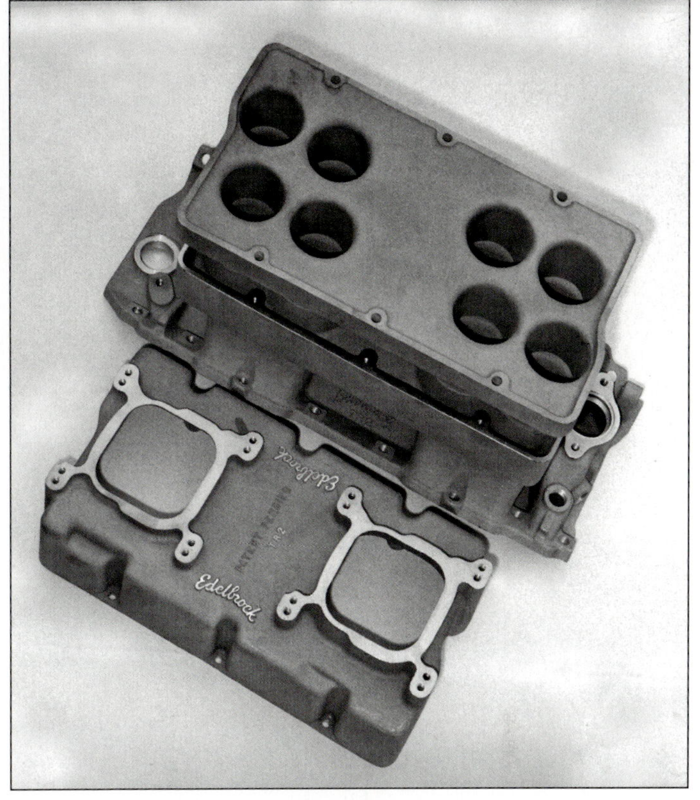

Edelbrock's TR-1 was a small-block intake, whereas the TR-2 was designed for use on 1965-and-newer big-block Chevys that were running a pair of Holley 4-barrels. Neither were ideal for the street. (Photo Courtesy Edelbrock Corp.)

As was the industry's modus operandi, Weiand was soon to market with its own tunnel ram, an example of which is on this small-block Chevy with a pair of Holleys.

Based on a design developed by Carroll Caudle of Amarillo, Texas, and shipped to Edelbrock, Bobby Meeks and Murray Jensen refined Caudle's design and developed it into the legendary TR-1. (Photo Courtesy Edelbrock Corp.)

Ban the Nitro

On February 3, 1957, drag racing took what many thought was a backward step and banned nitro methane as a racing fuel. Initiating this move was a run of 165.13 mph by Emory Cook in the Cook & Bedwell dragster at Lions Drag Strip. Officials were shocked. They checked their clocks, but Cook backed it up with an even quicker 166.97. Something had to be done.

The Cook & Bedwell rail was powered by a 354-ci Chrysler fitted with six Stromberg 48s on a new, fabricated tube-steel dual-log intake made by Bruce Crower.

Also new for the Hemi was an Isky 5-cycle cam. Iskenderian had come upon his A-505 cam design that typically leaves the intake valve open on the compression stroke longer than a normal engine. American engineer Ralph Miller patented the concept in 1957, and is it more correctly termed the "Miller cycle."

C.J. Hart, manager of Santa Ana, was the first to ban any fuel other than pump gas. Other tracks quickly followed suit but not all. There was also talk of banning superchargers and multi-engine cars. Of course, not all tracks signed on for the fuel ban. Drag racing was under a lot of pressure then, even though huge strides had been made in helping to curb endemic street racing.

The fuel ban caused a switch to supercharging in an effort to regain the power lost by the switch from fuel to gas. Racers just did not want to see their speeds drop, and a blower was an easy, bolt-on answer. A less-easy answer to more power was more engines, and in 1958, Glenn Ward driving the twice-blown, twin-engine Howard's Cams Special, later known as the *Twin-Bear*, set a new gas record with an elapsed time of 9.10 at 166 mph. Interestingly, it had a sheet of aerodynamic plywood running from the axle up to the blowers—no doubt to hopefully direct air over the engines.

As you can imagine, these developments translated to sales for the parts manufacturers. More engines meant more parts, and the market for blowers increased dramatically. It was given another boost in 1959 at the very first U.S. Fuel & Gas Championships.

This tribute to the famed Emery Cook & Cliff Bedwell Isky-U-Fab Special is owned by Ray Lake and is a faithful recreation of the Scotty Fenn–chassied slingshot that initiated the infamous fuel ban. (Photo Courtesy Steve Reyes)

Regardless of the furor the Cook & Bedwell dragster initiated with its 168.85-mph run at Lions Drag Strip, the industry made bank, as shown by this ad from Grant Piston Rings. (Photo Courtesy Scotty Gosson)

The original Cook & Bedwell was powered by an unblown Chrysler Hemi fitted with an Isky 5-cycle cam, Grant piston rings, a Bruce Crower U-Fab intake, and six Stromberg 48s.

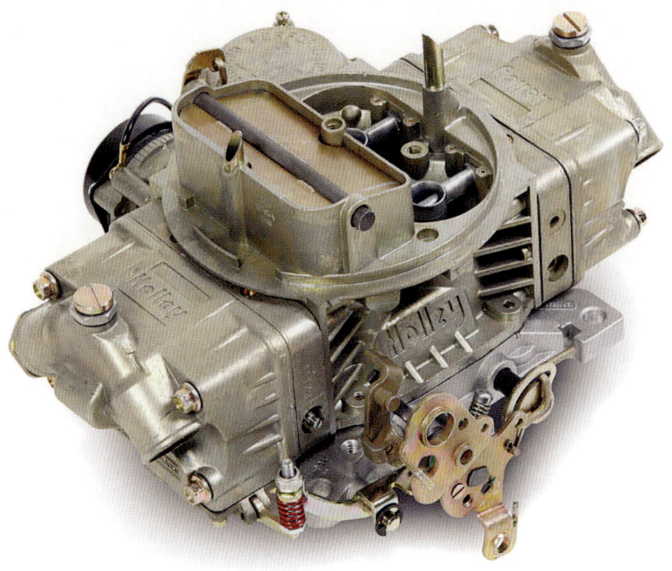

Holley's modular design 4150 benefitted from two metering blocks. One was for the primary and one was for the secondary circuit that enables the tuner to easily swap jets and power valves. (Photo Courtesy Holley Corporation)

You can't stop progress, and the fuel ban initiated more engines and more blowers, as was evidenced by the 1958 Howard's Cams twin-blown Bear that set a new gas record with an ET of 9.10 at 166 mph with Glenn Ward driving. (Photo Courtesy Steve Reyes)

Holley's Double

Estimates put the number of Holley carburetors produced since production began in 1903 at around 250,000,000—yes, 250 million. That's a staggering number, and in this world of electronic fuel injection, it's simply amazing.

Holley produced its first 4-barrel carburetor, the Model 2140, in 1953, just two years after it closed its Detroit plant and moved operations to the current facility in Bowling Green, Kentucky. Nicknamed the "teapot" because the bottom portion was the throttle body and the upper portion the float bowl. Incidentally, the first carburetor, introduced in 1904, was nicknamed the "iron pot."

Over in Ford country, the Thunderbird was doing well. Sales were buoyant at some 15,631 units for 1956, and for 1957, Ford planned a surprise. The surprise was even more horsepower. The base 292 Y-block now produced 212 hp, but in 1956, Ford had offered a 312-ci V-8 with a 465-cfm 4-barrel Holley 4000 rated at 245 hp.

The following year, there were even more options. The 312 could now be ordered with dual 4-barrel Holleys, which increased the horsepower to 270. The racing version was available with a long-duration Iskenderian E-2 cam and a dual-point distributor. A limited number of T-Birds were also offered with a McCulloch VR57 variable-ratio supercharger. However, the carburetor used was not the carburetor used on the naturally aspirated T-Birds.

The Holley 4150 was a modular design with ample airflow and astute fuel metering. It benefitted from two

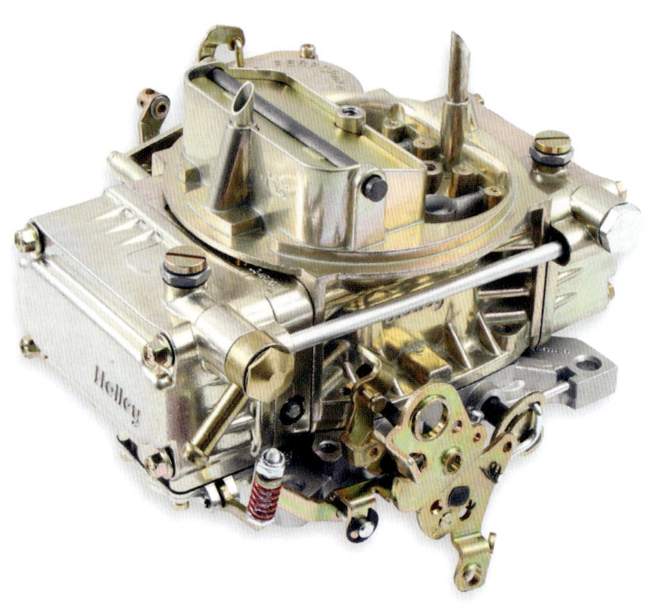

Introduced in 1958, the Holley 4160 is a basic manual choke, single-feed workman carburetor. (Photo Courtesy Holley Corporation)

metering blocks: one for the primary and one for the secondary circuit. What makes the 4150 unique, especially for its day, is that the second metering block enables the tuner to easily swap jets and power valves. They had both front and rear accelerator pumps. Consequently, the carburetors are referred to as "double-pumpers."

The 4150 could also be found on other vehicle brands, such as AMC. In 1958, Holley introduced the 4160, which is a basic manual choke, single-feed workman carburetor. Meanwhile in 1965, the 4150 was installed on Chevys with the 327 engine in 1965 and the 427 engine in 1966. From 1967 through 1972, these carburetors were used on 327, 396, 402, and 427 engines, while the El Camino and pickups used the 4150 through 1974.

Man-A-Fre

The story of the Man-A-Fre induction plate is perhaps the story of the world's most famous intake that no one ever heard of, as one was fitted to Milner's coupe in the movie *American Graffiti*. In spite of this, barely anyone knows what it is.

The system was developed in the early 1950s by Robert E. Patrick of Hapeville, Georgia, who filed for a patent on August 7, 1957, for a carburetor adapter. The patent was granted July 28, 1959. Initially, these intakes were made for the early small-block Chevys, and early castings said "MAN-A-FRE. MFG. CO. ATLANTA S. GA."

Somehow, Harold Graves took over the project and is the name most commonly associated with the brand. Graves worked at Offenhauser but learned his trade in the military. He was a draftsman and specialist in Rochester carburetors.

What was unusual about the Man-A-Fre, which stood for "manifold free of passages," was that it was primarily a multi-carburetor assembly but with the benefit of additional fuel induction that was engineered to cure fuel distribution problems. It was not an intake with a plenum chamber and runners but rather a low-profile induction plate, weighing just 9 pounds that placed a Rochester 2G 2-barrel carburetor directly over each intake port.

An optional "afterburner" unit positioned injector nozzles either in the base of the induction plate or in the top of each carburetor. At the press of a driver-operated button, typically above 4,000 rpm, additional fuel was delivered either directly into the port or directly into the carburetor.

By the early 1960s, Graves relocated to Southern California. The later plates cast at the Sheehan Foundry (which still exists in Sun Valley) were embossed with the words "CANOGA PARK." Graves went on to develop similar induction plates for engines other than small-blocks, including big-block Chevys.

Immortalized on Milner's coupe in the movie American Graffiti, *the Man-A-Fre induction system was invented by Robert Patrick in the early 1950s but put into production by Harold Graves.*

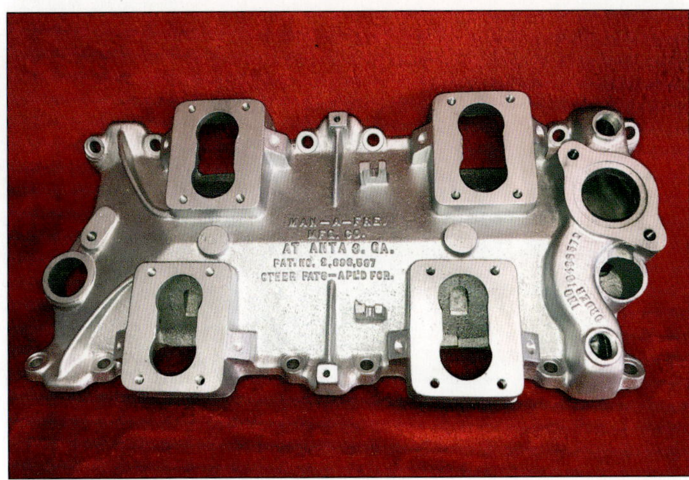

The Man-A-Fre induction plate was just that: a plate rather than a manifold with passages. Instead, the four Rochester 2G carburetors dumped directly into the intake ports. Additional fuel was injected into the carburetor or the manifold.

Traco Engineering

Like so many in the high-performance industry, Jim Travers and Frank Coon got their respective starts on the dry lake beds of Southern California. Indeed, there's a photo of Coon in his Deuce roadster in Veda Orr's *Hot Rod Pictorial*, and the caption says, "FRANK COON (Low Flyers) Fastest time 1946 122.78. Mercury engine stroked, filled heads, Evans manifold, Engle cam, Coon ignition."

During World War II, Coon served as a flight engineer, and Travers was an Army Air Force crew chief. After the war, Travers, known as "Crabby," joined Stu Hilborn working on the development of Hilborn's fuel injection

This Traco-badged 327 Chevy can often be seen sitting in the back of Dan Shaw's pickup. It's typical of the type of engines built by Jim Travers and Frank Coon at Traco Engineering.

system. In fact, the very first cast-aluminum production Hilborn injection units had their casting embossed with the names "HILBORN – TRAVERS." However, as Paul Smith pointed out, Travers was soon gone to "pursue his racing interests."

In 1948, horse and auto racing enthusiast Howard Keck, who owned Superior Oil Co., was famous for constructing the first offshore oil platform in the Gulf of

In-and-out boxes were used exclusively in direct-drive, clutchless race cars such as midgets and sprint cars so as to disconnect the drive. They were made by a number of companies, including Stelling.

The pump on Shaw's engine is a McGurk Cummins cam-driven tri-drive unit that pumps oil, water, and fuel separately.

Thunder Alley

Thunder Alley was the 11000 block of real estate on West Jefferson Boulevard in Culver City. It and the surrounding environs was home to not only Traco Engineering but also a host of other speed merchants at one time or another, including the following businesses.

It's now a row of stores and apartments

Business	Address
Ansen Automotive Eng.	3801 W. Jefferson
Baron's Automotive Service	4916 Venice Blvd., Los Angeles
Belond Exhaust	11142 Washington Place (behind Karl Orr's Speed Shop)
Belles Crankshaft Grinding	1051 W. Washington Blvd., Los Angeles
Edelbrock	4921 W. Jefferson Blvd., Los Angeles
Lou Falcon Frame & Axle Service	10417 W. Washington Blvd., Culver City
James Garner's American International Racing	11918 W. Jefferson Blvd., Culver City
Dick Guldstrand	11924 W. Jefferson Blvd., Culver City
Halibrand	5851 W. Washington Blvd., Culver City
Hedman Muffler & Mfg. Co.	11039–49 W. Washington Blvd., Culver City
Hilborn	3430 Caroline Ave., Culver City
Iskenderian	5977 Washington Blvd., Culver City
Mercury Tool & Die	5977 Washington Blvd., Culver City
Jim Nairn Pattern Maker	11930 W. Jefferson Blvd., Culver City (became Reventlow's shop)
Norden Machine Works	5453 W. Washington Blvd., Culver City
Karl Orr Speed Shop	11142 Washington Place, Culver City
Lance Reventlow Automobiles Inc.	11930 W. Jefferson Blvd., Culver City
Sky Lark Plating	350 W. Washington Blvd., Venice
Traco Engineering	11928 W. Jefferson Blvd., Culver City
Troutman and Barnes	4117 Overland Ave., Culver City

Karl and Veda Orr opened one of the very first post-World War II speed shops located at 11140 Washington Pl. in Culver City. That's Karl's roadster outside, and his Modified is in the window.

Edelbrock was located on 4921 W. Jefferson Blvd. in Los Angeles. Here in 1958, Vic Sr. adjusts Stromberg 97s on a X-1 Ram Log manifold that elicited 284 hp from a 283-ci Chevy. (Photo Courtesy Edelbrock)

Mexico. He hired Travers and Coon to wrangle his fleet of cars. Keck entered an Emil Deidt–built Offy in the 1948 Indy 500 that driver Jimmy Jackson drove to 193 laps before a spindle failure.

In 1949, the combination came in sixth and in 1950 was third with Mauri Rose driving and Hilborn injection handling fuel delivery. Indeed, 13 of that year's qualifiers ran Hilborn's injection, but only 5 were confident enough in the system to leave the fuel injectors in place for the race. The others reverted to carburetors.

For the 1952 race, Keck fielded a new Frank Kurtis 500A with a canted, offset Offy. Billy "Vuky" Vukovich was hired to drive the *Fuel Injection Special*. He qualified eighth with a speed of 138.212 but a steering failure sent him out. The following year, Vukovich qualified number one and went on to win the race and $89,497. In 1954, he qualified at 19 and again went on to win the race.

This string of success in America's premier motor-sports showcase put the name Traco, officially founded in 1957, on the map. Traco, located at 11928 West Jefferson Blvd. in Culver City, on what was known as Thunder Alley, went on to be hugely successful, building Trans-Am engines for Lance Reventlow's Scarabs, Roger Penske's Trans Am Camaros, and many of the Can-Am cars.

While Travers and Coon might not have developed any specific parts of which I am aware, they sure used a lot of speed equipment and elevated American engine building to an art.

I'd Rather Be Blown

Born in 1935, Donny Hampton, the son of a service-station owner, dreamed of racing. He began working in the service station in Bell, California, at age 13, and by the time he was 16, he had already built a 1929 roadster powered by a two-port Cragar-equipped banger that

Tampa Don Meets Jimmy

Despite what Barney Navarro and Tom Beatty had done to advance the acceptance of Jimmy supercharges on their lakes roadsters in the late 1940s, the Roots-type blower had not caught on with the drag racers. There were a few, but they weren't all that common. That is, until 1959 and the first U.S. Fuel & Gas Championship at Famoso Raceway, which is commonly known as "The Patch" north of Bakersfield.

The story goes that back east, "Big Daddy" Don Garlits had been recording some impressive quarter-mile times (low 8s at 176 mph) in his Hemi-powered *Swamp Rat* dragster with eight Stromberg carburetors. Garlits was persuaded to travel west for three events. Unfortunately, he suffered mechanical problems at the Patch and didn't make the final, where Art Chrisman's blown 392 Chrysler Hemi *Hustler* beat out Tony Waters in the blown DeSoto-powered Water-Sughrue-Guinn Modified roadster.

Garlits was no slouch. He knew what to do, and at the shop of his cam sponsor Ed "Isky" Iskenderian, they assembled a 354-ci Hemi with a hard-chromed crank from C-T Automotive, forged pistons, boxed rods, and a Jimmy blower. According to Robert C. Post, Isky provided a prototype belt-drive system that he was tooling up to make. Garlits cleaned up at the next two races at Kingdon, California, and Chandler, Arizona. There was no denying it now: top-mounted blowers were and still are drag racing's answer to horsepower.

"Big Daddy" Don Garlits was doing well on his own turf, but when he came west in 1959, his Swamp Rat *was running eight Strombergs but lacking in the blower department. (Photo Courtesy Dan Shannon)*

Barney Navarro, one of the first hot rodders to experiment with a GMC Jimmy blower, is seen here with four Strombergs atop his flathead Ford V-8. It took a while for drag racers to catch on. (Photo Courtesy HandHFlatheads.com)

Tampa Don looked around the field at the very first Bakersfield Fuel and Gas Championships and noticed that the guys to beat, Art Chrisman and Tony Waters, and others were all blown. (Photo Courtesy Dan Shannon)

he raced at the Santa Ana drags circa 1951. He quickly gained a reputation as a driver wheeling such rides as a rear-engine Buick V-8, Chet Herbert's Top Fuel dragster, and Kenny Lindley's *Miss Fire* dragster that he drove at the 1959 Nationals in Detroit.

Lindley was a diesel mechanic and knew all about GMC superchargers, and their friend Chuck Potvin made parts, so Hampton, Lindley, and Potvin combined their talents and assembled a few blowers. Eventually, Lindley moved away for work, and in 1957, Hampton purchased the equipment to put him in the blower business in a big building at the back of his house.

In a recent interview, Hampton said, "We didn't make kits: Cragar made drives and manifolds as did Weiand, and Isky made drives, so all I did was the blower."

The restored blown Chrysler Hemi is from the infamous Vulcan's Vicky *from* Hot Rod *January 1961. The original was an over-bored 1951 331-ci with a chain-driven 4-71 fed by two Strombergs.*

Over the years, like all race cars, the Vulcan's Vicky underwent many changes. The original car sported a chain-driven 4-71 Jimmy blower with a Cragar intake and snout and a Cirello magneto.

According to the original article in Hot Rod, *the carburetors were from a surplus landing craft. These are Stromberg-Bendix NAR-6-B updraft units. The car was restored by Jay and Joe Kennedy.*

In 1963, Hampton gained notoriety when he fielded the Dye & Hampton *Too Bad* AA/Comp Dragster with a pair of stroked 283 Chevys. In the mid-1960s, Hampton was the first to manufacture a magnesium blower.

In 1970, he won the Winternationals, sold the dragster, and used the money to build the similarly twin-engined, twin-blown *American Band Stand* Corvette.

The Corvette ran mid-7s at 180 mph but was unfortunately destroyed in Australia in 1974. The last time we spoke, Hampton was still in business (HamptonBlowers. com) at age 86.

M&H Drags Slicks

Along with the development of aftermarket wheels came the parallel development of high-performance tires. In the 1930s, Harry Rifchin opened a tire sales and recap business for passenger cars and trucks in the back of a Jenny Gas station on Main Street in Watertown, Massachusetts. After World War II, Harry's son Marvin, who had been an army intelligence officer deciphering enemy transcripts and codes, joined his father in the family business.

Marvin was a keen racing fan, and as the sport boomed, he reached out to their recap rubber supplier Denman Rubber Mfg. Co. of Warren, Ohio, to produce a new racing recap rubber using compounds Marvin had developed. Unfortunately, rubber was in short supply, and there weren't enough 12-inch tubes to meet demand. Marvin devised a way to cut

Before GM designer Larry Shinoda penned the 1963 Corvette Stingray, he was a hot rodder. Here he is at Santa Ana in 1951 with his Chopstick Special III. *Note the feathered recap slicks. (Photo Courtesy Dan Shannon)*

Incredibly, Don Moody won Top Eliminator honors at Lions Drag Strip eight weeks in a row. Then in 1962, he ran the first 7-second pass at Pomona. Obviously, the choice of slick was M&H Racemaster. (Photo Courtesy Dan Shannon)

For most of their formative years, hot rodding and drag racing were underground hobbies vilified by the press. No doubt, LIFE might have wanted to sensationalize the activities, but there is no bad publicity.

down 16-inch passenger tubes to make 12-inch tubes, making it possible to sell more midget tires and help the business flourish under the new name M&H Tire Co.

Although Marvin was an oval track fan, he saw what was happening on the country's drag strips, where racers were using smooth-tread recapped passenger tires, offering poor traction. Marvin's goal was to develop a purpose-built tire that could endure the incredible forces of acceleration. In 1958, he convinced a well-known drag racer named "Big Daddy" Don Garlits to try a set of his drag slicks for a race in South Carolina.

Garlits blistered the competition and won Top Eliminator that day. He went on to be the first to break the 8-second barrier on this innovative new tire. Later, he recorded the first officially recognized 200-mph run in Great Meadows using M&H tires. M&H was the brand to beat.

LIFE in the Fast Lane

On April 29, 1957, *LIFE* magazine published a shot of a starter leaping in the air, flagging off a drag race at Fort Worth, Texas. With a tagline "The Zoom in Drag Racing," the seven-page story did more to boost the sport to the general public than any number of buff books.

The article's introduction stated that there were 130 legal strips in 40 states, and in 1956, some 2.5 million spectators swarmed to the strips to watch 100,000 hot rods whose owners were members of 15,000 clubs. It wasn't all good news, though. The article highlighted the

Norm Grabowski's Kookie Kar, nee Lightnin' Bug, had kids glued to the TV watching 77 Sunset Strip to catch a glimpse of this radical T-bucket powered by a 1952 Cadillac engine fitted with a Horne intake and four Stromberg 97s. (Photo Courtesy Dan Shannon)

growing problems of street racing, and one whole spread was devoted to depicting racing in the Los Angeles riverbed—although, that's hardly street racing.

The last page was the iconic photo of Norm Grabowski in what became known at the *Kookie Kar,* eating a sandwich at Bob's Big Boy in Toluca Lake, California, a venue that remains a popular hangout more than 60 years later.

Hurst Performance

There's almost no brand that stands out in the hot rod psyche more than Hurst, as it was imprinted on the shaft of millions of shifters in the hands of millions of hot rodders. Born in Pennsylvania in 1927, George Hurst never went beyond the eighth grade and dropped out of school to join the U.S. Navy when he was 16.

Upon his return from the war, Hurst went into business with Bill Campbell, working out of a garage in Abington, outside Philadelphia, making engine mounts. Ripped off by a California company, Hurst and Campbell teamed up with Ed Almquist and Jonas Anchel to form Anco in Glenside, Pennsylvania. Their first product was an improved engine mount called the Adjusta-Torque. They then concentrated on making headers before deciding to develop an aftermarket shifter.

Almquist's design had an adjustable fulcrum, but Hurst was determined to build a more complicated dual-pattern design. According to his book *Hot Rod Pioneers,* Almquist recalled, "After my partner and I refused to provide $90,000 for tooling, a friendly disagreement triggered the buy-out offer."

Meanwhile, Jack "Doc" Watson had entered the fray. Doc's mother had a connection at Pontiac, and an order for floor shifters was secured complete with their signature curved, flat-chromed lever topped by a cue ball–style knob. Lawrence Greenwald supplied operating capital,

A lucky connection between Doc Watson's mother and Pontiac resulted in an order for Hurst-branded shifters with their signature curved, flat-chromed lever topped by a cue ball-style knob. (Photo Courtesy Scotty Gosson)

The first product from George Hurst and Bill Campbell was an engine mount. This original in Mike Williams's A-V8 allows the installation of a small-block Chevy in an early Ford chassis.

The Deuce sedan with setback Chevy indicates the Hurst support trailer is at a dragstrip somewhere, maybe Pomona with those bleachers, giving the racers support. (Photo Courtesy Dan Shannon)

and the new entity quickly tooled up to manufacture and supply the Hurst 4-speed shifter as a non-factory branded item for the 1961 Pontiac Catalina powered by the 421-ci Super Duty.

A myriad of new products erupted out of the Warminster, Pennsylvania, headquarters, from wheels for the 1965 GTO to the Jaws of Life rescue tool. Unfortunately, as so often happens today but not so much then, Hurst decided to take his company public. In 1970, Sunbeam Corp., known for countertop kitchen appliances, bought Campbell's share of the company. By the mid-1970s, Hurst was out. He passed away in 1986 at age 59. It had been a heck of a ride, though.

Tri-Y

We have seen that a catchy name worked wonders for some speed equipment. For example, there's Edelbrock's Slingshot and the Cherry Bomb, but changing the name of one's business is never a good idea. Unfortunately, due to some personal issues, Doug Thorley's header business changed from Doug's Headers to Headers by Doug to Doug Thorley Headers.

Whatever the name, Doug's header business, located at 5533 E. Whittier Blvd. in Los Angeles, had a long list of clients. According to author Bob McClurg in his book from CarTech titled *The History of AMC Motorsports*, clients included "Big" John Mazmanian; Stone, Woods, & Cook; K.S. Pittman; "Junior" Thompson; Sox & Martin, "Dandy" Dick Landy; Hubert Platt; Tom Hoover; and many more.

Doug Thorley, who was born in Cedar City, Utah, in 1929, graduated from Cedar High in 1947, and the following year migrated south to Long Beach, where he served in the U.S. Navy/Air Corp Reserves until 1949. Meanwhile, he discovered the new sport of drag racing and raced a 1938 Buick Century coupe at the Santa Ana drags, where he set numerous records in the Stock class.

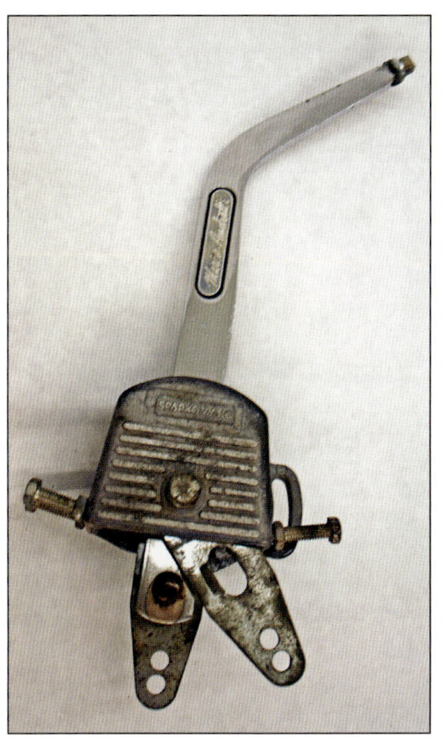

Hurst shifters were quickly copied by many, including Sparkomatic, which was owned by Jonas Anchel and son Edward who produced a line of accessories out of Milford, Pennsylvania, with an endorsement from Mario Andretti. (Photo Courtesy Scotty Gosson)

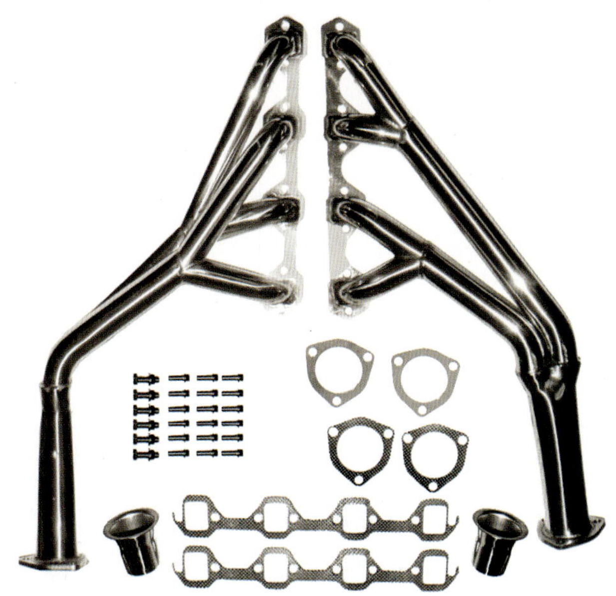

While new rather than old, this set of Mustang Tri-Y headers perfectly illustrates the design concept that takes advantage of the firing order to maximize exhaust scavenging.

Hundreds of race cars, such as the Thomas, Pritchard, & Harrison Beaver Hunter II AA/Fuel Altered seen here at Lions Drag Strip proudly carried a Headers by Doug decal. John Force once drove but crashed in the fire-up road. (Photo Courtesy Dan Shannon)

Drag racing wasn't his only passion though, and he was soon behind the wheel of Jack Lufkin's bright red, modified 1962 Corvette at Bonneville. The September 1964 issue of *Drag Racing* magazine said, "After installation of Doug's Headers, Jack Lufkin breezed to a new B/MSP record of 131.95 mph, won class at 11.83."

According to Phil Burgess writing in *National Dragster*, the Vette turned 204.248 on the salt in 1964. The words "DOUG'S HEADERS" were written in large letters along the front fenders. Besides racing at Bonneville, Doug's Headers also sponsored some trophies and advertised in the program.

Thorley was also getting some time behind the wheel of various race cars and was so impressed with Hubert Platt's stretched 1966 Mustang that he decided to build his own Funny Car. Thorley's *Chevy II Much* was built by Ted Brown and debuted in 1966. Running on alcohol, the altered-wheelbase Nova regularly ran in the 9s at 150 mph.

Not enough to compete with the fuel cars, Thorley trailered the *Chevy II* and commissioned Gary Slusser to build him a new tube-framed, front-motored, altered-wheelbase, steel-bodied Chevy Corvair. The car debuted in 1967 and ran high-7s and went on to win the 1967 U.S. Nation-

als with a 7.83. Thorley later said, "It was, without a doubt, the greatest day of my life." The Corvair also recorded the first (unofficial) 200-mph Funny Car pass at Lions Drag Strip.

The Nationals win resulted in a call from AMC, which wanted its own Javelin-based Funny Car. The company tried it with a 392 AMC Wedge, but it wasn't until it dropped it in Thorley's blown Chevy from the Corvair that AMC saw some success. That must have been a public relations nightmare for the AMC folks.

Thorley, who was given the 1968 *Car Craft* magazine All Star Drag Racing Team Funny Car Driver of the Year award, was offered the job of running AMC's factory Super Stock program. He declined but introduced AMC to H.L. and Shirley Shahan, who took the reins. Thorley, meanwhile, remained involved as the header supplier, and it was as a manufacturer that he really made a name for himself.

Thorley is generally credited with having invented the Tri-Y design, but that is difficult to confirm, as there were similar configurations on several Italian race cars of the 1950s, as there were rows of downdraft Webers. In a conversation with Cobra Daytona coupe designer Pete Brock, he recalled, "I think our engine team at Shelby developed those on the dyno and then first used them on CSX 2287, our first Daytona Coupe that ran at

Jack Chrisman, Art's uncle, debuted the Sachs & Sons Mercury Comet at the 1964 Nationals. With Headers by Doug, it was the world's first blown-fuel Funny Car clocking a best ET of 10.13 at 156.25 mph. (Photo Courtesy Dan Shannon)

Daytona in Feb. '64." Tri-Y headers certainly appeared on the 1966 Shelby Mustang GT350 and Cyclone Automotive Products located at 7040-A Lankershim Blvd. in North Hollywood, is often credited as Shelby's supplier.

According to the Doug Thorley Headers website (the company is now part of the PerTronix group), "The Tri-Y header was designed to match the synchronization of the engine firing order, thereby maximizing exhaust scavenging. This design creates the optimum torque and greatest horsepower gains in comparison to other designs." Whether Thorley invented the design is immaterial, as he was the one who popularized the term Tri-Y.

1958 Jardine Headers

As we have seen, the exhaust business was pretty much like the cam business in that it attracted a lot of players. This was because the exhaust business required minimal start-up investment: just take a long can and shove a perforated tube through it.

One name that surfaced in 1958 was that of Jerry Jardine. Jardine had been working part-time at Pearly's Muffler Shop on the corner of Colorado Boulevard and Madre Street in Pasadena.

By the time he finished high school, Jardine had saved enough to buy a new 1958 Impala powered by a 315-hp 348. He raced it at El Mirage and at the San Gabriel

Steve Bovan of Chevy II fame is installing headers at Blair's Speed Shop on a 1964 Plymouth Fury with a Max Wedge evidenced by the twin holes in the underside of the hood. (Photo Courtesy Dan Shannon)

Some Jardine Tri-Y headers were placed on a small-block 301 Chevy in Larry "Quicksilver" Fator's 1959 Apache. Notice how the 6 and 8 pipes are joined. The third Y is actually in the fender well.

The passenger's side of Fator's 1955 truck shows that the header tubes take a different route, where 1 and 2 are joined, as are 3 and 4. Again, the third Y is in the fender well.

drags. According to Doug Boyce's book from CarTech titled *"Dyno" Don*, Jardine cleaned up at the drags, beating several cars prepared by Les Ritchey's Performance Unlimited. "The next day, he drove out to 'Dyno' Don Nicholson's shop in Monrovia looking for some help in making the Chevy go even faster."

At first, Nicholson wasn't interested, but when Jardine told him of his success, Nicholson warmed to him, and the pair formed a friendship. Jardine apparently built his first set of headers on the floor of Nicholson's garage in Duarte. They were a Tri-Y design based, some have said, on an Italian Maserati that Jardine had studied.

Jardine began his business out of a sheet-metal shop owned by the father of a friend in Pasadena. As soon as he could, he moved to his own shop at 7565 Acacia Ave. in Garden Grove, California. Located on Nelson Street and Garden Grove Boulevard, it was a shack next to Ray Alley's Engine Masters.

Soon, Jardine's racing success was translated into his advertising. He began citing big-name clients, such as Don Nicholson, Eddie Schartman, and Al Joniec. Every design was dyno tested and guaranteed two years. According to Doug Boyce, "At his peak, Jardine Headers was producing roughly 100 sets of headers a day." Jardine was also one of the first to sell bolt-on headers in a box.

Tommy Ivo and the Nailheads

In his book *"TV" Tommy Ivo Drag Racing's Master Showman*, author Tom Cotter quotes Ivo as saying, "These were not timed injectors but were basically a metered leak." Despite the description, Ivo enjoyed huge success with his Hilborn-injected Buicks, whether they had one, two, or four engines.

Child actor Tommy Ivo, who made more than 100 movies, might have had it a little easier than many others, but there was no one with more enthusiasm. He walked away from his lucrative acting career to go drag racing full time.

Ivo was a Buick guy, and his first big influencer was seeing Norm Grabowski's Cadillac-powered T-bucket at

Ivo settled on Hilborn fuel injection for his Buick Nailhead when he began to race it more than drive it on the street. Ivo described the system as "really just a metered leak."

the drive-in at Bob's Big Boy in Toluca Lake, California. Of course, Grabowski's bucket went on to star in the hit TV show *77 Sunset Strip* as the *Kookie Kar*.

Taking an abandoned T tourer that he found in the desert, Ivo spent a year building his rod using a Model A frame and, of course, a Buick Nailhead. He had no intention of racing but was soon off to the Saugus drags, where he ran 104 mph, just beating Grabowski.

Striving to go faster, Ivo tried various induction systems until he settled on a Hilborn stack injection, and the car became more of a racer than a roadster. His mentor in all of this was Max "Old Yeller" Balchowsky, who was a "wizard of building Buick racing engines," Ivo said. "Nobody was building parts for the Buicks back then, so I had to 'woo' manufacturers into making parts for this engine, which they considered an orphan."

Two Is Better than One

Metered leak or not, Ivo was far from done with Hilborn-injected Buick Nailheads. In fact, he'd only just started when Don "the Beachcomber" Johnson offered him a Kent Fuller dragster chassis. Ivo threw in his injected Buick, and he was hooked by the win. He ordered his own chassis from Fuller and went on to set the World Elapsed Time Gas record at 9.5 seconds.

After measuring the Kookie Kar, *Ivo built his own T-bucket powered by a Buick Nailhead. He tried various induction systems: 6x2s, 3x2s, and this dual-quad setup that was on the car in the 1957 movie* Dragstrip Girl. *(Photo Courtesy Tommy Ivo)*

Eventually, Ivo got the rail down to 9.16 but realized he was never going to go faster with one engine. His next thought was, "How about two?" The single-engine rail was sold to Don "the Snake" Prudhomme, and Ivo embarked on mating two Nailheads in one rail.

Once again, the chassis was built by Kent Fuller, while Ivo built front and rear engine plates to cradle the engines. The two starter ring gears of the two flywheels were meshed, and Ivo reversed the flow of one engine so that they worked together. Only one engine had the bell-housing and driveshaft that was connected to an offset differential.

"TV" Tommy Ivo's first dragster built in 1958 was powered by the injected Buick engine out of his T-bucket and shoehorned into the very first chassis built by Kent Fuller, who had recently left C-T Automotive. (Photo Courtesy Dan Shannon)

Ivo couldn't get the single-engine car any faster than 9.16, so he figured two Nailhead engines had to be better. In 1960, he built this twin side-by-side that at times he ran with a blower on one engine. (Photo Courtesy Dan Shannon)

If two is good, then four must be better. In 1961, Ivo fielded Showboat a four-engine 1,856-ci 4WD monster that wowed the crowds as it smoked all four tires. Unfortunately, it was relegated to exhibition only. (Photo Courtesy Tommy Ivo)

Considering Ivo's lack of mechanical engineering schooling, that is to say none, the assembly worked extremely well and looked wicked. According to Ivo in Tom Cotter's book, "The twin-motor car was the baddest bear in the woods." It became the first gas-powered dragster to run in the 8s and was the first to hit 170 and then 180 mph.

Four Is Better than Two

Ever the showman, Ivo rightly concluded that if two engines pleased the crowd, four would double the fun. According to Tom Cotter's book, "His rationale was that if you could double the horsepower of the twin-engine car and only add 50 percent more weight, you couldn't be beaten by any gas-powered car." When complete, the four-engine car cost $4,000 and weighed 3,100 pounds compared to the twin-engine car that weighed 1,850 pounds.

Kent Fuller was paid $15 an hour to build the chassis, and Buick supplied the engines that were bored and stroked to 464 ci each (1,856 ci combined). There were 32 Jahns pistons, four Isky cams, and 16 exhaust pipes, two of which angled down between the engines.

The engines were coupled in pairs: The left-side engines faced the rear and drove the front Halibrand quick-change while the right-side faced forward as normal and drove the rear Halibrand differential. It was simple but effective. However, Ivo recalled to Cotter that adjusting the 64 valves was a tedious operation.

Unfortunately, as he completed *Showboat*, the NHRA banned all four-engine cars except his, relegating

Many onlookers scratched their heads as Ivo's Showboat *morphed into the Buick-bodied* Wagon Master, *but it remained a crowd pleaser. Today it survives along with a tribute to the original.*

Note the Irvin logo on the chute can of this early-1960s dragster at Bakersfield for the U.S. Fuel and Gas Championships. I wonder where these three kids are today. (Photo Courtesy Dan Shannon)

it to exhibition runs only. To make matters worse, the sanctioning body also began to reinstate the use of fuel, making *Showboat* an instant dinosaur. Nevertheless, the car was a huge success, making Ivo an international star even though he rarely drove it, turning over the control to Don Prudhomme, Ron Pelligrini, and eventually Tom McCurry. If you never saw it run, watch the movie *Bikini Beach*; it's awesome.

Chute

While Ivo's evil twin was running 180 on a good day, the comparative fuel dragsters were running 190. Stopping, especially on some of the shorter strips, was a real problem. Ivo remembered, "I heard about a guy named Jim Deist who had a parachute that had been used to

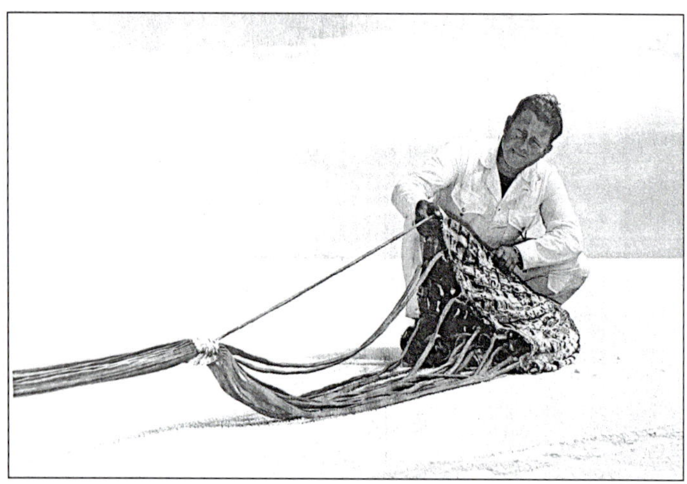

Taking a job at the Irvin Air Chute Co. was prophetic for a young Jim Deist, who soon found himself in the racing parachute business thanks to encouragement from Mickey Thompson. (Photo Courtesy Dan Shannon)

slow jet aircraft during landing, and he was experimenting with it at the drag strip."

Deist grew up in Los Angeles, where in 1939 his dad built a gas station. It was there that Deist built his first hot rod. After graduating high school, he began a career as a fabricator but in 1948 took a job at the Irvin Air Chute Co. in Glendale. In 1939, Irvin (sometimes spelled "Irving") was the world's largest manufacturer of parachutes.

According to the American Hot Rod Foundation, in 1956, Deist was introduced to Abe Carson, who was running a dragster but having trouble stopping. While running at San Fernando, their efforts were spotted by Mickey Thompson. Thompson encouraged Deist to start making the chutes commercially.

Deist founded Deist Safety in 1958 and was soon making chutes for all the leading racers, including Art Chrisman and Ed Pink. Deist also worked with Thompson on chutes for the then-unblown *Challenger I* that ran at Bonneville in 1959. From then on, there was no stopping him.

The Big-Block

Gas was cheap at around 30 cents per gallon in 1958, but cars and trucks were getting bigger as were the truck loads. Something needed to be done, and as a consequence, Chevrolet began developing the W-series of big-block engines. The first, a 348 ci, debuted in 1958 and is easily identifiable because of its distinct "dub-ya"-shaped interchangeable cylinder heads.

Conventional in most respects, the Turbo Thrust or Super Turbo Thrust 348 was unusual in that the

With its W-shaped heads and Moon no-name valve covers, Chevy's 348-ci big-block that debuted in 1958 was a game changer. Its Wedge design was created by not having the surface of the cylinder head square to the bore. (Photo Courtesy Dan Shannon)

The 348-ci 1958 W-motor in Colby Martin's Model A coupe is equipped with Weiand valve covers, a factory Tri-Power intake, and triple factory Rochester carburetors. (Photo Courtesy Colby Martin)

combustion chamber was in the upper part of the cylinder rather than in the head that only had small recesses for the valves. This so-called Wedge design was created by not having the surface of the cylinder head square to the bore. Instead, the block decks were at 74 degrees rather than 90 degrees to the bore. This made for a 16-degree, wedge-shaped combustion chamber.

The Turbo Thrust sported a single Rochester 4GC carburetor for 250 hp and 355 ft-lbs of torque at 2,800 rpm. Meanwhile, the Super Turbo Thrust enjoyed a triumvirate of Rochester carburetors to produce 280 hp and 355 ft-lbs of torque at 3,200 rpm. Under normal operation, only the center carburetor worked, but operation of what was known as the foot feed was opened to 60 degrees, and a vacuum switch operated the other two carbs. The Tri-Power assembly added $70 to the price.

Hot on the heels of the initial 348 came a Police Cruiser 348 with a solid-lifter hi-performance cam, 11:1 compression ratio. Horsepower was rated at 315 at 5,600 rpm with 356 ft-lbs of torque at 3,600 rpm. The following year, Chevrolet offered seven different 348 series engines.

Mickey Thompson Enterprises

By the time he became famous as the first American to go 400 mph, Marion Lee "Mickey" Thompson had already lived the life of three people. Thompson was born in Alhambra, California, in 1928, and his father was for many years a no-nonsense chief of detectives.

"He only had to look at you," Thompson's son Danny said.

At age 14, Thompson bought a 1927 Chevy for $7.50 and embarked on an amazing journey.

Thompson's name first appeared in the Bonneville Nationals program in 1951. He was racing a 296-ci flattie-powered 1936 coupe and went 141.065 mph, winning the award for Most Determined Effort. Hooked on salt, he returned the following year with a long-nose yellow Austin Bantam coupe with not one but two flathead Ford V-8s with a total of 592 ci. It went a staggering 196.72 mph. In 1953, he swapped the back flathead for a $40 Chrysler Hemi fitted with a $10 4-71 blower. Possibly the first to blow up a blown Hemi, he earned the meet's Hard Luck award.

Thompson's push car was a 6-cylinder 1953 Ford that he had raced in that year's Carrera Pan Americana. It was sponsored by Ellico Ford of Alhambra, and the Bantam coupe was sponsored by Harry Weber's Weber Cams. You could already tell Thompson was no ordinary racer. He was off in all directions like a dervish trying his hand at sports car racing and drag racing.

In 1954, Thompson fielded what many regard as the first slingshot dragster, but in fact, there had been others (much like Garlits and the rear-engine dragster). For example, there was the Bean Bandits' 1951 twin-flathead engine rail. No matter, Thompson was an innovator, and his full-bodied *Panorama City Special* (it was sponsored by planned community Panorama City, a suburb of Los Angeles) had a narrowed rear axle and the engine connected directly to the axle.

Thompson tried many engines in that car. At the San Fernando Drag Strip on September 4, 1955, using a 302-ci Chrysler Hemi borrowed from Ray Brown, Thompson was the first to break 150 mph with a single engine with a run of 151.26 mph.

At the time, Thompson had a full-time job as a pressman at the *L.A. Times* and was running a repair garage on the side. Somehow, he found the time to build and manage Lions Drag Strip. Although pretty basic when it opened on October 6, 1955, 10,000 people showed up. Thompson continued to improve the facility and bring innovative new ideas to the track for the next eight years.

In 1958, Thompson and his mechanic Fritz Voigt were heading to Oklahoma City for the Nationals when they decided to take a small detour to the Bonneville Salt Flats. It's not exactly on the way, but with a Bob Sorrell body over the 4WD twin Hemi beast, Thompson ran 294 mph. Not quite the 300 he needed for a deal with Firestone, but it was, nevertheless, the "world's fastest hot rod."

At that point, Thompson's focus shifted back to the salt and the challenge of being the first to 400. He immediately went home and began chalking on the garage floor of his El Monte home a vehicle with four engines, four Cadillac transmissions, four overdrives, and four

With some Las Vegas gambling winnings, Mickey Thompson quit his night job at the L.A. Times and purchased this building at 1410 Coat Ave. in Long Beach and dived into the speed equipment business. (Photo Courtesy Danny Thompson)

quick-changes.

On August 9, 1959, test runs were made at Edwards Air Force Base, which was formerly Muroc dry lake. While accelerating, Thompson hit an unseen bump, went airborne for 60 feet, and spun out at over 200 mph. He was shaken but learned a lot. The acceleration and handling exceeded even Mickey's expectations, and the tires and wheels withstood tremendous forces.

At the Bonneville Nationals, Thompson made several runs and discovered and cured a severe fishtailing problem caused by the length of the parachute towline. With the gremlins sorted, he made a one-way run at 362.31 mph—some 68 mph faster than any American had ever traveled on land.

After Bonneville, Thompson bought a lot at 1410 Coat Ave. in Long Beach with Las Vegas gambling winnings. He quit the *L.A. Times* and launched his own speed equipment business. The first product was forged-aluminum pistons. Then, there were forged aluminum connecting rods, and eventually more than 1,100 products, including manifolds, blower kits, valve and timing gear covers, and on and on. The first Mickey Thompson catalog appeared in 1962.

With the addition of four GMC 6-71 superchargers and a reconfigured nose and tail, the *Challenger I* returned to the Salt in 1960. The morning of September 9, everything worked perfectly, and Thompson drove faster than any man in history at 406.60 mph. On the return run, a driveshaft broke, ending the effort. As Thompson said, "I did it with equipment that is American down to the last cotter pin."

In 1959, Mickey Thompson took the 7,000-pound Challenger I *to Bonneville and used a plane wing for shade. The four used Hilborn-injected 389-ci Pontiacs powered the beast to a new record of 362 mph. (Photo Courtesy Danny Thompson)*

Seen before but nevertheless this is a fantastic visual of what typical dragster parts cost circa 1961. Sadly, prices have not stayed the same. This simple build might cost ten times as much today. (Photo Courtesy Danny Thompson)

Thompson was forever experimenting with different ways to make power. Here, he tries twin Jimmies on an unusual V-8 that has intake ports on the outside of the heads. Note the pulley-operated injectors. (Photo Courtesy Danny Thompson)

Thompson liked to experiment with his Ponchos, and in this instance, he cut one in half and made a 4-cylinder fitted with an Enderle-injected Jimmy blower mounted to a custom, one-off cast intake.

Not content with cutting an eight in half, Thompson went on to cut a four in half, making a 2-cylinder engine that was likewise injected and blown but this time with a fabricated manifold.

For the most part, Thompson was a Pontiac guy, but in the early 1960s, Tommy Ivo supplied the chassis for the Ford-powered Harvey Aluminum Special, seen here at Lions with Wally Parks. (Photo Courtesy Danny Thompson)

In 1963, Thompson shipped the dragster to the UK for a series of match races against the Mooneyes dragster. It stayed in the UK, morphed into the Commuter, and retained the 4-bolt 427-ci Wedge.

The one part of the Mickey Thompson empire that endures is Mickey Thompson Tires. This Super Stock tire circa 1966 offered "exclusive tread compound gives you lightning recovery from starting-line slip." It was all for about $50.

Mickey Thompson wasn't the only one forging a new business with aluminum. On the left is an early Howard billet rod from the Stone, Woods, & Cook Gasser, and on the right is a forged rod from the Howard Twin-Bear dragster.

Hooker

Gary Ronald Hooker was born in 1941 in Sioux City, Iowa. When he was five years old, the family moved to Pomona, California, which back then was known for citrus growing but was also a hot bed of hot rodding and racing, being surrounded by racetracks.

At school, Hooker excelled in sports, playing basketball, baseball, and football. His school also had an industrial arts department, and he admits he drew a lot of cars in class. An avid mechanic, his first hot rod was a $175 1940 Ford coupe that he soon tore down and rebuilt with a three-quarter race cam.

After high school and junior college, Hooker volunteered for the draft but was persuaded to join the National Guard where he did six months active duty. At age 20, he went to work as an electronics engineer at General Dynamics, which was located in Pomona at the time. He earned good money, enough to buy a brand-new 1962 409 Chevy.

Hooker immediately ripped into the Chevy and began making his own headers in his parents' garage. His apparent secret was to use large-diameter tubing that helps produce more horsepower and long tubes that help produce more torque. Hooker took the Chevy along to renowned engine builder Jack Bayer Racing Engine Co. (one time mechanic for Dave MacDonald) located then at 9645 Rush St. in South El Monte, California. Bayer had just finished dyno'ing a customer's car with a similar engine. Well, Hooker's made more power.

"It's got to be those headers," said Bayer. "Can you get me some of those?"

"No," replied Hooker, "those are the only ones I've made. But if you give me a ride home, we can take the headers off my car and put them on your customer's."

"I more or less went into business right then," said Hooker in an interview for the SEMA Hall of Fame.

Hooker soon sold the 409 to buy equipment and began building headers at his parents' home. He then rented a small space that he shared with Elwin Westbrook, a welder and fabricator who also built roll cages. Westbrook was a record holder in a 1962 Biscayne sponsored by Airline Auto Sales.

"Within a few months, 6 of the top 10 Super Stock racers had my headers," said Hooker.

In the summer of 1965, Hooker rented a larger building, but an explosion caused by some faulty welding bottles caused the shop to be razed. Hooker had no insurance, but his neighbor was Bill Casler of Casler Tire Service in Ontario who made Casler Cheater Slicks. The two businessmen partnered, and Casler purchased 50-percent of Hooker Headers.

A manufacturing facility was established at 1032 West Brooks St. in Ontario, California. Between 1966 and 1969, Hooker Headers grew from a $100,000 company to $3 million. By 1975, it was doing $10 million. Around that time, Casler and Hooker parted ways.

The growth came from natural growth within the industry but also because of its distinctive logo, a red heart with the large word "Hooker." The decals proclaiming "I Love My Hooker Headers" were in the windows of many cars, and their advertising had catchy taglines, such as, "Dick Landy would rather go without his cigar than his Hooker Headers." Hooker was known as one of the winningest brands in drag racing history.

The company soon branched out into other exhaust systems and parts. It also had a line of fiberglass accessories, such as spoilers and fender flares for trucks and vans. The company was sold to Holley in 2000.

Side Pipes

If General Motors Vice President of Design Bill Mitchell had not gone fishing off the coast of Florida, we might never have enjoyed the visceral benefits of the side pipe. However, the experimental Mako Shark Corvette show car of 1961 had four chrome pipes exiting through the fender and entering a ribbed aluminum side pipe. Little did Mitchell realize what impact he would have on the cognoscenti.

A more purposeful, racy-looking side exhaust appeared on the 1963 Grand Sport, and low and behold, the pipes became a factory option from 1965 through 1967. Not to be outdone, Carroll Shelby fitted some to his early 427 Cobra comp and semi-comp cars.

Like so many, electronics engineer Gary Hooker kind of fell into the performance business when Jack Bayer asked if he could buy some 409 headers Hooker had made. "No, but I can make some more," said Hooker.

We have GM's head of styling Bill Mitchell to thank for the side pipes that debuted on the 1958 XP 700 and are seen here on the SS that was built on the tube frame of one of Duntov's 1957 race cars.

Side pipes were nothing new. They had been fitted to hot rods as far back as 1940 and called "lakes" or "lake pipes" even though they were not typically seen on lakes cars. Heck, Ed Iskenderian had a version on his famous 1924 Model T built in 1940, and there were plenty installed on other contemporary hot rods.

Unwittingly, perhaps, Bill Mitchell had given the aftermarket a new meal ticket. Soon, side pipes were appearing on everything that had four wheels. No doubt the most unanticipated market came with the van craze that blossomed in the early 1970s. They were unceremoniously thrown

The *Beatnik Bandit*

It's interesting to note that trends in racing tended to trickle down to the street. One of the first to perpetuate this in the "Swingin' Sixties" was Ed "Big Daddy" Roth. Roth landed on earth like a big meteorite that bounced through life oblivious to the rules. It took a while for Roth to get into his stride, but once he found the kryptonite formula, there was no stopping him.

The first car that Roth didn't buy but built himself was the *Outlaw*, and it looked for all intents and purposes like a stumpy dragster from its brakeless wire front wheels and chrome lakes pipes to its slick-like rear tires.

While the *Outlaw* was outrageous for 1960, it was not as out there as Roth's next car: the *Beatnik Bandit*. Based on a 1950 Oldsmobile, the *Bandit* featured a blown Oldsmobile engine, a bubble top, and tiller steering.

No, Roth never was a maker of parts—except T-shirts. He was strictly a one-off man, but he was undoubtedly an influencer of his day, showing and thereby encouraging the public to try something different.

Millions of kids, me being one of them, were turned on to the hot rod hobby by Ed "Big Daddy" Roth and creations such as the Beatnik Bandit. He might not have sold parts, but he sold inspiration.

down the side of everything, and I even saw them used as bumpers on the backs of vans.

221-260-289

Ford was behind the eight ball, as it often was, when it came to technical developments or so it seemed. For example, take its small-block that was introduced in July 1961, six years after the small-block Chevy. In the hot rodder's opinion, it was never quite the engine the Chevy was. Sure, it went on to power a lot of hot rods, including Carroll Shelby's Cobra, and a lot of people love it, but it was just not quite as swappable as a small-block Chevy.

That said, the "The New Size Ford" Falcon of 1960 was only the second American compact after the Rambler American, but it was the first small car from one of the Big Three manufacturers. Initially powered by a variety of sixes, the Falcon was seen as a woman's car in the United

Constantly struggling with the fact that hot rodders liked to drop Chevys into their Fords, Ford Motorsport initiated a "Ford in a Ford" program that included Dan Fink installing one in his 1932 Woody.

States. Elsewhere, the Falcon literally flew.

Ford struggled with the fact that most hot rodders swapped a small-block Chevy into early Ford hot rods and not a small-block Ford. Consequently, in the late 1980s and early 1990s, Angelo Giampetroni, who once operated Detroit's Gratiot Auto Supply but was at the time a manager at Ford Motorsports SVO, launched a "Ford-in-a-Ford" marketing program. Aided on the outside by Roy Brizio Street Rods, Ford Motorsports SVO engineered and promoted some components to make a small-block Ford a more palatable swap. The primary focus was complete crate engines, but the list also included T-5 transmissions, oil filter relocators, EFI kits, headers, instruments, etc.

Despite its cast-iron construction, the 221 (3.6L) weighed only 470 pounds due to its thin-wall casting. It was the lightest and most compact engine in its class. With wedge combustion chambers and a 2-barrel carburetor, it was rated at 164 hp at 4,400 rpm and 258 ft-lbs of torque at 2,200 rpm. It was initially offered for the 1962 model year as an option in the Ford Fairlane and the Mercury Meteor. The 221 was destined for a short life, as it was discontinued in April 1963 after only 270,000 were produced. Of course, one infamous 221 went to AC Cars in the United Kingdom (UK), where it was shoehorned into an AC Ace sports car destined to become the Cobra.

Meanwhile, Ford had bored it out from 3.5 inches to 3.8, increasing the displacement to 260 ci. Introduced in March 1962, the 260 became the base engine for all full-size Ford sedans. Later in the year, it was optional for the Ford Falcon and the Mercury Comet. It was also offered in early Mustangs. While not yet out of the corral, the 260 was definitely ponying up to be a contender.

Ford was about to enter the international motorsports scene. In the UK, Alan Mann, a young garage-owning racing driver, was building a reputation and an alliance with Ford.

Mann's success with Andrew's Racing led to an invitation from Ford USA to compete in the Marlboro 12-hour race in August 1963 in Maryland. The 4-cylinder Ford Cortinas of Willment and Andrews finished first and second outright, beating the Holman & Moody–built Falcon V-8 that came third.

Mann returned to the UK and set up his own shop, Alan Mann Racing (AMR). His first big contract with Ford was to build Falcons for the Monte Carlo Rally. While they did not win, they set fastest time on every stage.

Another Falcon driven by Sir John Whitmore was the first to set a 100+ mph lap at Silverstone GP circuit. AMR went on to prepare six Mustangs, but it had proven that the little small-block Ford could hold its own. As a consequence, Ford introduced the XHP-260,

Lynn Park's original (as found) 289 Cobra came with the finned aluminum "Cobra Powered by Ford" valve covers, an optional $71 aluminum intake, a stock Holley 600-cfm carburetor, and an original Autolite air filter.

Obviously, some of the early 289 Cobras came with pressed tin valve covers, but what look like Weber carburetors is actually a late-model Borla electronic fuel injection system.

The "Enderle Special" is a bit of a misnomer. However, this injected 289 did come out of one of the spec Can Am cars that Shelby built. It features Enderle injection, a Hilborn pump, and a Vertex magneto.

The small-block Ford was a boon to the speed equipment business and remains so with everything from rotating assemblies to headers, such as these made by Jerry and Gaston Belanger of West Covina, California.

a high-performance version of the 260 with higher compression, solid valve lifters, larger valves, an aggressive cam, and a 4-barrel carburetor. The letters XHP-260 were painted on the valve covers. Photographs of the first Cobra assembled at Dean Moon's shop clearly show the letters "XHP-260-1" on the pressed steel valve covers.

This kit gave the aftermarket a blueprint for how to tune the 260 and what to make. A parts catalog soon followed. For example, the August 1962 issue of *Sports Car Graphic* had a road test and technical report of the 260-powered Cobra. In it, John Christy said, "There is a standard four-throat unit as on the test car, a dual-quad, a triple two-throat setup and, finally, the very hairy looking quadruple twin-choke Weber combination on a ram-tuned manifold."

The test went on to say that the addition of the Webers alone increased the output from 242 to 282 bhp. The story continued to say that with one of four optional cams and an 11:1 compression ratio, the engine developed 300 ft-lbs of torque (31 more than standard). Power for the full-option engine is pegged at 335 sustained horses. There's all of this, and we haven't even got to the 289 yet.

Sidedraft Webers were installed on some early Cobras, but they had to be removed to adjust the valves and were soon replaced with the downdrafts. Likewise, the Spalding ignition was also used on some early Cobras.

The 260 had a little more shelf life than the 221 but not much. After approximately 604,000 had been built, Ford upped the ante and introduced the 289 in April 1963. While the stroke remained at 2.87, the same as the original 221, the bore was cranked out to 4 inches and the compression ratio raised to 8.7:1. Weight increased to 506 pounds while base output was rated at 195 hp at 4,400 rpm and 285 ft-lbs of torque at 2,200 rpm.

There followed a whole string of what were called coded options: D-Code, C-Code, A-Code, and K-Code. All added a little juice to the blender, but the big news came late in the 1963 model year when Ford introduced the 289 Hi-Po (K-Code).

The Hi-Po was built using selected, flaw-free blocks that had thicker main bearing caps. The cranks featured 80-percent nodular iron (regular cranks were 40 percent) with increased counterweighting to compensate for the heavier connecting-rod big ends. It had a hotter, solid-lifter cam; 10.5:1 compression ratio; small combustion chamber heads with cast spring cups and screw-in studs; free-flow exhaust manifolds; and a dual-point centrifugal advance distributor. Finally, it had a bigger manual-choke 595-cfm Autolite 4100 carburetor. All of this and more resulted in 271 bhp at 6,000 rpm and 312 ft-lbs of torque at 3,400 rpm.

Exact numbers are not known, but apparently around 25,000 K-Code Hi-Po 289s were produced in Cleveland between March 1963 and June 1967. The story does not end there though because Shelby upped the ante again in 1965 with tube headers, an aluminum intake, and a 750-cfm Holley. Output was rated at 306 bhp at 6,000 rpm and 329 ft-lbs of torque at 4,200 rpm.

To reiterate, Ford showed the speed equipment manufacturers the road to victory, and the aftermarket went on to produce a vast array of performance and dress-up parts for the small-block Ford inspired by the Cobra and the Mustang.

"Gentleman" Joe

As were so many, Joe Schubeck from Lakewood, Ohio, was influenced by reading *Hot Rod* magazine. As soon as he was able, Schubeck began racing a flathead Ford V-8-powered dragster that had been abandoned by his buddy Jack Harris. Harris had opened Speed Equipment Company on Madison Avenue in Lakewood and didn't have time to finish the rail. He went on to be the largest warehouse distributor in sales volume in the country at the time. Schubeck, meanwhile, dumped in some $1.50-a-gallon nitro and faced off against Walt Arfons.

In his SEMA Hall of Fame interview, Schubeck said, "They lined me up next to Walt's *Bologna Slicer* that was propelled by an Allison V-12-driven propeller. Arfons had a really big engine, and it looked like a locomotive next to me. When I looked over, all I saw were the blades of his propellers spinning next to my head, and I thought, 'If I don't get the hell out of here, I'm going to be sliced bologna.'" It was a prophetic start to Schubeck's career in the industry.

Schubeck lost his first race, but in 1957, he teamed up with mechanic Butch Scarpelli, who was knowledgeable about Chrysler Hemis. Schubeck and Scarpelli fielded an AA/Gas dragster with a blown Hemi. "In '58, I had built my own tube chassis," Schubeck said, "and the following year, I rounded up a bunch of people who wanted them, and suddenly, I was in business. I called it Lakewood Chassis Co. I started it at home in Lakewood, Ohio, but soon moved to a one-stall shop on 117th on the Cleveland/Lakewood boundary line."

In 1959, the pair won the International Timing Association World Gas Dragster title with a 170-mph run. In the early 1960s, drag race car builders struggled with fabricating a new, deeper bellhousing, which was needed to house the flywheel and a double-disk clutch for the high-powered dragsters. The direct-drive method without a transmission was known as "high gear only." Typically, a cylinder was rolled from aluminum plate and capped with a circular aluminum plate. The block end also received a drilled flange. With enough length added to accommodate two and even three clutch disks and their floater plates, the new housing solved the depth problem. However, the amount of weld time needed to complete this deeper clutch was almost equal to welding an entire new tubular chassis.

Before Joe Schubeck hydroformed bellhousings, they were often cast iron, such as this Chevy unit from Ansen. Of course, cast iron can shatter, especially when a clutch explodes, but this one was NHRA approved.

Cast iron was one way of containing an exploding clutch, as was a fabricated aluminum can. However, there had to be a better way.

"The aluminum bellhousing that I assembled from welding various pieces together was my biggest headache," said Schubeck. "I looked at stamping and metal spinning but discovered the Hydra-form process in a Cleveland metal fabricating shop. They only had a small version of the machine required to do my job but pointed me in the right direction. Lucky for me, a machine of adequate size was recently installed at Westinghouse Electric in Cleveland to produce streetlight shades, and the chief engineer was a car enthusiast. We struck a deal in 1963 to produce the first Lakewood bellhousings."

The Hydra-forming process hydraulically produced the deep-drawn housing from a circle of aluminum in just 22 seconds. It needed only the drilled engine mounting holes to be complete. This process revolutionized the production of housings for both direct-drive dragsters and

The tag on the fabricated aluminum can says "A Product of Dye Engineering Co. 1500 So. Broadway, Gardena, Calif." It was no doubt a copy of the Donovan bellhousing.

In 1978, product quality and safety issues initiated the formation of the SEMA Foundation Inc. (SFI). Eventually, SFI split from SEMA but continues to monitor and test the quality of speed equipment.

"Gentleman" Joe Schubeck saw a need in the drag racing world for a better scattershield, or bellhousing as they are more commonly known today, and discovered a way of hydroforming them in steel. (Photo Courtesy Holley Corporation)

bellhousing scatter-shields for Sportsman class cars. The Sportsman class cars needed to replace the die-cast aluminum factory housings that failed to contain the clutch and flywheel blowups that were plaguing full-body cars at that time.

"We built a test machine in our shop," continued Schubeck, "and actually exploded flywheels to find that the ductility and strength of our Hydra-formed housing would contain all the shrapnel. Long story short, the NHRA made them mandatory, and all I had to do was produce."

Midway through the 1965 season, at the urging of Jack Harris, Schubeck sold the dragster, quit building chassis, and launched Lakewood Industries.

An article by Terry Cook in the March 1968 issue of *Car Craft* gave a detailed overview of scattershields from Ansen; Cyclone-Wedge; Russ Ciphers's RC Industries of Medina, Ohio; and Joe Schubeck's Lakewood Chassis. Cook went on to say that the Lakewood can was lighter than any of the competitors and probably stronger.

The Lakewood scattershield soon became the industry standard. Schubeck, meanwhile, had been christened "Gentlemen" Joe by Ed "Isky" Iskenderian. So, when Schubeck drove George Hurst's twin-engine *Hurst Hairy Oldsmobile*, Jim Deist made him a custom-fitted tuxedo-styled fire suit complete with a bow tie and top hat.

Besides being a safety innovator, Joe Schubeck also drove the Hurst Hairy Olds powered by two Joe Mondello-built supercharged 425-ci Oldsmobiles with Hilborn injection running on straight alcohol. (Photo Courtesy Bob McClurg)

1963-1966
MUSCLE BOUND

The voluntary racing ban in 1957 by the Automobile Manufacturers Association that resulted from the horrific crash at Le Mans in 1955 was largely ignored, certainly after a year or so. However, in 1961, when President John F. Kennedy took office, his brother Robert Kennedy, attorney general, picked up on anti-trust allegations against General Motors that Robert Bicks of the Eisenhower government had initiated.

The GM Racing Ban

General Motors wasn't the first or only target; there were antitrust suits against other industry giants, most notably General Electric. However, the antitrust suit against General Motors was never actually filed, and soon Kennedy was being criticized for his lack of action regarding General Motors and AT&T in particular. Perhaps there just wasn't a case to answer.

Meanwhile, in April 1961, Ford had purchased Electric Autolite Co. for $28 million, and that purchase included Autolite's $2 million racing program. Henry Ford II reasoned that Autolite, which became Ford's Motorcraft Division, was not an automobile manufacturer because it primarily made spark plugs and batteries. Since the sponsorship program had been initiated before Ford's acquisition, then Autolite's program was not subject to the 1957 AMA agreement. To

In 1957, as a result of a horrific crash at Le Mans in 1955 and ongoing mayhem, the Automobile Manufacturers Association initiated an auto racing ban that was ignored at will. (Photo Courtesy Dan Shannon)

Despite the racing ban, Pontiac was cleaning up in NASCAR. Glenn "Fireball" Roberts won both the Daytona 500 and the Firecracker 250 in 1962 in this Smokey Yunick-built car. (Photo Courtesy Dan Shannon)

throw the cat among the pigeons, Ford was elected president of the AMA on June 15, 1961.

Meanwhile, GM's Chevrolet and Pontiac divisions were cleaning up at the races. In the June 2, 1962, issue of the *Detroit Free Press,* Henry Ford II "revealed that he had notified the AMA that the No. 2 auto manufacturer would no longer be bound by the resolution." The story went on to say, "A spokesman for Chrysler Corp. quickly pointed out that Ford's decision made the resolution inoperative."

On June 11, 1962, General Motors officially responded that it would continue endorsing the AMA resolution, but the writing was on the wall—or was it? General Motors ultimately decided to continue its racing ban.

A small article in the February 2, 1963, issue of *The Charlotte News* said, "Pontiac's new 421-inch engine with solid lifters will now be available only with hydraulic lifters and Chevy's new 427-incher and possibly its 409-inch engines." The story went on to say, "The move is in sharp contrast to new performance programs announced by Ford, Mercury and Chrysler Corp."

The Wide World of Sports (1961)

If you were a motorsports fan watching TV on Saturday, April 29, 1961, your prayers were about to be answered when ABC launched its *Wide World of Sports.* The show was the creation of Edgar Scherick, who owned Sports Program Inc. but sold it to ABC. Hosted for the most part by Jim McKay, the TV program covered the gamut from the Oklahoma Rattlesnake Hunt Championships to the 1967 Monaco Grand Prix.

For the most part, the auto action was covered by Chris Economaki, who began editing *National Speed Sport News* in 1950. Economaki was also a track announcer and joined ABC on July 4, 1961, covering the NASCAR Firecracker 250 at Daytona. He went on to cover everything from demolition derbies to the 24 Hours of Le Mans until 1984, when he moved to CBS. ABC's *Wide World of Sports* put international motorsports into every American living room. In 2007, *Time* magazine listed the *Wide World of Sports* as one of the 100 best television programs of all time.

SEMA

The acronym SEMA originally stood for Speed Equipment Manufacturers Association, and the group was formed when Henry Blankfort of Revell Models was looking to license industry logos for Revell's popular model kits. When meeting with Dean Moon of Moon Equipment and Roy Richter of Bell Auto Parts and Cragar, Blankfort was shocked to find there was no association to protect the group's interests and no one entity to deal with.

With help from Blankfort, John Bartlett of Grant Industries drew up the bylaws, and the first meeting was

Pete Chapouris and Jim Jacobs of Pete & Jake's Hot Rod Parts were filmed in 1985 at the Chrysler Shelby Performance Center in Santa Fe Springs, California, for a Wide World of Sports *segment. Chapouris, of course, owned the California Kid.*

If it hadn't been for the boom in building plastic model kits and the resultant need to license logos, there might never have been a Speed Equipment Manufacturers Association.

Dean Moon (center) was one of the founding fathers of SEMA and in 1964 the second president. This early 1960s show booth has a sign for MacKay manifolds on the left-hand side. (Photo Courtesy Mooneyes)

actually held at Revell. SEMA was incorporated in May 1963, and the first president was Ed Iskenderian.

The 13 founders of SEMA were Louie Senter, Ansen Automotive; Bob Spar, B&M Automotive; Roy Richter, Cragar Industries; Els Lohn, Eelco Manufacturing; John Bartlett, Grant Industries; Ed Iskenderian, Ed Iskender-

ian Racing Cams; Don Alderson, Milodon Engineering; Paul Schiefer, Schiefer Manufacturing; Willie Garner, Trans Dapt; Harry Weber, Weber Speed Equipment; Phil Weiand, Weiand Power & Racing; Dempsey Wilson, Wilson Racing Cams; and Dean Moon, Moon Equipment.

The first SEMA show was produced by Robert E. Petersen of Petersen Publishing under the title *Hot Rod Industry News,* which was edited by Alex Xydias, who had previously operated the So-Cal Speed Shop. The first show was held under the cold and damp grandstands of Dodger Stadium in Los Angeles. The following year, the show was moved to the new Anaheim Stadium, and in 1977, it moved permanently to Las Vegas.

Meanwhile, the industry as a whole was struggling with quality issues. Product performance specs became one of the chief functions of SEMA. The intent was to improve performance quality and the reliability of the racing products, which would hopefully translate to safety on the track.

Eventually, due to the need to focus on anti-hobbyist legislation, the SEMA Specs program was spun off. It is now a totally separate organization called the SFI Foundation. It can be said that product failures have been greatly reduced over the decades as a result of SFI's contributions to the motorsports industry.

Pontiac GTO

Coinciding with the formation of SEMA was the muscle car boom that is often erroneously credited to Pontiac. While Pontiac played a huge part in the creation of the muscle car, it was not alone.

Nonetheless, as we have seen, Bunkie Knudson got the ball rolling when he became general manager of Pontiac in 1955. Knudson was a youthful 43 at the time, and he steered Pontiac away from the sleepy family division onto performance road, transforming the tired "tin Indian" division into the "Performance Division." It was a genuine transformation that had been signaled by the Tri-Power carburetor setup introduced for 1957 and the adoption of wide track for 1959.

By the early 1960s, General Motors was in the spotlight, under scrutiny for antitrust violations, which included the great streetcar conspiracy in which

Noel Carpenter's 1966 SEMA-sponsored show was in Anaheim, California. Here in front of the Dode Martin and Jim Nelson Dragmaster display was the Rollin' Rice Bowl III *built in Pasadena, California, by Paul Horning, Ernie Murashige, and Gray Baskerville. (Photo Courtesy Mooneyes)*

At the end of October 1962, Junior Johnson, driving the #3 Fox racing Pontiac, placed first at Charlotte. It was his first win of the year, but he crashed at Atlanta two weeks later. It set the stage for the GTO. (Photo Courtesy Dan Shannon)

General Motors and others conspired to monopolize the sale of buses and control transit systems. DuPont's ownership of 63 million GM shares when it was the largest paint supplier to General Motors created perceived favoritism toward GMAC over local banks for auto financing. The list went on, and there were calls in particular in January 1961 by Attorney General Robert Kennedy to dismantle the GM conglomerate and divest itself of all but one division.

Meanwhile, Pontiac was doing well at the track, placing first, second, and third in the 1957 NASCAR Flying Mile and first and second in the NASCAR Acceleration Tests. Meanwhile, GM President Harlow Curtice was asking to deemphasize performance and emphasize safety. It was a confusing time, as in June 1962 Henry Ford II announced the company's withdrawal from the AMA's 1957 racing ban.

Arguably America's first muscle car, the 1964 Pontiac GTO, was a lot of engine (a 389-ci trophy engine) in a relatively small car, the LeMans. Pictured here is a 1965 model, which shared the same bodystyle but adopted the vertical stacked headlights that were becoming popular in the mid-1960s.

Chrysler quickly followed, but General Motors sat on the fence until early 1963. Then, it decided that all divisions were to immediately cease all racing activity and discontinue supplying engines such as Chevy's 427 mystery motor and Pontiac's Super Duty 421.

Funnily enough, in an internal memo G.S. Stephens wrote to "All Zone Car Distributors": "Effectively today January 24, 1963, 389 and 421 Super Duty engines are canceled, and no further orders will be accepted (421 HO engines are still available.)"

The directive threw everyone involved with Chevy and Pontiac racing for a loop. Chrysler and Ford were going at it full speed, so what were they to do? The answer, of course, was to put it on the street.

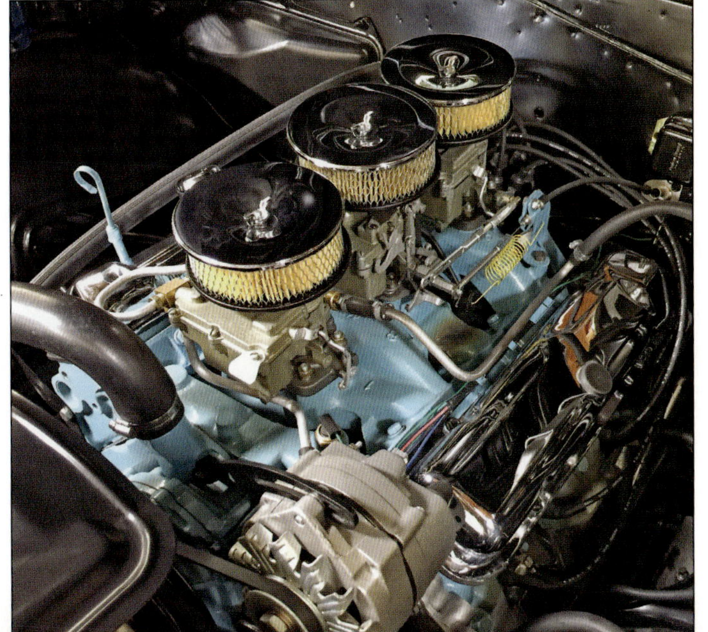

With a single Carter AFB, the 389's output was rated at 325 hp at 4,800 rpm, but with the Tri-Power shown here on Jaydee Maness's car, horsepower was rated at 348 hp.

Built when he was just a teenager, Dan Woods's Milk Truck *debuted in 1965. It was his first show car, and like many, Woods chose a 1957 347 Poncho fitted with an Isky cam, an Edelbrock 6x2 intake, and chrome Stromberg 97s. (Photo Courtesy Dan Shannon)*

There was yet another GM directive that vehicles should have 10 pounds of weight per cubic inch. The proposed Tempest LeMans coupe with a Grand Prix 389 fitted with 421 HO heads exceeded that mandate until the team spotted a loophole. The edict referred to the base model, and as long as the GTO was an option, it would not violate company policy. So that's what it was in 1963, but in 1964 buyers could purchase a GTO.

With a single Carter AFB atop the 389, output was 325 hp at 4,800 rpm, but the Tri-Power version was rated at 348 hp. However, the brakes were antiquated drums for a car weighing in at around 3,700 pounds. *Motor Trend* said the 1963 Tempest required more stopping distance than any other car tested. Nevertheless, it set the mold for the American muscle car.

Cragar S/S

As we have seen, the first mag wheels were just that: magnesium wheels built primarily for racing. They were lightweight, but they were expensive and corroded before your very eyes as fast as you could clean them. They were not for the man on the street.

Several companies, including of course American Racing, jumped into the fray and began producing a

Cragar launched the two-piece S/S in 1964 with a strong marketing campaign including point-of-purchase displays, such as this one seen in a typical speed shop setting.

This recent UK build by Miles Sherlock of Jackhammer Hot Rod & Kustom Supply typifies the 1960s look of Cragar S/S five spokes fronting a big-block Chevy and some headers dumping into the fender well. (Photo Courtesy Mile Sherlock/Jackhammer)

This advertisement from the early 1970s highlights how popular aftermarket wheels had become by this point. As you can see in the ad, Cragar also sold headers and ignitions, but wheels were what they were known for.

As wheel casting technology improved, Cragar moved into making a one-piece, five-spoke, non-plated aluminum wheel called the G/T. Typically, the cap infield was painted red whereas the S/S was blue.

An Elephant in the Room

more cost- and maintenance-friendly cast-aluminum wheel. The problem with aluminum is that it has to be kept shiny, and it's never as shiny as chrome. By 1957, both "TV" Tommy Ivo and Norm Grabowski had chrome-reverse rims on their iconic T-buckets. It quickly became obvious that it was possible to split the rims, chrome the two parts, and assemble them into a glittering wheel.

Next to appear on the scene was a chrome rim riveted to a sand-cast aluminum center. It was an improvement of sorts, but Bell Auto Parts's Roy Richter decided that a die-cast center, while expensive to develop because of the up-front permanent mold tooling costs, the unit price would be lower and the finish better. According to Art Bagnall in his Roy Richter book, "Up to this point, no one had made a die-cast custom wheel."

After almost two years of development and a lot of destruction testing, the S/S Super Sport became Cragar's first wheel. Initial marketing began in 1964, and almost overnight the S/S became a classic.

The original 426 Hemi was introduced in February 1964 for NASCAR racing after a winter of discontent trying to cast serviceable blocks. Chrysler engineers apparently worked around the clock to assemble engines for the February race at Daytona. Mum was the word, but by mid-February all of the Mopar teams had received the new Hemi V-8, including Richard Petty.

When it came to race day, Chrysler dominated with Petty's Plymouth first (it was his first Daytona 500 win) Jim Pardue's Plymouth second, and Paul Goldsmith's Plymouth third. Ford managed fourth place. Petty set a new average speed record of 154.334 mph and went on to be NASCAR's champion for 1964.

Next on Mopar's target was the quarter mile, and again records fell, causing a surge in showroom traffic with the public demanding the new elephant in the room. Production ramped up until Chrysler was building 50 to 60 engines a week, but the engines were not yet available to the public. It didn't matter because NASCAR outlawed the 426 along with Ford's 427 SOHC Cammer for the 1965 season. In an effort to appease NASCAR, the 426 was offered in the Dodge Coronet and the Plymouth Belvedere, as "off-road" options not suitable for street use. NASCAR was unmoved, and the ban continued.

It was a different story over on the drag strip, where "Big Daddy" Don Garlits, the Ramchargers, and Roger Lindamood's *Color Me Gone* embraced the new 426 as they had the old 392. However, the Elephant had tough skin and could take much more abuse than its forebearer. It would be the basis for the drag racing engine of the future.

Chrysler, meanwhile, was forced to make the 426 available to the public to placate NASCAR and for 1966 offered a much-detuned Street 426 in its intermediate-size cars. Petty, of course, went on to win the 1966 Daytona 500 in a Plymouth Satellite/Belvedere. The cat, or in this case the elephant, was out of the bag.

Needless to say, the 426 was the Farah Fawcett of the racing fraternity. While it was the poster child, it only resided in the garages of a select few.

Speed & Custom Equipment Show

There had, of course, been the Hot Rod Exposition and Automotive Equipment Display sponsored by the SCTA in 1948, but after three events, it just petered out. It wasn't until 1965, two years after the formation of SEMA, that Los Angeles promoter and publisher of *Speed Equipment Directory* Noel Carpenter produced the Speed & Custom Equipment trade show. It was apparently inspired by Mickey Thompson, who needed a venue to promote his products prior to the Indy 500.

Carpenter started his own show in the second-floor ballroom of the Disneyland Hotel in Anaheim. The show, which was held between the Winternationals and the

Unable to buy Noel Carpenter's Speed Equipment Directory, Robert E. Petersen launched his own publication Hot Rod Industry News and aligned with SEMA. (Photo Courtesy Dan Shannon)

U.S. Fuel & Gas Championship when there were a lot of industry people in the Los Angeles region, attracted 77 displaying companies and 1,200 attendees.

Not to be left out, SEMA hitched up to Carpenter's wagon and participated the following year. SEMA received $535 for showing up. For 1967, Carpenter moved his show to Las Vegas, but SEMA had switched allegiances and joined Robert E. Petersen, who had failed to buy *Speed Equipment Directory* and instead launched his own publication *Hot Rod Industry News*.

With the backing of SEMA and Wally Parks, Petersen put on the High Performance & Custom Trade Show in the concession area under the grandstands of Los Angeles's Dodgers Stadium. With 98 exhibitors and some 3,000 attendees, it is regarded as the first official SEMA Show. In 1977, the SEMA Show was moved to its current location in Las Vegas, and in 1982, SEMA took control of the show from Petersen.

Thrush and the Cherry Bombs

As we have seen, the exhaust business was relatively easy to get into with no expensive patterns and castings to deal with. It can also be a relatively lucrative business.

Linda Vaughn "The First Lady of Motorsports" enjoyed a long and distinguished career as Miss Hurst. Here, she's working the Hurst booth with her cousin Billie Whitner at an early trade show. (Photo Courtesy Dan Shannon)

We've already seen that getting it right in the muffler business could be very lucrative. In 1966, Gidon Industries introduced the Thrush muffler with its famous woodpecker logo.

No wonder then, with the explosion in muscle cars, that the segment would begin to boom.

Gidon Industries of 22 Iron St. in Rexdale, Ontario, Canada, filed for a patent of its Thrush muffler on November 16, 1966. It was a simple, zinc-coated double-wrap can emblazoned with its famous woodpecker logo that was close to the Clay Smith Cams logo but minus the cigar. It promised "to deliver specific low back-pressure, reading, [and was] computed for maximum engine performance."

Mufflers are a commodity, but clever marketing made some brands household names, such as the catchily named and cleverly designed Cherry Bomb by Maremont. They are still in production.

Interestingly, Thrush listed a U.S. address at 513 E. Washington Blvd. in Los Angeles. It did one heck of a marketing job with four-color, full-page ads in many of the big enthusiast books saying, "It's straight-thru. No fiberglass to burn out."

As the exhaust market developed and enthusiasts got turned on to side pipes first seen on the 1965 Corvette, they and the industry decided that side pipes could be fitted to just about every automobile on the road. Gidon applied for the Sidekick trademark on March 11, 1976. In 1993, Tenneco purchased Performance Industries, whose brands included Cyclone, Blackjack Headers, and Thrush Mufflers.

Two years after the 1966 introduction of Thrush Mufflers, the distinctive red Cherry Bomb brand was introduced. It is quite often touted as being the inventor of the glasspack, but there are many ads for fiberglass-packed mufflers prior to that date, even in the Pep Boys catalog of 1965. Mitchell may well have been one of the first to pack its mufflers with "America's FIRST and FINEST FiberGlass" in the late 1940s. No matter, like the Thrush before it, the Cherry Bomb, no doubt because of its catchy name and cool design, captured the public's attention and favor.

The parent of Cherry Bomb, Maremont, was founded in 1877 in Chicago as a supplier to the wagon industry. As the automobile developed, Maremont moved into that market and eventually into the aftermarket. Unfortunately, in 1953, Maremont apparently began using asbestos in the production of brake parts under the Grizzly and Leland brands.

In 1954, Maremont began making aftermarket mufflers using asbestos-wrapped sealing components. Eventually, a trust was established to deal with the claims.

Meanwhile, the Cherry Bomb, made in Loudon, Tennessee, was distinctive from other mufflers in that the cans had rounded ends that they described as "bullet-shaped" and advertised as "It's Boss, Man." In a 2007 interview, Robert Mater Jr., former marketing director at Maremont responsible for launching the Cherry Bomb brand, said, "Those were great times. It was the heyday of the hot rod and any muscle car worth its salt had to have a pair of 'Bombs.' We couldn't manufacture them fast enough."

Meyers's Manx

Bruce Meyers was born on March 1, 1926, and grew up in the beautiful Southern California coastal town of Newport Beach. One of five children, it must have been idyllic, as his father worked for Ford Motor Co. setting up dealerships. Meyers was a surfer before it was cool

Dune buggies were another California phenomenon that resulted from the beach scene of Pismo Beach. Here is a pair of Model A Ford rails and the powertrain from an Oldsmobile Rocket including the hubcaps. (Photo Courtesy Dan Shannon)

Still stylish after all these years, Bruce Meyers's VW Beetle-based Meyers Manx *was revolutionary in design and simple in execution. It helped spark a whole tuning industry based around the Bug. (Photo Courtesy Philippe Danh)*

and attended Los Angeles's Chouinard Art Institute, where he studied fine art. Interestingly, Meyers is not listed in their roster of notable alumni—shame.

In 1944, at age 18, he was drafted into the U.S. Navy, and he was aboard the aircraft carrier USS *Bunker Hill* when two Japanese kamikaze pilots attacked it off Okinawa. When everybody abandoned ship, Meyers gave his life jacket to a sailor without one and then proceeded to haul another sailor for two hours through burning oil to safety. You would never have known that Meyers was that kind of hero though. To him, it was all in a day's work.

When the war ended, he returned to Newport Beach (why wouldn't you?) where he enjoyed a unique perspective on the needs of beach bums. He shaped surfboards and paddleboards and made fiberglass boats—a skill that would prove prophetic.

Like most surfers in search of the perfect wave, his search took him south to Baja, Mexico, but it was on a trip north to Pismo Beach, California, where he had his epiphany. While trying to figure out a means of transporting surfboards to remote Baja beaches, he saw some early buggies that were little more than cut down cars with balloon tires driving around the Pismo dunes. He could see that the Volkswagen Beetle, which was enjoying huge popularity, was the most versatile.

The off-road or dune buggy phenomenon, as it became known, was depicted in several contemporary magazines. *Hot Rod* covered it in the March 1961 issue, calling it the "Zaniest Rod Craze." Calling on all his talents, Meyers figured out how to shorten a VW Bug floorpan and, using his boat-making skills, craft a tub-like body to sit on top. His *Meyers Manx* concept and design was nothing short of brilliant, and he created a whole motoring segment that has survived for more than half a century.

Unfortunately, Bruce suffered all sorts of growing pains due to demand. Pretty soon, he was unable to protect his invention and was being knocked off by dozens of companies. An industry had been spawned, and to go with the various kits, there followed a plethora of aftermarket parts and speed equipment for the Volkswagen 4-cylinder engine. No, it wasn't an American engine, but American speed merchants exploited it.

1964½ Mustang

Around the same time Meyers debuted his dune buggy, Ford introduced the Seabiscuit of pony cars: the

Just as Ford's Model T and Model 18 did before it, the 1964½ Mustang was a shot in the arm for the aftermarket. In 1965, Gas Ronda fielded this injected 427-powered Mustang and ran mid-10s. (Photo Courtesy Dan Shannon)

Mustang—a clear winner. Designed by the team of John Najjar, Phillip Clark, Joe Oros, and Gale Halderman (who rarely receive credit because Lee Iacocca, Ford Division general manager, is generally credited as the father of the Mustang), the car was known internally as T-5.

The Mustang was gestated quickly in just 18 months and was predicted to sell 100,000 units. However, subsequent to its introduction on April 17, 1964, it went on to sell more than 400,000 units that year. Within two years, Ford had sold one million ponies. The Mustang was the flathead Ford V-8 of its day, comparable to the '55 Chevy, it provided enthusiasts with an amazing blank canvas that could be painted a myriad of styles.

The Mustang's first V-8 was the lowly 260, but that was quickly supplanted by the 289 that became Ford's equivalent of the small-block Chevy. Though perhaps not quite as versatile as the Chevy, the Ford was the go-to engine for Carroll Shelby's Cobra, Sunbeam's Tiger, the TVR Griffith, and of course, various De Tomaso sports cars.

Above all, Carroll Shelby was Ford's champion, particularly with the introduction of the 1965 Shelby Mustang GT350. What the GT350 did was give the speed merchants a blueprint for how to modify the Mustang with everything from finned valve covers to suspension components and disc brakes. The vast majority of Mustangs sold came with drum brakes on all four corners. There was barely a part of the car that wasn't modified for racing and therefore copied for eager enthusiasts.

Some of the most popular upgrades back in the day were, disc brakes and matching finned aluminum engine accessories, including valve covers, air cleaners, and oil pans. There were also aluminum intakes from everyone who had a foundry, the export brace that tied the shock towers to the cowl and the corresponding shock brace, and of course, Tri-Y headers. For the exterior, there was the R-Model front valence, rear window louvers, and outside mirrors because the Mustang only came with a driver-side mirror. That's not to mention rims and tires.

Ford's 427 SOHC hemi was variously hailed as "Ford's greatest engine," and the "90-day wonder" was intended for NASCAR in 1964 but was soon banned. It found a home, of sorts, on the strip with Lou Baney and Don Prudhomme.

Quad-Weber Intake for S-B Ford

One of the most exotic pieces of speed equipment to appear as a result of the whole Cobra and Mustang phenomenon was the quad Weber intake for the small-block Ford.

Edoardo Weber was born in Turin, Italy, on November 29, 1889, into an engineering family—his father was Swiss. He graduated in mechanical engineering from the university in 1904 and in 1907 moved to Bologna to work for Fiat. By 1912, he was promoted to the position of inspector. After World War I, he continued to work for Fiat until 1923, when he founded Fabbrica Italiana Carburatori Weber Co. with three partners. Their first product was a twin-choke sidedraft that in turn was bolted to a supercharged, OHV conversion for the Fiat 501. Soon, Weber became an OEM supplier to Fiat, Alfa Romeo, Maserati, and Ferrari. By 1940, it had 400 employees.

It appears that Weber himself was a member of Mussolini's Italian Fascist Party, from which he received several decorations. Unfortunately for them, the fascists lost the war and Bologna was liberated on April 21, 1945. Just three weeks later on May 17, he was picked up, possibly by the Italian resistance, and was never seen again. In 1952, the company was acquired by Fiat.

As early as 1951, the F.T. Griswold Manufacturing Co. of Wayne, Pennsylvania, was importing Weber carburetors priced from $50. Griswold also sold imported Scintilla mags priced from $75 to $195.

In the post-World War II motor racing boom, Weber was the racing carburetor. Nothing looked nor ran better than a row of six lined up in the valley of a Ferrari V-12 engine. And so it was that the Shelby entry for the 1963 Daytona Continental three-hour race debuted the 289 engine fitted with four Webers. Also debuting on the car were some mag wheels from Ted Halibrand.

The intake for the four Webers was probably supplied by Shelby's friend Dean Moon (the first Cobra having been assembled in Moon's shop in Santa Fe Springs), as

In the late 1960s, Shelby advertised in *Hot Rod* with an endorsement from the Snake himself, Don Prudhomme. In 1967, Prudhomme was running Lou Baney's AA/Top Fuel dragster under Shelby's Super Snake banner. Products listed included cams, a 4V air cleaner, tuned headers, and pop-up pistons with deep valve relief, but there was a whole catalog full of goodies for modifying your Mustang—a market that continues to this day. Unfortunately, by 1968, they were discounting parts.

Incidentally, Prudhomme's front engine dragster was powered by Ford's SOHC 427 Cammer that had been developed but soon banned for NASCAR in response to Chrysler's 426 Hemi.

This is a rare Dean Moon photo of L. Brier MacKay, who developed the downdraft intake to accept 45DCOE Webers. It's a pity that someone chopped off the bottom of the picture. (Photo Courtesy Mooneyes)

The initial Weber carburetor intakes were of a low-profile cross-ram design. The design required removing the carburetors to adjust the valves, which was no good in a race situation.

Dean Moon and L. Brier MacKay worked together to develop the Weber intakes not only for the small-block Ford but also for the small-block Chevy, as shown here in Moon's shop where the first Cobra was assembled. (Photo Courtesy Mooneyes)

Moon was friends with L. Brier MacKay. Indeed, there is plenty of photographic evidence that Moon supplied the Weber-equipped intake, but in a July 1966 *Hot Rod* ad, Moon advertised MacKay "Iso-Ram" Weber kits with 48 IDA-1 carburetors. Besides small-block Fords, they were also available for small- and big-block Chevys. Initially, the intakes were of a cross-ram design, but due to the fact that the carburetors had to be removed to adjust the valves, the manifolds were redesigned to use 45DCOE downdraft Webers.

Today, several companies continue to make Weber manifolds, but many people feel they are too difficult to tune and have switched to look-alike fuel injection.

As the cross-ram design necessitated the removal of the carburetors to adjust the valves, the manifold design was revised to stand the 45DCOE carburetors upright. (Photo Courtesy Scotty Gosson)

Carroll Shelby's GT350

The story of the Shelby Mustang GT350 has been told many times, but we can't leave it out. Carroll Shelby ordered a bunch of Wimbledon White fastback Mustangs to turn into race cars. Those first cars were used for development and were known as advanced prototype (AP) cars.

The iconic John Christy was editor of *Sports Car Graphic* magazine and known as the Godfather of the Cobra because of all the enthusiastic articles he wrote extolling its virtues. Christy changed the game when he pitched Shelby American the idea of an extended road test of the new GT350. He started his article for the June 1965 issue saying, "This report marks a first . . . it isn't easy to get a manufacturer to turn loose a car for the extensive testing we had in mind." Christy's

Powering the original GT350 publicity car (shown here) was a 289 that had a 11.5:1 compression ratio. It was fitted with a single center-pivot float 715-cfm Holley atop a Cobra high-rise aluminum intake. There were also Tri-Y headers.

Ford's Mustang was a surprise hit, selling four times its prediction and quickly becoming a performance icon, especially when Carroll Shelby applied his magic. It became a template for the performance industry.

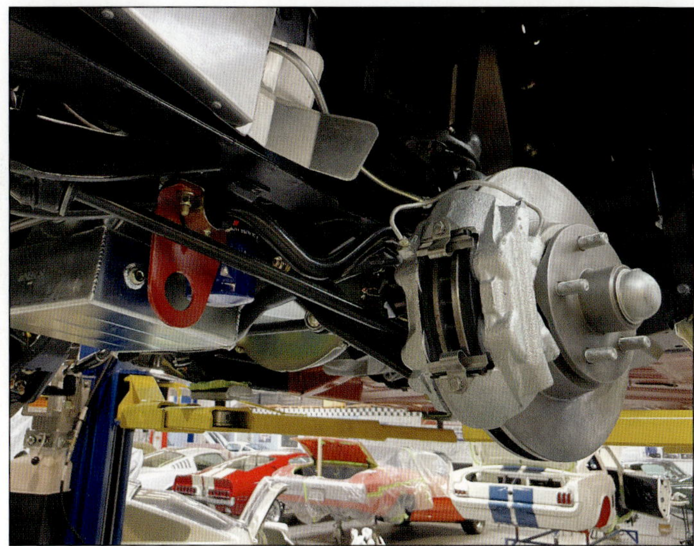

One of the important upgrades to the GT350 was the addition of 11.375-inch Kelsey Hayes vented front discs plus quickened steering, Koni shocks, and a heavy anti-roll bar.

In 1966, Mustangs and Shelbys were available with a belt-driven Paxton SN-60 centrifugal supercharger that blew through the carburetor that was enclosed in a large, cast-aluminum box. It was good for a 68-hp increase.

Various wheels were available on the GT350, including cast magnesium wheels. The original two-piece wheels were cast for Cragar at Buddy Bar Casting in South Gate, California, where they are still made.

unique and rare extended story was titled: "10,000 Mile Road Test, SHELBY MUSTANG 350 GT."

In the story, Christy wrote, "We fell in love with the Shelby Mustang 350 GT." He went on to say, "All in all, the Shelby Mustang proved to be one of the most reliable sports cars we have tested."

The article not only bolstered sales of Shelby's Mustangs but also did wonders for the speed equipment industry. We've seen how the Cobra endorsed and enhanced sales of speed equipment for Ford's 289 family of engines, but the GT350 initiated sales of suspension components and dress-up accessories that continues to this day. This list, of course, included everything from Holley carburetors and Koni shocks to Goodyear Blue Dot tires.

Three Ninety Six

While Ford was killing it with its new Mustang pony car, selling 121,500 units in the second half of 1964, Chevy's Corvette was doing less well in the marketplace. Obviously a different car, it was nevertheless not going anywhere with sales stagnant at a little over 22,000 units. Something was needed, and that something came in the form of the L78 396.

The 396, nicknamed the Rat motor but originally the Porcupine, appeared midyear in the Corvette and full-size Chevrolets. It was factory rated at 425 hp at 5,800 rpm with 415 ft-lbs of torque at 3,600 rpm. However, it would only be rated as such for that one year. In 1966, it was down rated by the factory to 375 hp.

Of course, Chevy fans always believed that it was just factory speak, and the engines still produced 425. Years later, in 2016, Steve Magnante tested an L78 396 (bored to 402) for *Hot Rod* and declared that the engine in fact made 50 hp more than the factory stated. What the test went on to show was that a set of headers replacing the stock exhaust bumped horsepower to an impressive 457.5 at 5,800 rpm with 464.4 ft-lbs of torque at 3,600 rpm.

Interestingly, the 1970 396 was, in fact, a 402, and there were some 402 decals on 1970 air cleaners. Technically, the last year of the 396-ci 396 was 1969.

Bullitt

Hot on the heels of Shelby's Mustang offerings, Ford offered the GT and hit "Number One with a Bullitt" when a Highland Green 390 2+2 fastback appeared in the 1968 Steve McQueen movie *Bullitt*. The Bullitt Mustang is arguably one of the most famous cars of all time (there were actually two used in making the movie) and did more for the performance industry than perhaps any other production car.

From the factory, the 390-ci car was equipped with a choice of either a 2-barrel or 4-barrel carburetor delivering 270 and 325 hp, respectively. The two cars used in the movie were built in January 1968 at Ford's San Jose plant. After Warner brothers purchased the cars, they were shipped to Max Balchowsky's Hollywood Motors located at 4905 Hollywood Blvd. in Hollywood.

Balchowsky modified both Mustangs as well as the two Dodge Chargers used in filming. Besides campaigning his famous string of Old Yeller sports racers, Balchowsky, who was also a stunt driver, worked on a string of car movies from *It's a Mad, Mad, Mad, Mad World* to *Brain Donors* in 1992 and 1971's *Vanishing Point*.

Externally, the Bullitt was fairly stock, but the movie did wonders for the sale of American Racing Torq Thrust D wheels that were initially shod with Wide Oval white-sidewall nylon tires. These were later changed for Dunlop and then Firestone tires. Meanwhile, the badging and backup lights were removed, and the gas filler was painted black.

Under the hood was the factory S-code 390 backed by heavy-duty BorgWarner 4-speed with a BorgWarner clutch and a Hurst 4-speed shifter. Also installed for the movie were heavy-duty coil springs, Koni shocks, and Hellwig sway bars. To enable the stunt work, Balchowsky also beefed up the frame and the shock mounts and installed strut braces, all of which worked wonders for aftermarket sales when people became obsessed with the cars.

One of the original Mustangs used in the movie and unrestored sold in auction at the end of 2019 for $3.74 million.

The Also Rans

The Bullitt Mustang was not the first nor would it be the last vehicle that drove the enthusiast market (puns intended). Everything from the Model Ts of the *Keystone Cops* through the Batmobile, the Munster's Coach, *Drag-U-La*, innumerable Bond

Early-era BB Chevys often had Weber-fed induction, aluminum M/T valve covers with tall breathers, and white-painted headers. A few years later, everything had changed. Polished aluminum gave away to chrome valve covers, a tall Weiand tunnel-ram intake, a pair of Holleys with chrome float covers, and that yellow Accel ignition.

cars, *The Saint*'s Volvo P1800, *Starsky and Hutch*'s Torino, Christine, Herbie, *Knight Rider*'s K.I.T.T., the Pink Panthermobile, *Grease*, Eleanor, *Mad Max*, the A-Team van, and the Duke's *General Lee*, the fake Ferraris of *Miami Vice*, the Monkeemobile all the way to Kowalski's Challenger in *Vanishing Point* have all played a major role in establishing, reinforcing, and legitimizing the car culture that helped form our hobby and in so doing create an industry.

Camaro

It took General Motors a long time, more than two years, to give the public its answer to the Ford Mustang. The Camaro, code named XP-836 and originally named Panther, was unveiled in September 1966. For the performance market, the Z28 was the option to have if you knew the secret to unlock its delivery.

Obviously, not many did, as only 602 were built. Vince Piggins's Cheetah package included a 302.4-ci engine made by using the 4-inch bore 327 block with the 3-inch stroke 283 crank to meet the SCCA 305-ci ceiling for Trans Am racing. A forged steel crank, 11:1 domed pistons, and a 30/30 camshaft from the 375 HO Corvette 327 completed the package. Atop was an 800-cfm Holley carburetor, helping to produce the shockingly underrated 290 hp and 290 ft-lbs of torque. In reality, it produced more than 375 hp.

The 302 was mated to a heavy-duty Muncie F41 transmission, power-assisted discs and sintered metallic drums handled the stopping, and a fast-ratio box was used for the steering. Automatic boxes, air conditioning, and convertible tops were not tick-able options. Not part of the Z28 package but available was a rear deck spoiler styled by hot rodder-turned-designer Larry Shinoda.

Car and Driver magazine said of the Z28, "Chevy is on the way toward making the gutsy stormer the Camaro should have been in the first place." What the Camaro and the Z28 in particular did was give the Chevy drivers what Ford had given its fans: a platform on which to build enthusiasm.

When Smokey Yunick saw the 1967 Camaro, he saw the potential to break records, maybe 300 of them. This is one of three Z28-branded, far-from-stock Camaros that broke hundreds of records. (Photo Courtesy Dan Shannon)

CHAPTER 8

1967–1973
CHANGE IS IN THE AIR

Ever since Romeo Palamides invented American Racing Wheels, the wheel business had boomed. Heck, everybody needs four for every car. The designs kept rolling and people kept buying. The first OEM to offer cast-aluminum wheels was Ettore Bugatti in 1924. It would be 30 years before Cadillac introduced its Sabre-Spoke wheel made by Kelsey-Hayes in 1954. It was standard on the 1955 Eldorado and an option on all other models.

In 1960, Pontiac offered an odd, eight-lug wheel with an integrated brake drum that needed a special adapter plate so that the wheels could be balanced. It was not a popular option. Four years later, the 1964 Corvette was available with a center-lock cast-aluminum wheel with a radial spoke design. Some years later, in conversation with Chuck Blum, who was president of SEMA at the time, he remembered that the aftermarket companies were worried that the OEM move to cast-aluminum wheels would kill the aftermarket.

"Instead," Blum said, "the aftermarket increased dramatically because the factory had, by using them, endorsed them." In addition, of course, alloy rims were generally lighter than steelies, so they offered a racing advantage.

Center Line

In 1970, Ray Lipper, owner of Center Line Tool Corporation located at 13521 Freeway Dr. in Santa Fe Springs, California, introduced Center Line Wheels that were revolutionary, light, and strong. Lipper was born on December 8, 1933, in Newport Beach, California.

According to Bill Holland, whose Holland Communications was Center Line's advertising agency, "Ray was initially a tool and die maker who got into the stamping business and was a supplier to Cragar. He suggested to Cragar that it rivet rather than bolt their 'Super Trick' wheels together, but Cragar wasn't interested. Consequently, Ray decided to go into the wheel business."

Rather than being cast or spun, Center Lines were eventually rotary forged. Invented in 1914, rotary forging is a cold-forming process used to make round shapes (i.e., wheels) by deforming a metal blank using a combination of rotation, rolling, and axial compression. It offers excellent accuracy, smooth surface finish, and optimized grain structure for strength. It also offered an efficient use of materials.

Initially, Center Line Wheels were essentially a two-piece wheel riveted together using Grade-8

In 1970, Ray Lipper of Center Line Tool Corp. and a supplier to Cragar suggested riveting rather than bolting the wheels together. Cragar declined, and the Center Line Auto Drag Wheel was born.

Ray Lipper's next big contribution to the wheel industry was the Convo Pro that had strengthening convolutions in the rotary-formed rim. They were light and strong and ideal for racing.

stainless-steel rivets with a patented centering device. Its first wheel was the Auto Drag, but that was eclipsed by the Convo Pro that was further strengthened by convolutions in the rims. Apparently, it took a million pounds of pressure to form the 6061 aluminum in one of Center Line's multi-story tall hydraulic presses.

In 1980, the Champ 500 model became the only multipiece wheel approved for the Indy 500. They were fitted to Dan Gurney's AAR *Gurney Eagle* race cars. Center Lines were also used on Craig Breedlove's *Spirit of America III* that unfortunately crashed at an unofficial 675 mph in 1996.

Half a Foot

Maybe we were going too fast? Top Fuel dragsters were banging on the 230-mph door and would soon be through it. But first, "Big Daddy" Don Garlits took a dramatic step that changed the look of drag racing forever. Coming off the line at Lions Drag Strip on March 8, 1970, in *Swamp Rat XIII*, the experimental 2-speed transmission exploded, dramatically broke the car in half, and took half of Garlits's right foot with it.

Recovering in hospital, Garlits decided that his future lay sitting in front of rather than behind the engine. He wasn't the first to try this, but he was Big Daddy, and his opinion held a lot of sway. In 1971, he was back in California with *Swamp Rat XIV*. He lost at Lions, but he put everyone else on the trailer at the Pomona Winternationals and then Bakersfield. Just like that, front-engine dragsters were obsolete.

The top speed record was set by Larry Hendrickson driving John Blanchard's *The Gladiator* at 232.55 in 1970. It was not eclipsed until 1972 when Tony Nancy went 233.16. Garlits set the ET record at 6.21 at the U.S. Nationals.

Act Before It's Too Late

It could be argued that New Year's Day 1970 did not signal a good year for automobile enthusiasts, but it could also be argued that the environment needed attention. On that day in 1970, the National Environmental Policy Act (NEPA) was signed into law. It was one of the first laws ever written that established the wide national framework for protecting the environment.

There were many reasons for the signing of NEPA. One was a reaction to the highway revolts of the 1960s, when citizens protested the bulldozing of many communities and environmentally sensitive areas during the building of the Interstate Highway System.

NEPA required that all branches of government give due consideration to the environment when proposing major developments of highways, airports, military bases, etc. NEPA didn't directly impact the automobile, but it sure did signal what was coming down the pike.

Donovan

There was good news on the horizon, however, as Ed Donovan of Donovan Engineering in Torrance, California, was about to introduce the first cast-aluminum 417-ci block.

"Big Daddy" Don Garlits was not the first to build a rear-engine Top Fuel dragster, but after this foot-severing explosion at Lions Drag Strip in 1970, he championed back-motored rails. (Photo Courtesy Don Garlits)

It revolutionized the racing industry.

Donovan was born in Los Angeles in 1928, which was the same year Ford introduced the Model A. He loved four-banger Fords and raced a Winfield-equipped banger at the lakes in the 1940s. When Santa Ana opened in 1950, Donovan was right there racing the Howmann Bros. Model T roadster with a hopped-up B-banger set-back under the cowl.

After a stint in the army, Donovan returned to Los Angeles, where he worked on Offys as a machinist at Meyer & Drake Engineering Corp. From 1947 through 1964, every winner of the Indy 500 was powered by an Offy 4-cylinder. In turbocharged form, Offys won in 1968 and from 1972 through 1976. For banger-fan Donovan it must have been heaven.

Through his experience working on Offy engines, Donovan realized there was a need for high-strength stainless-steel valves. According to Fred Seay, who worked for Donovan from 1976, "Chrysler valves were not very good, and we really needed some stainless valves, but a set of dies were too expensive. Ed went to a surplus store, where he found some valves covered in wax paper. They were Nash valves for landing craft, and the heads were huge. Ed had them ground and reshaped and put grooves in them. They were perfect for the Chrysler Hemi."

Apparently, Donovan made these valves after working hours. However, business soon ramped up, and Donovan set up shop on the side of his sister-in-law's garage. That first shop had no windows and was very dark, so it earned the nickname "the Mole Hole" because, according to Seay, "Ed wore glasses, and folks said he was almost blind."

When his side business got too big, Donovan finally left Meyer & Drake and went into business for himself, making stainless valves, axle shafts, and bellhousings. From these humble beginnings, Donovan built a reputation as the most perfect machinist in drag racing.

In 1962, Donovan fielded a dragster powered by a 6-71 Jimmy-blown DOHC 270-ci Offy 4-cylinder with Hilborn injection. It eventually ran 186 mph, just 4 mph short of the class record at that time. The rail was also featured in an issue of *Hot Rod*.

Also that year, Donovan and partner Frank Startup started Donovan Engineering in Inglewood, California, before eventually settling at 2305 Border Ave. in Torrance. As Meyer & Drake wound down, Donovan was able to pick up some of its employees. One of his main employees was lakes racer Arnold J. Birner, who was a very talented pattern maker.

Ten years later, the new Donovan

We all require clean air, but the 1970 National Environmental Policy Act sent shock waves through the industry that continue to ripple more than 50 years later. (Photo Courtesy Dan Shannon)

Donovan soon graduated to a rail job, albeit with an early Ford front end and a Model B-based four-banger. Santa Ana remained the venue. (Photo Courtesy Donovan Engineering)

417 graced the cover of the February 1972 issue of *Hot Rod* surrounded by John Wiebe, Don Prudhomme, Donovan, and "Big Daddy" Don Garlits. Later in the year, on December 1 and 2, at The Last Drag Race at Lions Drag Strip, the Top Fuel final saw Jeb Allen face Carl Olson, who went on to win.

Donovan celebrated the victory with an advertisement announcing Kuhl & Olson's "Low ET of 6.09." The ad quoted Mike Kuhl, "On the National circuit this summer, we were able to make good money because we didn't have so much downtime on our engine." The ad went on to say the engine developments for 1973 will see bore size increased to 515 ci, and the 417 is "proven to be the strongest engine built specifically for drag racing."

Gas Crisis

On October 19, 1973, as a result of the Yom Kippur War initiated by Egypt and Syria, members of the Organization of Arab Petroleum Exporting Countries (OPEC) enacted an oil embargo targeted at nations assumed to be supporting Israel. Basically, OPEC stopped shipping oil to the United States because President Nixon requested $2.2 billion in military aid for Israel.

Before the embargo, oil was $2.90 a barrel, and by the time the action ended in March 1974, oil was at $11.65 a barrel. At the pumps, gas prices jumped to 55 cents per gallon from around 29 cents, and they never really went down. Meanwhile, congress enacted a mandatory national 55-mph speed limit, known as the "double nickel," in an effort to conserve oil.

OPEC had proven that it had the Western world in a stranglehold. Mess with us and we'll cut you off at the pumps. It was not a good feeling, and it caused a knee-jerk reaction that put a nail in the muscle car coffin.

Moving on up, Donovan's next rail was powered by an 800-hp dry-sump DOHC 230-ci Offy with a Hilborn-injected 6-71 blower that provided 25 pounds of boost. With a 25-percent nitro load, it ran the quarter mile in 8.37 at 181 mph. (Photo Courtesy Donovan Engineering)

Keith Black 426

The name Keith Black is synonymous with the Chrysler Hemi and the 426 in particular, but Black got his start in the performance industry racing flathead Ford-powered boats on California's Salton Sea. Indeed, he set a record on only his second time out with a Hallet hull and a flathead Ford V-8 of his own tuning.

Black was born in 1927 in Huntington Park, a suburb southeast of Los Angeles. His father operated an auto parts business, and Black eventually went to work there after spending

With the introduction of Donovan's aluminum 417-ci hemi, the business really took off, which is evident here with this shot of the machine shop. (Photo Courtesy Donovan Engineering)

A factory promo photograph shows the 417 billet block that incorporates a modular girdle that reduces downtime between runs. It also uses drop-in sleeves for fast repairs. (Photo Courtesy Donovan Engineering)

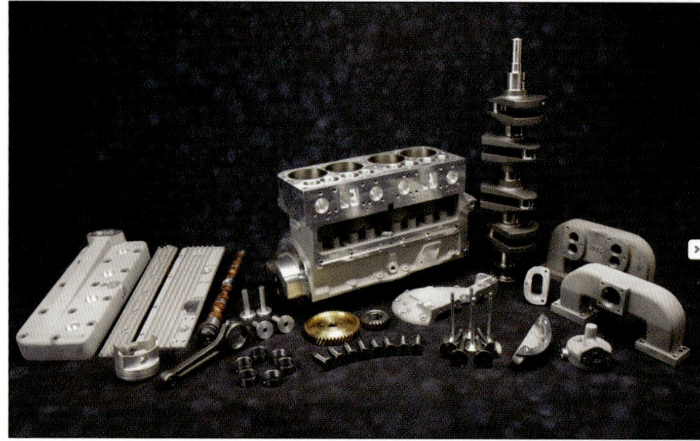

Donovan never let go of his roots and came full circle when he developed this 70-pound cast-aluminum Model D block. It was his take on the next-generation Model B block and cured all its ills. (Photo Courtesy Donovan Engineering)

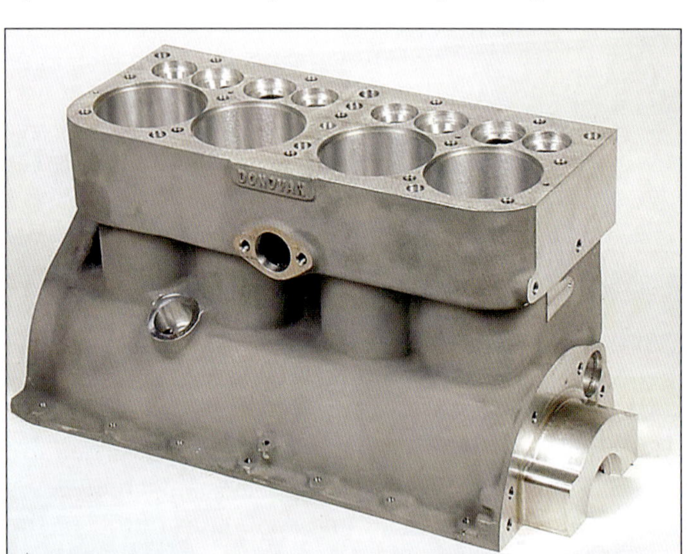

Donovan's Model D uses ductile iron liners and enjoys the benefit of five four-bolt main bearings and five cam bearings compared to the stock three. It also uses a 4340 billet steel crank and rods. (Photo Courtesy Donovan Engineering)

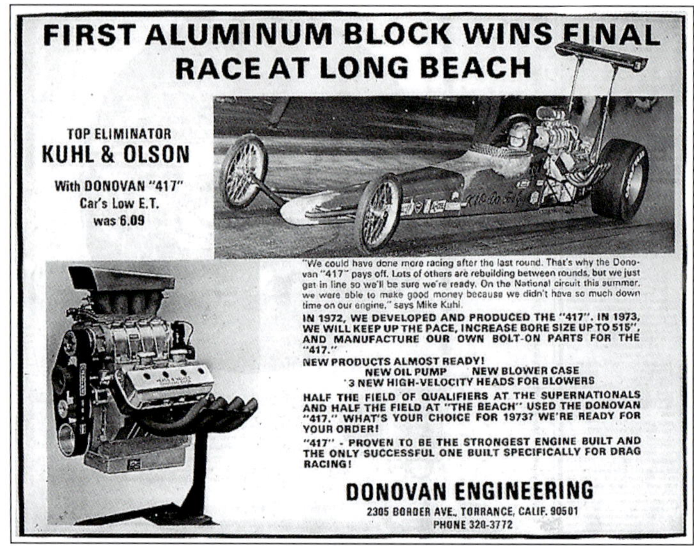

Donovan capitalized on Kuhl & Olson's success in 1972 and advertised that for 1973 the 417 would be bored out to 515 ci and that they would be making their own heads, blowers, oil pumps, etc. (Photo Courtesy Donovan Engineering)

some time working with both Clay Smith and Cliff Collins of Harman & Collins cam fame.

Black, who was an avid boat racer with almost 50 national and international records, decided that he was a better engine builder than he was boat driver. That said, we found his name listed in the September 1951 issue of *Hop Up* as the third place of the E Racing Runabout class with his Mercury-powered *Honey Bee Too*. Interestingly, at the same Long Beach Marine Stadium event, Louis Meyer Jr. came third in the Crosley-powered 48-ci Hydroplane *Lou-Kay*, and Eddie and Bud Meyer came in second and third in the 135-ci Hydroplanes *Avenger II* and *III*, both with V-8-60 power.

Eventually, Black was building engines for other boat racers. His first was in 1956 for the Black, Hallet, and Greer *Seven Grand*. The fuel-injected engine made 375 hp and set a competition record of 86.455 mph. By 1959, Black was able to open his own shop on Atlantic Boulevard in South Gate before eventually moving to a piece of property purchased at 11120 Scott Ave. in South Gate.

Of course, it wasn't long before drag racers heard of Black's abilities and the reliability of his engines. His friend Tommy Greer who operated Greer Machinery in Los Angeles (Greer moved to Huntington Beach in 1984) wanted Black to partner in a Top Fuel dragster with Greer paying the bills.

December 1 and 2, 1972, will go down in the annals of drag racing history as the dates of The Last Drag Race at Lions Drag Strip. The Top Fuel final saw Jeb Allen lose to Kuhl & Olson's 417 Donovan-powered RED. (Photo Courtesy Carl Olson)

Prudhomme trifecta was born.

According to Robert C. Post in his book *High Performance*, "The team debuted in the summer of 1962. They seldom raced out of state and never won a California meet the likes of Bakersfield or the Winternationals, but in week-in, week-out competition, they were almost unbeatable."

According to Lou Hart in his book *Slingshot Dragsters*, "The team won over 80 percent of its races." In the two and a half years the team was together, they won something like 270 races. In February 1963, Prudhomme ran an unprecedented 7.77 ET at 190 mph.

Black had found his development driver. Prudhomme was consistent and could tell Black how the car was reacting. He could also follow instructions as the team developed slipper clutches in conjunction with Schiefer. Unfortunately, Greer got into financial trouble, and Prudhomme switched camps to Roland Leong's *Hawaiian*. Black had found a new challenge.

Having seen Black's success, Chrysler came calling, asking if he could help with its Hemi marine program.

Initially, Chuck Gireth drove, but he wasn't able to tell Black what was going on. Black needed what we now call a development driver: a driver who knew and could explain what was happening with the car. With Gireth gone, Greer and Black purchased a 112-inch-wheelbase chassis that Kent Fuller had assembled in early 1961.

It was raced by Rod Stuckey, who won the American Hot Rod Association's Winternationals. However, Stuckey lasted little longer than Gireth. In his place, Greer and Black hired Don Prudhomme, who would get 50-percent of any earnings. It was a deal, and the Greer, Black, and

The year 1962 was a seminal year for drag racing with the debut of the Greer, Black, and Prudhomme dragster restored here by Steve Davis with a 392-ci Chrysler that ran an incredible 7.77 at over 191 mph.

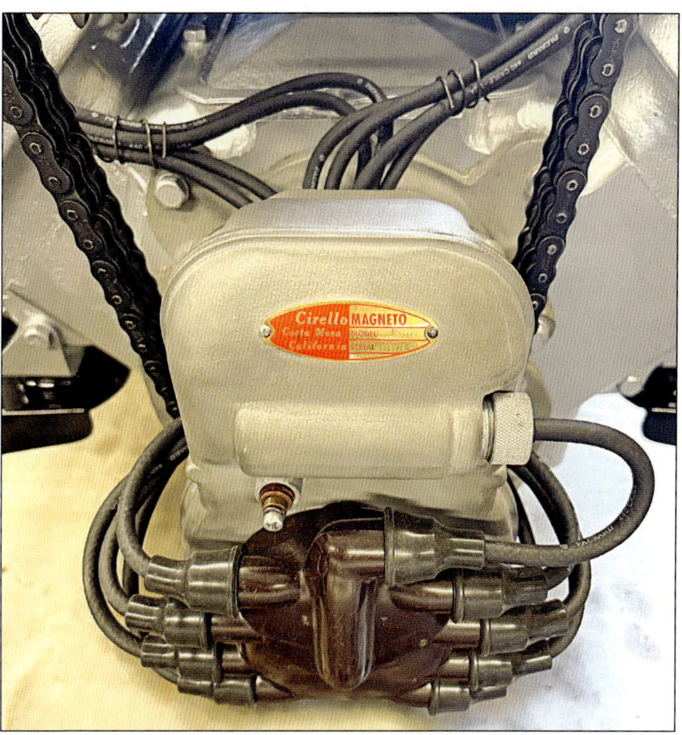

Typical magnetos used on early 1960s Top Fuel engines were Cirello units made by Tony Cirello. This one is crank driven, but the later ones, nicknamed Frankenstein, were cam driven.

It's hard to tell what driver Don Prudhomme might be thinking here as he sits in Roland Leong's Hawaiian waiting to make a pass. Engine builder Keith Black and Leong look on. (Photo Courtesy Dan Shannon)

This is a typical cast-aluminum Keith Black block, in this case out of Geoff Stilwell's 7707 Lucas Oil land speed racer that set a blown fuel rear-engine Modified roadster record at 258.569 mph.

American Graffiti

Most notably, Black used two blown 426 Chrysler Hemis in the Unlimited Hydroplane *Miss Chrysler Crew* that won the UIM World Championship Regatta in 1967.

Suitable 392 Hemi blocks were getting harder to find. Racers were using them up just like they had used up the dry lake beds—they couldn't help themselves. The last year for sales of Chrysler's Street Hemi was 1971. Something had to be done.

That same year, Ed Donovan began production of his Hemi, but that was no use to Black. How could he be an engine builder if Donovan's name was cast right into the block? Ever his own man, Black embarked on casting his own block based on the Chrysler 426 Elephant introduced in 1966.

According to Post, "The design work was done by Bob Tarozzi, a former Chrysler engineer, and Black's 426, designed specifically for racing was introduced in 1973 (according to his 1975 catalog)." Black's block was 130 pounds lighter than the factory cast-iron block. It had quickly removable cast-iron liners, improved structural rigidity, and improved oiling.

Very soon, the KB 426 block became the only block on the block. Between 1967 and 1981, Black was voted Best Dragster Engine Builder 10 times, Best Funny Car Engine Builder 3 times, Best Fuel Racing Manufacturer twice, and in 1978, he was the recipient of the prestigious Ollie Award for overall contribution to the sport. His contribution to the speed equipment industry is immeasurable.

It was *Easy Rider* for hot rodders and just as important. I am, of course, talking about George Lucas's seminal movie *American Graffiti*, released in the United States on August 1, 1973. It cost around $777,000 to make, and to date it has grossed $115 million.

According to imbd.com, the fake working title was *Another Slow Night in Modesto*, which is the central California town where writer/director George Lucas was born and raised. Lucas was born in 1944 and would have been just 18 in 1962, when *Graffiti* is supposed to have

Keith Black was an avid and winning boat racer. Life came full circle when Chrysler asked if he could help with its Hemi marine program. (Photo Courtesy Dan Shannon)

taken place. Interestingly, his nostalgic look back was made only a dozen years after when it was set. Barely worth it one would think, but *Graffiti* went on to be a huge cult and cultural hit. It touched the American psyche, as even urbanites could relate to cruising, catcalling members of the opposite sex, raising a little hell, and maybe a little street racing before the night faded to black.

Graffiti made a lot of stars, but to most car enthusiasts, the stars were John Milner's "piss yellow" coupe and Bob Falfa's '55 Chevy. Bookending the cruising and racing scenes, those two cars polarized the audience: you either loved the hot rod or you loved the Chevy.

Chopped hiboy coupes were not the thing when the movie came out; hot rodders were mostly into resto-rods: stockish-looking early Fords with plenty of doodad accessories but modern powertrains beneath their full fenders. It didn't reflect what rodders were building in 1974, but it perfectly reflected what rodders were building in 1962.

Car guy Lucas, who owned at least one Chevy-powered Deuce hiboy roadster, dictated the look of the coupe down to the cycle fenders up front, bobbed fenders in back, and chrome-reverse rims. Power came from a mid-1960s 327 Chevy fitted with a rare Man-A-Fre intake and four Rochester 2G carburetors. Incidentally, Man-A-Fre, made by Harold Graves in Canoga Park, California, stood for "free from manifold passage." The transmission was a Super T-10, and the axle was from a '57 Chevy.

There were actually three '55 Chevys used, two of which had already appeared in the 1971 movie *Two Lane Blacktop* when they were cast for *American Graffiti*. The third car was used in the "burn" scene. The cars were prepared by Richard Ruth's Competition Engineering, then located on Lankershim Boulevard in North Hollywood. One of the Chevys was fitted with a 1969 427-ci L88 while the others received 454s—all crate engines supplied by General Motors. Weiand tunnel rams and a pair of Holley carburetors were installed on the two lead cars while the main car was painted shiny black and fitted with chrome-reverse rims.

Both the coupe and the Chevy continue to enjoy worldwide celebrity status. *American Graffiti* reinforced the legitimacy of what hot rodders were doing despite the ills of the world caused by the gas crisis and oncoming regulatory actions aimed at curtailing motorsports. It was a booster shot that enthusiasts continue to take nearly 60 years later.

Pete Chapouris's California Kid *is one of the three iconic hot rods along with the* American Graffiti *coupe and ZZ Top's* Eliminator. *Beyond the made-for-TV movie, Chapouris drove the snot out of it.*

The *California Kid*

Another reason 1973 wasn't all bad is because the November issue of *Rod and Custom* magazine (the "chopped top" issue) featured the controversial 1934 coupes of Pete Chapouris and Jim "Jake" Jacobs. They were controversial because at the time the prevailing hot rod trend was for resto-rods: rods that had modern powertrains between their rails but externally they looked almost original except for numerous added accessories and geegaws. Some people were vehemently against chopping up good cars.

At the time, Chapouris was working at Blair's Speed

Under the hood of the California Kid *was a typical 1970s, almost-stock 302 Ford with a Weiand intake and a Holley. However, that's not the engine shown in the movie. Instead, the movie featured the Man-A-Fre Chevy from the* American Graffiti *coupe.*

Shop in Pasadena while Jacobs worked at *Rod and Custom* magazine, which was temporarily shuttered. The two joined forces and opened Pete and Jake's Hot Rod Parts at 8827 E. Las Tunas Dr. in Temple City, California. As the pair cranked up their welders, they shifted the direction of street rodding, put the "hot" back in hot rodding, and gave the sport/hobby a much-needed boost.

That boost was reinforced the following year when Chapouris's black and flamed '34 was chosen by Howie Horwitz, producer of TV's *Batman*, for ABC's 200th Movie of the Week production titled *The California Kid*. Starring a young Martin Sheen, Vic Morrow, Michelle Phillips, and Nick Nolte, *The California Kid* was about a deranged sheriff who forced speeders off the highway to their deaths.

Martin Sheen arrives in *The Kid* to avenge his brother's death. *The Kid* was another 1970s car movie that helped validate the public's love of automobiles in general and hot rods in particular. As an aside, when they throw back the hood to look at the engine, it's actually a shot of the Man-A-Fre-equipped engine of the *American Graffiti* coupe and not Chapouris's engine at all.

While Chapouris and Jacob never made any speed equipment, they made a lot of hot rod chassis parts. In a small way, they helped revolutionize their part of the industry with an international dealer network and a philosophy that supported their dealers rather than competing with them.

Vans

Vans (no, not the shoe brand) was the mode of transport chosen by many Americans in the 1970s. It wasn't exactly the fault of *Hot Rod* magazine, but as with so many automotive trends, *Hot Rod* publicized it, legitimized it, and in so doing caused it to grow.

Because of their extracurricular purpose, vans had a lot of nicknames—none of which are printable here. They became just another one of those car crazes that appeared to emanate from California, similar to drag racing, dune buggies, and go-karts. Whether it did or not is irrelevant because the media was based in Los Angeles. Therefore, it looked like the trends originated there.

The craze really got off the ground because surfers had gravitated from woodies to vans as a reliable means of getting themselves and their boards to the beach. They also gave surfers somewhere to change, to crash, and to copulate. According to Dave Wallace writing for *MotorTrend*, *Hot Rod* editors Don Evans and A.B. Shuman "initially added vans to the mix of 'Everybody's Automotive Magazine.'" As they vacated *Hot Rod,* Terry Cook took the editor's seat and proved to management that covers with vans spiked in sales. Terry said, "So, I put vans in, and sales went nuts. In the next two years, we sold a million more magazines than in the previous two years."

The van-in lasted a decade, employing the R. Crumb "Keep on Truckin'" as its logo and motto. While the group was not necessarily consumers of genuine speed equipment, it did purchase a heck of a lot of accessories—everything from side pipes by the van load to side windows to acres of shag carpet. Vans were a boost the aftermarket needed when it was struggling on other fronts.

The appropriately named Van Nuys Boulevard was the home to Los Angeles cruising from the 1950s through the 1960s until the police cracked down. There was even a movie titled Van Nuys Boulevard.

Most vans were not as radical as Yosemite Sam Radoff's angle-chopped 1971 Dodge Tradesman slant-6 seen here at the 1975 Bowling Green Truck-In. Note the side pipes.

Before he realized how easy it was to make wheels, hot rod builder Boyd Coddington used Center Line wheels on some of his builds, such as the seminal Vern Luce coupe. (Photo Courtesy Chris Coddington)

Amazingly talented, Lil' John Buttera initially modified Center Line wheels before machining his own centers and inserting them into spun aluminum rims. He revolutionized the wheel business.

Boyd Coddington is at home on the lathe in his Hot Rods by Boyd shop at 10541 Ashdale St. in Stanton, California. Here, he's turning up Lil' John-designed hubs for the Boydster.

Hot Rods by Boyd

If the custom wheel business had been successful before, it was nothing compared to when Boyd Coddington arrived on the scene in 1978. He grew up in Idaho, where he took a body and fender class after graduation but gravitated toward machining and eventually took a three-year apprenticeship at May Machine in Salt Lake City, Utah.

Boyd moved to Southern California in 1967 and worked for Western Gear in Lynwood. By 1971, he had married Diane Ragone and embarked on the build of a Model T coupe, the first of several Model Ts. To fund the projects, he worked part-time for Larry and Roger Jongerius's J&J Chassis. Eventually, he left Western and was hired on as a machinist at Disneyland, where he worked until 1978, when he hung out the Hot Rods by Boyd shingle.

Mentoring this shy magician with a milling machine was Lil' John Buttera, a truly gifted machinist and fabricator with a string of dragsters and Funny Cars to his credit. Buttera is generally regarded as the "father of the billet" because he could make his mill do things it was not designed to do. When asked how he had made a billet mirror, Buttera replied, "Take a piece of aluminum and machine away everything that doesn't look like a mirror."

That first mirror machined from a hunk of billet aluminum was made for Boyd Coddington. Pretty soon, the two Midwesterners were collaborating on a string of iconic and influential hot rods. If Buttera could make something rather than buy it, and he could, then he would. It was inevitable that he would soon turn his hand to making wheels.

The hot wheel of the time that was to Buttera's liking was Ray Lipper's Center Line, being both light and strong. Being a two-piece design, the centers lent themselves to customization, and pretty soon Buttera was machining up centers of his own design and bolting them into spun or forged rims.

According to folklore, Buttera was only ever really interested in producing one of anything. Boyd, however, understood right from the beginning that the real money

In the early 1960s, Bill Huth, Dick Flynn, and Jack Hordemann teamed up to market nitrous oxide systems under the Second Wind brand. Their ad in the May 20, 1961, issue of Drag News *told it all. (Photo Courtesy Dave Wallace)*

was in duplicating his work and selling it. Within a few years, Boyd had purchased four Takisawa CNC machines, each costing $150,000, and installed them at 8151 Electric Ave. in Stanton, California. The wholesale production of billet wheels had begun. The wheel industry was changed forever, and fleets of trucks plied the freeways of Southern California, hauling centers, rims, and castings from shop to shop.

According to Boyd writing in his book *Hot Rods by Boyd*, "We originally made true knock-off, racing-style wheels but that style wasn't for everybody and soon we made wheels with conventional bolt patterns." A set of Boyd Wheels retailed for an unprecedented $1,695, and while Boyd Wheels were not for everyone, everyone wanted a set.

Throttle in a Bottle

Perhaps, and arguably the last great performance invention of the 1970s, nitrous oxide (N_2O) was actually invented in 1772 by Joseph Priestly. Its psychotropic properties were explored by Humphrey Davy in the late 1790s, and in 1844 Horace Wells, a dentist, discovered nitrous oxide's anesthetic qualities. It was known as "laughing gas."

Fast-forward, literally, to 1914 when Robert H. Goddard, an American engineer and rocket pioneer, patented the idea of nitrous oxide combined with gasoline as a potential rocket fuel. It was also found to work in internal combustion engines, where it enables the engine to burn more fuel by providing more oxygen. This fact was first put to use by the German Luftwaffe during World War II, when its Goring Mishung 1 system was used to inject nitrous oxide into Messerschmitt 109 engines. Methanol-water injection was tried at the same time.

The next recorded occurrence, according to Gary Hordemann writing for *Hot Rod News,* came on September

7, 1958, when Gary Harms filled an oxygen bottle with nitrous oxide and laid it in the tool tray of his supercharged 1940 Ford. A hose ran from the bottle to an air-gun nozzle set on his thigh. From there, another hose ran to a nipple at the base of a Stromberg jetted extra rich. The jerry-rigged device worked, and Harms won B/Gas.

Somewhere hereabouts in 1953, Bill Huth, builder of Willow Springs International Raceway in California, teamed with Pacific Northwesterners Dick Flynn and Jack Hordemann to market nitrous oxide systems under the Second Wind brand.

Over the next few years, the Pacific Northwest (PNW) racers experimented and refined the system. At the 1961 Bakersfield Fuel and Gas Championships, several PNW cars were equipped with nitrous oxide. The gas was out of the bottle, so to speak, and no one was laughing. The May 20, 1961, issue of *Drag News* spilled the beans.

The center spread was a thinly disguised ad for Speed Power Suspension Second Wind and featured the PNW boys and "This New Fuel" . . . "Safe as Gas." For a hefty $225, a complete kit could be purchased to "install on any engine and absolutely guaranteed to add 20 mph top speed." It didn't take off.

Ron Hammel, another PNW transplant, entered the picture in 1962. Hammel worked for Tony Capanna's Wilcap at 10215 S. San Pedro St. in Los Angeles, and Jack Hordemann gave him a nitrous oxide kit to test on Capanna's dyno, where they were running Zane Shubert's Chevy. The results were encouraging, and in 1964, Hammel founded 10,000 RPM Speed Equipment, supplying nitrous oxide and racing clutches from a facility on Sepulveda Boulevard in Torrance, California.

Meanwhile, Shubert ran nitrous oxide concealed in a fire extinguisher disguised with black paint. Unfortunately, they grenaded three blowers before abandoning the laughing gas—it wasn't funny.

Later in life, Hammel built one of the only high-horsepower dynos in existence. It was capable of testing an 8,000-hp engine.

Although Hammel sold a lot of nitrous oxide kits, the name 10,000 RPM might have been too tricky and not catchy enough to market. It sure wasn't as catchy as the letters NOS. In 1978, inspired by one of the 10,000 RPM kits, Mike Thermos and friend Dale Vaznaian joined forces

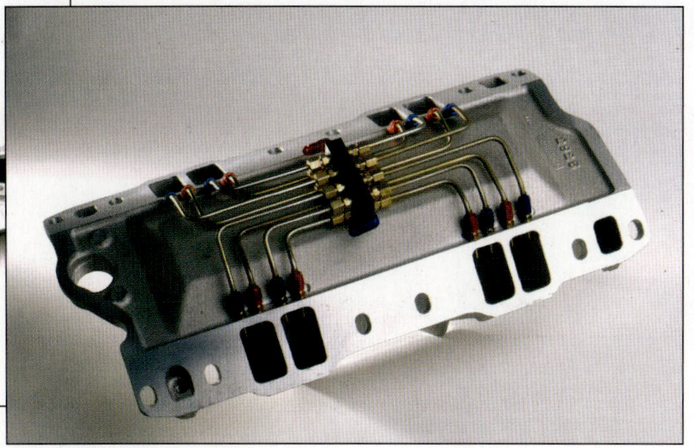

The underside of the Weiand 1922 tunnel-ram intake has a two-stage, direct-port NOS system with some Big Shot solenoids. (Photo Courtesy Mike Thermos)

Nitrous oxide was actually invented in 1772, but it was hot rodders Mike Thermos and Dale Vaznaian who popularized its use on high-performance automobiles. (Photo Courtesy Mike Thermos)

to develop their own nitrous oxide kits under the Nitrous Oxide Systems or simply, and far catchier, NOS brand. They had a cool logo to boot, and they took it to market.

Located at 5930 Lakeshore Drive in Cypress, California, NOS revolutionized the delivery of nitrous oxide, which in Hammel's time had primarily been a mechanical device. However, the advent of electronic solenoid control made the gas delivery completely controllable.

In July 1981, *Hot Rod* published a nitrous oxide shoot-out article by David Vizard. Vizard tested three systems from Internal Combustion Engines, NOS, and 10,000 RPM on a well-prepared 350 Chevy-powered Camaro Z28 running on 92-octane pump gas on a computerized Superflow 800 chassic dyno. NOS won, producing 491 hp at 5,120 rpm and 562 ft-lbs of torque at 4,100 rpm. With 102-octane gas and open pipes, they recorded 529 hp at 5,500 rpm and 570 ft-lbs of torque at 4,000 rpm.

Sales of NOS took off like a bullet, but Thermos and Vaznaian continued with their product development, and NOS became the performance adder of the decade. There was more to come in 2001 (after NOS was sold to Holley) with the release of the first film of the hugely popular and influential *Fast & Furious* franchise.

EPILOGUE

The 1973 oil crisis was not a nail in the coffin of the performance industry nor did the decade itself signal the end. Speed may have taken a back seat to fuel economy for a while as we became used to a different world. The price of a barrel of oil quadrupled from a pre-embargo $2.90 per barrel to $11.65 per barrel in January 1974, and prices at the pump nearly doubled from 29 cents per gallon to 55. It is similar to what is happening today, although perhaps for different reasons.

As we have seen, the 1970s actually saw some great strides forward for the industry with the introduction of "new" hemi-based blocks from Keith Black and Ed Donovan, and toward the end of the decade, Mike Thermos and Dale Vaznaian launched their Throttle in a Bottle nitrous-oxide systems that revolutionized the speed business and continues to do so. Meanwhile, we all flocked to the movies to see George Lucas's *American Graffiti* or huddled around the haunted fishbowl to watch Martin Sheen outfox the nasty sheriff in TV's The *California Kid*.

It was all grist for the mill, and these developments kept a generation of enthusiasts hungry for the foot-to-the-floor, wide-open-throttle days of the 1960s. They came back with a vengeance, though, and one has to say things have never been better for the industry, which grew from about $10 billion in 1970 to around $50 billion today.

Many companies saw record sales through the two-year Covid-19 pandemic, as people apparently had money and time to work on their projects. However, if the powers that be have their way, there could be an electric vehicle in all of our futures, and I'm not sure what that spells for our hobby. I truly believe that we will always want to mess with our cars and make them go faster. Indeed, there are plenty of companies making speed equipment and hopping up electric vehicles. I'm just not sure if that will be allowed and we don't all turn into bit players in a real-life *Mad Max* scenario where we are foraging for gasoline to keep our "infernal combustion engines" running. Only time will tell.

Additional books that may interest you...

HOW TO BUILD AFFORDABLE HOT RODS
by Tony Thacker
In *How to Build Affordable Hot Rods*, author and lifelong hot rod aficionado Tony Thacker takes you through the process of building a hot rod on a budget. Drawing on his own extensive experience of both buying and building rods, Thacker explores the good, the bad and the ugly. 8.5 x 11", 176 pgs, 558 photos, Sftbd. ISBN 9781613255285 Part # SA477

THE AMERICAN SPEED SHOP: Birth and Evolution of Hot Rodding *by Bob McClurg*
Longtime hot rodder and industry veteran Bob McClurg brings you the story of the era and the culture of speed shops as told through individual shop histories and compelling vintage photography. 8.5 x 11", 192 pgs, 400 photos, Hdbd. ISBN 9781613253342
Part # CT595

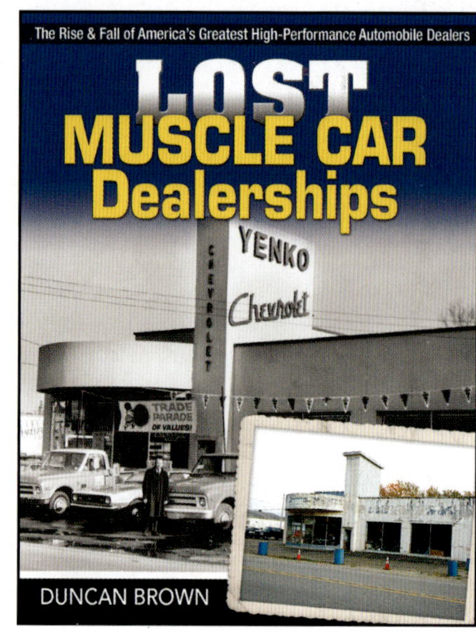

LOST MUSCLE CAR DEALERSHIPS
by Duncan Brown
Revisit the glorious 1960s and early 1970s, when cars from Reynolds Buick, Yeakel Chrysler-Plymouth, Mel Burns Ford, and others created the lasting muscle car legacy through innovative advertising and over-the-top performance. Detailed text and more than 250 historic photos and illustrations provide the history of those dealerships. 8.5 x 11", 192 pgs, 360 photos, Sftbd. ISBN 9781613254516 Part # CT644

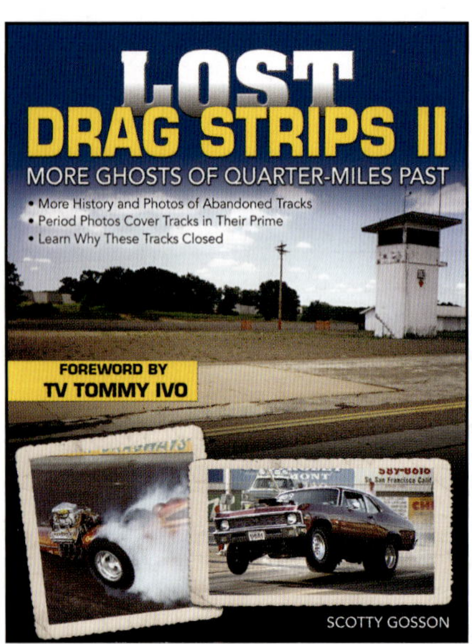

LOST DRAG STRIPS II: More Ghosts of Quarter-Miles Past
by Scotty Gosson
Lost Drag Strips II picks up where the first volume left off, covering even more tracks with archival photos of racing in the tracks' heyday, the cars that ran there, and coverage of the tracks as they exist today. This volume also includes some of the tracks that survived, those that fought off the economic demons and the urban sprawl and continue to run today. 8.5 x 11", 176 pgs, 249 photos, Sftbd. ISBN 9781613252239
Part # CT550

www.cartechbooks.com or 1-800-551-4754